Edward John Hopkins, W. H Smyth

The Choral Psalter

Containing the Authorized Version of the Psalms, and Other Portions... Ninth

Edition

Edward John Hopkins, W. H Smyth

The Choral Psalter
Containing the Authorized Version of the Psalms, and Other Portions... Ninth Edition

ISBN/EAN: 9783337080495

Printed in Europe, USA, Canada, Australia, Japan

Cover: Foto ©Thomas Meinert / pixelio.de

More available books at **www.hansebooks.com**

THE CHORAL PSALTER.

CONTAINING THE AUTHORIZED VERSION OF THE PSALMS, AND OTHER PORTIONS OF SCRIPTURE, POINTED FOR CHANTING, WITH A SELECTION OF CHANTS.

BY

E. J. HOPKINS,

ORGANIST TO THE HON. SOCIETIES OF THE INNER AND MIDDLE TEMPLE, LONDON;

AND

W. H. SMYTH,

ORGANIST OF SANDYFORD CHURCH, GLASGOW;

WITH A RECOMMENDATORY NOTE FROM THE REV. DR. MACDUFF.

"I open the Book of Psalms, and there I find words which seem to issue from the soul of the ages. . . . . There we see David, or rather the human heart itself, with all its God-given notes of grief, joy, tears, and adoration—poetry sanctified to its highest expression; a vase of perfume broken on the steps of the Temple and shedding abroad its odours from the soul of the Sweet Singer of Israel to the heart of all humanity."—LAMARTINE.

NINTH EDITION.

LONDON:
JAMES NISBET & CO., 21 BERNERS STREET.
EDINBURGH: OLIVER & BOYD.   GLASGOW: DAVID BRYCE & SON.

NOTE.

WHATEVER diversities may exist, in other respects, in the Ritual of the different portions of the Christian Church, the Psalms must ever occupy a conspicuous place in her Devotional Services.

Sacred as are our traditional and time-honoured associations with our metrical rendering, none who have made a fair and unprejudiced trial, can refuse to concede a preference in Public Worship to the use of the literal, undiluted, unmutilated Prose Version.

In the sister Church of England, the Prayer-book Version (unquestionably inferior in fidelity of rendering, if not in beauty and rhythm, to the authorized Bible one[*]) has, by various skilful hands, been adapted for the purpose of Chanting. The present Work is the first attempt to supply, in full, the same boon with respect to the other.

In these few prefatory words, I gladly record my humble testimony as to the successful introduction (now for some years) of the Prose Chanting in the service of my own Church; as well as to the careful and painstaking labours of the compilers of this Volume to make it one of standard and permanent value. Their joint names will be a guarantee, alike as to the taste and accuracy with which they have fulfilled their undertaking.

I have only farther to express an earnest and confident hope that other Congregations, among the many "Aids to Worship," may find this production eminently helpful; and that, as its highest end, it may tend to endear and consecrate more than ever, in the services of the Sanctuary, the use of the Great Hymn-book and Liturgy of the Universal Church.

J. R. M.

[*] The Prayer-book Version is rendered from the Septuagint, and contains and perpetuates many of its inaccuracies; the Authorized Version is from the original Hebrew.

The Compilers of THE CHORAL PSALTER have much pleasure in acknowledging their obligations to the following Gentlemen, for their kindness in allowing the use of valuable Copyright Chants, and for Original Contributions to the work:—To Messrs. Novello, Ewer, & Co., for the use of Chants, Nos. 36, 110, 111, 112, 139; to Mr. Henry Smart, for Nos. 120, 121; to the Rev. W. H. Havergal, M.A., for Nos. 39, 95, 131; to Dr. G. J. Elvey, for Nos. 70, 135; to Dr. S. Elvey, for No. 134; to Professor Herbert S. Oakeley, for Nos. 136, 137, 138, 140; to Mr. A. L. Peace, for Nos. 33, 102, 103; and to Mr. B. Whitham, for No. 71.

The Compilers have endeavoured, in all cases, to ascertain where copyright existed, in order to obtain the necessary permission; but if they have unconsciously trespassed on any copyrights, they trust to the forbearance of those who are interested.

They would, in a special manner, gratefully record their thanks to the Rev. J. R. Macduff, D.D., for his valuable counsel and hearty co-operation in the production of this work.

In preparing a Second Edition of THE CHORAL PSALTER, the Compilers, with a view to make the work more complete, have added special Music for the Te Deum—Jackson, in F— so universally known; and a beautiful setting by Rev. Dr. Dykes, the latter through the kindness of Messrs. Novello, Ewer, & Co. They also append the words of a selection of Anthems, which they believe will add much to the usefulness of the work.

ALPHABETICAL INDEX.

SINGLE CHANTS.

COMPOSER.	KEY.	NO.	COMPOSER.	KEY.	NO.
Alcock, Dr.,	G,	32	Gregorian Peregrine tone, G,		51
Aldrich, Dr.,	B flat,	25	Havergal, Rev. W. H.,	E,	39
,, ,,	G,	38	Hayes, Dr. P.,	E,	23
Battishill, J.,	A,	15	Hayes, Dr. W.,	B flat,	20
,, ,,	E flat,	18	Hine, W.,	G min.,	21
,, ,,	D,	27	Hopkins, E. J.,	E,	44
Bennett, A.,	F,	31	Humphreys, P.,	C,	4
Blow, Dr.,	E min.,	7	Kelway,	D,	24
Cooke, Dr. B.,	F,	13	Langdon, R.,	G min.,	30
Croft, Dr.,	B min.,	10	Nares, Dr.,	A,	41
,, ,,	F min.,	34	Oakeley, H. S.,	E flat,	140
Crotch, Dr.,	A,	6	Peace, A. L.,	E,	33
,, ,,	F,	22	Purcell, D.,	G,	11
,, ,,	D,	29	Purcell, H.,	G min.,	14
Dupuis, Dr.,	B flat,	42	Purcell, T.,	G,	3
Farrant, R.,	F,	1	Russell, W.,	C,	12
Felton, Rev. W.,	C min.,	9	Smyth, W. H.,	G,	28
Gibbons, C.,	G,	16	Tallis, T.,	F,	2
Goodson,	C,	26	,, ,,	A min.,	43
Greene, Dr.,	B flat,	40	Travers,	E,	35
Gregorian, 1st tone,	F,	45	Tucker, Rev. W.,	A,	19
,, 3rd ,,	A,	46	Turle, J.,	C,	36
,, 5th ,,	E,	47	Turner, Dr.,	A,	37
,, 7th ,,	F,	48	Weldon, J.,	G min.,	17
,, 8th ,,	B flat,	49	Woodward, Dr.,	C,	8
,, 8th ,,	B flat,	50	Anonymous,	F,	5

DOUBLE CHANTS.

COMPOSER.	KEY.	NO.	COMPOSER.	KEY.	NO.
Abel, C. F.,	G,	74	Hopkins, E. J.,	F,	118
Aldrich, Dr.,	F,	72	,, ,,	G min.,	119
Attwood, Thomas,	A,	83	Jackson, W.,	E,	96
,, ,,	E,	122	Jones, J.,	D,	94
,, ,,	D,	128	Langdon, R.,	F,	100
Alyward, Dr.,	G,	124	Lawes, H.,	C,	59
Barrow, T.,	F,	107	Lemon, Colonel,	A flat,	86
Battishill, J.,	A min.,	69	Luther (from),	C,	75
,, ,,	D,	78	Marsh, John,	E min.,	125
Beethoven (by J. Goss),	C min.,	90	Marsh, W.,	A,	85
Bennett, A.,	F,	97	Mornington, Lord,	E flat,	65
Boyce, Dr. W.,	E,	79	,, ,,	E,	73
,, ,,	D,	82	Morley W.,	D min,	60
Cambridge Chant,	A min.,	105	Nares, Dr.,	D,	123
Camidge, M.,	E min.,	55	Norris, T.,	A,	56
Cooke, Robert,	G,	84	Oakeley, H. S.,	E flat,	136
,, ,,	B min.,	127	,, ,,	G,	137
,, ,,	G,	129	,, ,,	D min.,	138
Cooper, G., sen.,	D,	130	Peace, A. L.,	F,	102
Crotch, Dr. W.,	G,	58	,, ,,	A min.,	103
,, ,,	A,	89	Pring, Dr.,	G,	109
,, ,,	C,	92	Randall, Dr.,	E,	53
Dupuis, Dr. T. S.,	A,	68	Robinson, John,	E flat,	52
,, ,,	C,	88	Russell, W.,	E,	61
,, ,,	E,	91	Smart, Henry,	F,	120
Elvey, Dr. G. J.,	E flat,	70	,, ,,	D,	121
,, ,,	A,	135	Smith, Dr.,	A flat,	104
Elvey, Dr. S.,	F,	134	Smith, J. S.,	G,	114
Fitzherbert, Rev. W.,	F,	132	Smyth, W. H.,	E,	63
Flintoft, Rev. L.,	G min.,	67	,, ,,	D min.,	126
Goodenough, Rev. R. P.,	A,	98	Soaper, J.,	A,	76
,, ,,	F,	113	Spohr (by W. H. Smyth),	G,	106
Gregory, Rev. T.,	E flat,	99	Troyte, A. H. D.,	F,	139
Handel, G. F.,	G,	77	Turle, J.,	F,	110
Havergal, Rev. W. H.,	D,	95	,, ,,	D min.,	111
,, ,,	E,	131	,, ,,	C,	112
Hayes, Dr. P.,	E,	80	Wesley, S.,	G,	62
Hayes, Dr. W.,	G,	57	,, ,,	F,	101
Heathcote,	A,	66	Whitham, B.,	E flat,	71
Henley, Rev. P.,	F,	54	Wood, G.,	A,	133
Higgins, E.,	F,	81	Woodward, Dr.,	C,	64
Hopkins, E. J.,	B flat,	115	,, ,,	D,	87
,, ,,	C,	116	,, ,,	B flat,	93
,, ,,	B flat,	117	Worgan, Dr.,	E flat,	108

INDEX OF PSALMS, ANTHEMS, &c.

	PAGE
Psalms i.–cl.,	3–214
Exodus xv.,	215
Ecclesiastes xii.,	216
Isaiah xii.,	217
,, xl.,	218
,, liii.,	219
,, lx.,	221
Hab. iii.,	222
Luke i. 46,	224
,, i. 68,	225
1 Cor. xv. 20,	226
"Glory be to God on high,"	229
O all ye works of the Lord,	230

Te Deum Laudamus, pointed for Chanting,	227
Te Deum Laudamus, by William Jackson, of Exeter,	233
Te Deum Laudamus, by the Rev. John B. Dykes, M.A., Mus. D.,	243

ANTHEMS.

No.		PAGE
7.	Arise, shine; for thy light is come,	255
,, 45.	Blessed be the Lord God,	263
,, 20.	Blessed for ever are they that die trusting in God,	258
,, 35.	Blessed is he that considereth the poor and needy,	261
,, 23.	Christ is risen from the dead,	258
,, 17.	Come unto Me, all ye that labour and are heavy laden,	257
,, 8.	Enter not into judgment with Thy servant, O Lord,	255
,, 51.	For our offences, Jesus took upon Him humility,	264
,, 28.	God be merciful unto us, and bless us,	260
,, 52.	Hallelujah! for the Lord God Omnipotent reigneth,	264
,, 6.	Hear my prayer, O Lord,	255
,, 22.	Hear the voice and prayer of Thy servants,	258
,, 4.	How beautiful upon the mountains,	254
,, 29.	How dear are Thy counsels unto me, O God,	260
,, 33.	How goodly are thy tents, O Jacob,	261
,, 1.	I will arise, and go to my Father,	254

ANTHEMS.

			PAGE
No.	16. I will alway give thanks unto the Lord,		257
,,	10. I will lift up mine eyes unto the hills,		255
,,	34. Let us now go even unto Bethlehem,		261
,,	38. Like as the hart desireth the water-brooks,		261
,,	19. Lord, for Thy tender mercies' sake,		257
,,	12. Lord, now lettest Thou Thy servant depart in peace,		256
,,	50. Lord, on our offences in justice look not,		264
,,	25. My God, look upon me: why hast thou forsaken me?		259
,,	11. My soul doth magnify the Lord,		256
,,	43. O come, ye servants of the Lord,		263
,,	40. O give thanks unto the Lord,		262
,,	32. O Holy Ghost, into our minds send down Thy heav'nly light,		260
,,	47. O how amiable are Thy dwellings, Thou Lord of hosts,		263
,,	24. O Lord God, Thou strength of my health,		258
,,	44. O Lord, we trust alone in Thee,		263
,,	14. O Lord my God, hear Thou the prayer Thy servant prayeth,		256
,,	42. O love the Lord, all ye His saints,		262
,,	3. O praise God in His holiness,		254
,,	2. O praise the Lord,		254
,,	31. O praise the Lord, all ye heathen,		260
,,	27. O sing unto the Lord a new song,		259
,,	13. O taste and see how gracious the Lord is,		256
,,	30. Ponder my words, O Lord; consider my meditation,		260
,,	18. Praise the Lord, O Jerusalem,		257
,,	48. Rejoice, O ye people of earth,		264
,,	15. Rend your heart, and not your garments,		257
,,	37. Saviour, source of ev'ry blessing,		261
,,	5. Teach me, O Lord, the way of Thy statutes,		255
,,	21. The Lord descended from above,		258
,,	46. The Lord is King,		263
,,	39. The Lord is loving unto every man,		262
,,	26. The Lord is my shepherd,		259
,,	9. Thine, O Lord, is the greatness,		255
,,	41. This is the day which the Lord hath made,		262
,,	36. Thou knowest, Lord, the secrets of our hearts,		261
,,	49. Thou Lord our refuge hast been from age to age,		264

SINGLE CHANTS.

PSALM I.

BLESSED is the | man that | walketh not in the | counSEL | of the-un|godly, || nor | standeth in the | way of sinners, nor | sitTETH in the | seat | of the | scornful:

2 But | his delight is in the | LAW | of the | Lord; || and in his | LAW doth he | meditate | day and | night.

3 And | he shall be | like a tree | planted by the | rivers of water, that | bringeth forth his | FRUIT | in his | season: || his | leaf also | shall not wither: and | WHATso|ever he | doeth shall | prosper.

4 The ungodLY | are not | so: || but are like the | CHAFF which the | wind | driveth a|way.

5 Therefore the ungodly shall not STAND | in the | judgment, || nor sinners in the | CONgre|gation | of the | righteous.

6 For the | Lord knoweth the | WAY | of the | righteous: || but the | way of the UN|godly | shall | perish.

GLORY BE TO THE FATHER, AND | TO THE | SON, || AND | TO THE | HOLY | GHOST;

AS IT WAS IN THE BEGINNING, IS NOW, AND | EVER | SHALL BE; || WORLD | WITHOUT | END. A|MEN.

PSALM II.

WHY DO the | heathen | rage, || and the | peoPLE i|magine-a | vain | thing?

2 The | kings of the earth | set themselves, and the | ruLERS take | | counsel to|gether, || against the Lord, and | AGAINST | his A-| nointed, | saying,

1.

3 Let us | BREAK their | bands a|s⟨…⟩
their | cords from | us.

4 He that sitTETH in the | heavens ⟨…⟩
shall | have them | in de|rision.

5 Then shall he| speak unto THEM ⟨…⟩
THEM | in his | sore dis|pleasure.

6 YET have I | set my | King ‖ upON ⟨…⟩

7 I will declare the decree: the Lord ⟨…⟩
Thou art my Son; this DAY have | I be⟨…⟩

8 Ask of me, and | I shall give thee t⟨…⟩
in|heritance, ‖ and the \ uttermost PART⟨…⟩
pos|session.

9 Thou shalt break THEM with a | ⟨…⟩
dash them in pieCES, | like a | potter's | ⟨…⟩

10 Be| wise now thereFORE, | O ye ⟨…⟩
ye | judges | of the | earth.

11 SERVE the | Lord with | fear, ‖ ⟨…⟩
trem|bling.

12 Kiss the Son, lest he be angry, and⟨…⟩
when his wrath is kindLED † but a | ⟨…⟩
THEY that | put their | trust in | him⟨…⟩

PSALM III.

LORD, how are they increasED that | ⟨…⟩
   they that RISE | up a|gainst | ⟨…⟩

2 Many there be which SAY | of my⟨…⟩
help for | him in | God.

2. Tallis.

3 But thou, O Lord, ART a | shield for | me; || my glory, AND the | lifter | up-of mine | head.

4 I cried unto the LORD | with my | voice, || and he heard ME | out of-his | holy | hill.

5 I laid ME | down and | slept; || I awaked: FOR the | Lord sus|tained | me.

6 I will not be afraid of TEN | thousands of | people, || that have set themSELVES a|gainst me | round a|bout.

7 Arise, O Lord; save ME, | O my | God: || for thou hast smitten all mine enemies upon the cheek-bone; thou hast broKEN the | teeth of | the un|godly.

8 Salvation belongETH | unto the | Lord: || thy blessING | is up|on thy | people.   GLORY BE, ETC.

PSALM IV.

HEAR me when I call, O GOD | of my | righteousness: || thou hast enlarged me when I was in distress; have mercy up- ON | me, and | hear my | prayer.

2 O ye sons of men, how long will ye turn my gloRY | into | shame? || how long will ye love vaniTY, and | seek | after | leasing?

3 But know that the Lord hath set apart him that is godLY | for him|self: || the Lord will HEAR | when I | call unto | him.

4 Stand in AWE, and | sin | not: || commune with your own heart upon YOUR | bed, | and be | still.

5 Offer the sacrifiCES of | righteous|ness; || AND | put your | trust in-the | Lord.

3. *T. Purcell.*

6 There be many that say, Who will show US | any | good? ||
Lord, lift thou up the light of THY | counte|nance up|on-us.

7 Thou hast put gladNESS | in my | heart, || more than in the
time that THEIR | corn and-their | wine in|creased.

8 I will both lay me DOWN in | peace, and | sleep: || for
thou, Lord, onLY | makest me | dwell in | safety.

GLORY BE, ETC.

PSALM V.

GIVE ear to MY | words, O | Lord; || CON|sider my | medi-|
tation.

2 Hearken unto the voice of my cry, my KING, | and my |
God: || FOR | unto thee | will I | pray.

3 My voice shalt thou hear IN the | morning, O | Lord; || in the
morning will I direct my prayer unTO | thee, and | will look | up.

4 For thou art not a God that hath pleaSURE in | wicked-|
ness; || neither SHALL | evil | dwell with | thee.

5 The foolish shall not STAND | in thy | sight: || thou hatest
ALL | workers | of in|iquity.

6 Thou shalt destroy THEM that | speak | leasing: || the Lord
will abhor the bloodY | and de|ceitful | man.

7 But as for me, I will come into thy house in the multi-
TUDE | of thy | mercy; || and in thy fear will I worSHIP |
toward thy | holy | temple.

8 Lead me, O Lord, in thy righteousness, beCAUSE | of
mine | enemies; || make thy WAY | straight be|fore my | face.

9 For there is no faithfulness in their mouth; their inward

4.

PART is | very | wickedness; ‖ their throat is an open sepul-CHRE; they | flatter | with their | tongue.

10 Destroy thou them, O God; let them FALL by | their own | counsels; ‖ cast them out in the multitude of their transgressions; FOR they | have re|belled a|gainst-thee.

11 But let all those that put their TRUST in | thee re|joice: ‖ let them ever shout for joy, because thou defendest them: let them also that LOVE thy | name be | joyful in | thee.

12 For thou, LORD, wilt | bless the | righteous; ‖ with favour wilt thou comPASS | him as | with a | shield.

GLORY BE, ETC.

PSALM VI.

O LORD, rebuke me NOT | in thine | anger, ‖ neither chasten ME | in thy | hot dis|pleasure.

2 Have mercy upon me, O LORD; for | I am | weak: ‖ O Lord, heal ME; | for my | bones are | vexed.

3 My soul is alSO | sore | vexed: ‖ BUT | thou, O | Lord, how | long?

4 Return, O LORD, de|liver my | soul: ‖ Oh save ME | for thy | mercies' | sake.

5 For in death there is NO re|membrance of | thee: ‖ in the GRAVE | who shall | give thee | thanks?

6 I am weaRY | with my | groaning; ‖ all the night make I my bed to swim; I waTER my | couch | with my | tears.

7 Mine eye is consumED be|cause of | grief; ‖ it waxeth OLD be|cause of | all mine | enemies.

5.

8 Depart from me, all ye workERS | of in|iquity; || for the Lord hath HEARD the | voice | of my | weeping.

9 The Lord hath HEARD my | suppli|cation; || the LORD | will re|ceive my | prayer.

10 Let all mine enemies be ashamED and | sore | vexed: || let them reTURN and | be a|shamed | suddenly. GLORY BE, ETC.

PSALM VII.

O LORD my God, in thee do I | put my | trust: || save me from all them that persecute ME, | and de|liver | me:

2 Lest he tear my soul like a lion, rendING | it in | pieces, || WHILE | there is | none to-de|liver.

3 O Lord my God, if I | have done | this; || if there BE in-|iquity | in my | hands;

4 If I have rewarded evil unto him that WAS at | peace with | me; || (yea, I have delivered him that withOUT | cause | is mine | enemy;)

5 Let the enemy perseCUTE my | soul, and | take-it; || yea, let him tread down my life upon the earth, and LAY mine | honour | in the | dust.

6 Arise, O Lord, in thine anger; lift up thyself because of the RAGE | of mine | enemies: || and awake for me to the judg-MENT | that thou | hast com|manded.

7 So shall the congregation of the people comPASS | thee a-|bout: || for their sakes thereFORE re|turn | thou on | high

8 The LORD shall | judge the | people: || judge me, O Lord, according to my righteousness, and according to MINE in-|tegrity | that is | in-me.

6. *Dr. Crotch.*

9 Oh let the wickedness of the wicked come to an end; BUT es|tablish the | just: ‖ for the righteous GOD | trieth the | hearts and | reins.

10 My deFENCE | is of | God, ‖ which savETH | the up-|right in | heart.

11 GOD | judgeth the | righteous, ‖ and God is anGRY with the | wicked | every | day.

12 If he turn NOT, he will | whet his | sword; ‖ he hath BENT his | bow, and | made it | ready.

13 He hath also prepared for HIM the | instruments of | death; ‖ he ordaineth his arROWS a'gainst the | perse|cutors.

14 Behold, he travailETH | with in|iquity, ‖ and hath conceivED | mischief, and | brought forth | falsehood.

15 He made a PIT, and | digged | it, ‖ and is fallen inTO the | ditch | which he | made.

16 His mischief shall return upON | his own | head, ‖ and his violent dealing shall COME | down upon | his own | pate.

17 I will praise the Lord according to HIS | righteous|ness; ‖ and will sing praise to the NAME | of the | Lord most | high.

GLORY BE, ETC.

PSALM VIII.

O LORD our Lord, how excellent is thy NAME in | all the | earth! ‖ who hast SET thy | glory a|bove the | heavens.

2 Out of the mouth of babes and sucklings hast thou ordained strength beCAUSE | of thine | enemies, ‖ that thou mightest STILL the | enemy | and the-a|venger.

7.   *Dr. Blow.*

3 When I consider thy heavens, the WORK | of thy | fingers, ‖ the moon and the STARS, | which thou | hast or|dained;

4 What is man, that THOU art | mindful of | him? ‖ and the son of MAN, | that thou | visitest | him?

5 For thou hast made him a little lowER | than the | angels, ‖ and hast crownED | him with | glory and | honour.

6 Thou madest him to have dominion over the WORKS | of thy | hands; ‖ thou hast PUT | all things | under his | feet:

7 ALL | sheep and | oxen, ‖ YEA, | and the | beasts of-the | field;

8 The fowl of the air, and the FISH | of the | sea, ‖ and whatsoever passETH | through the | paths of-the | seas.

9 O | Lord our | Lord, ‖ how excellent is THY | name in | all the | earth!   Glory be, etc.

PSALM IX.

I WILL praise thee, O Lord, WITH my | whole | heart: ‖ I will show FORTH | all thy | marvellous | works.

2 I will be glad AND re|joice in | thee: ‖ I will sing praise to THY | name, O | thou most | High.

3 When mine eneMIES are | turned | back, ‖ they shall FALL and | perish | at thy | presence.

4 For thou hast maintained my RIGHT | and my | cause; ‖ thou sattest IN the | throne | judging | right.

5 Thou hast rebuked the heathen, thou HAST de|stroyed the | wicked, ‖ thou hast put OUT their | name for | ever and | ever.

6 O thou enemy, destructions are come to A per|petual | end: ‖

8.

Dr. *Woodward.*

and thou hast destroyed ciTIES; their me|morial is | perished with | them.

7 But the LORD shall en|dure for | ever: || he HATH pre-| pared his | throne for | judgment;

8 And he shall judge the WORLD in | righteous|ness, || he shall minister judgMENT to the | people | in up|rightness.

9 The Lord also will be a reFUGE | for the-op|pressed, || A | refuge in | times of | trouble.

10 And they that know thy name will PUT their | trust in | thee: || for thou, Lord, hast NOT for|saken | them that | seek-thee.

11 Sing praises to the LORD, which | dwelleth in | Zion: || de-CLARE a|mong the | people his | doings.

12 When he maketh inquisition for BLOOD, he re|membereth | them: || he forgetteth NOT the | cry | of the | humble.

13 Have merCY upon | me, O | Lord: || consider my trouble which I suffer of them that hate me, thou that liftest me UP | from the | gates of | death;

14 That I may show forth all thy praise in the GATES of the | daughter of | Zion: || I will re|joice in | thy sal|vation.

15 The heathen are sunk down in the PIT | that they | made: || in the net which they HID | is their | own foot | taken.

16 The Lord is known by the judgMENT which he | exe-| cuteth: || the wicked is snarED in the | work of | his own | hands.

17 The wicked shall be turnED | into | hell, || and all the naTIONS | that for|get | God.

18 For the needy shall not alWAY | be for|gotten: || the ex-pectation of the POOR | shall not | perish for | ever.

9. *Felton.*

19 Arise, O Lord; let NOT | man pre|vail: ‖ let the hea-THEN be | judged | in thy | sight.

20 Put THEM in | fear, O | Lord; ‖ that the nations may KNOW them|selves to | be but | men. Glory be, etc.

PSALM X.

WHY standest thou aFAR | off, O | Lord? ‖ why hidest THOU thy|self in | times of | trouble?

2 The wicked in his pride doth perSE|cute the | poor: ‖ let them be taken in the deviCES | that they | have i|magined.

3 For the wicked boasteth of HIS | heart's de|sire, ‖ and blesseth the covetOUS, | whom the | Lord ab|horreth.

4 The wicked, through the pride of his countenance, will not SEEK | after | God: ‖ GOD is | not in | all his | thoughts.

5 His ways are always grievous; thy judgments are far aBOVE | out of-his | sight: ‖ as for all his eneMIES, | he | puffeth at | them.

6 He hath said in his heart, I shall | not be | moved: ‖ for I shall | never be | in ad|versity.

7 His mouth is full of cursing, AND de|ceit, and | fraud: ‖ unDER his | tongue is | mischief and | vanity.

8 He sitteth in the lurking places of the villages; in the secret places DOTH he | murder the | innocent: ‖ his eyes are priviLY | set a|gainst the | poor.

9 He lieth in wait secretly as a lion in his den: he lieth in WAIT to | catch the | poor: ‖ he doth catch the poor, when he drawETH | him in|to his | net.

10. Dr. Croft.

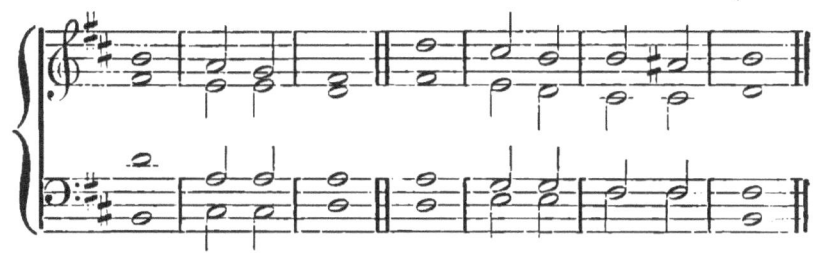

10 He crouchETH, and | humbleth him|self, || that the POOR may | fall by | his strong | ones.

11. He hath said in his heart, GOD | hath for|gotten : || he hideth his FACE ; | he will | never | see-it.

12 Arise, O Lord; O GOD, lift | up thine | hand : || FOR|get | not the | humble.

13 Wherefore doth the wickED con|temn | God ? || he hath said in his HEART, | Thou wilt | not re|quire-it.

14 Thou hast seen it; for thou beholdest mischief and spite, to reQUIRE it | with thy | hand : || the poor committeth himself unto thee; thou ART the | helper | of the | fatherless.

15 Break thou the arm of the wicked AND the | evil | man : || seek out his wickedNESS | till thou | find | none.

16 The Lord is KING for | ever and | ever : || the heaTHEN are | perished | out of-his | land.

17 Lord, thou hast heard the deSIRE | of the | humble : || thou wilt prepare their heart, THOU wilt | cause thine | ear to | hear;

18 To judge the fatherLESS | and the-op|pressed, || that the man of the EARTH | may no | more op'press. GLORY BE, ETC.

PSALM XI.

IN the LORD put | I my | trust : || how say ye to my soul, Flee AS a | bird | to your | mountain?

2 For, lo, the wicked bend their bow, they make ready their arROW up|on the | string, || that they may privily SHOOT | at the | upright in | heart.

11. *Daniel Purcell.*

---

3 If the foundaTIONS | be de|stroyed, ‖ WHAT | can the | righteous | do?

4 The Lord is in his holy temple, the Lord's THRONE | is in | heaven: ‖ his eyes behold, his eyeLIDS | try, the | children of | men.

5 The LORD | trieth the | righteous: ‖ but the wicked, and him that lovETH | violence, his | soul | hateth.

6 Upon the wicked he shall rain snares, fire and brimstone, AND an | horrible | tempest: ‖ this shall BE the | portion | of their | cup.

7 For the righteous Lord lovETH | righteous|ness; ‖ his counteNANCE | doth be|hold the | upright. GLORY BE, ETC.

PSALM XII.

HELP, Lord; for the godLY | man | ceaseth; ‖ for the faithful fail FROM a|mong the | children of | men.

2 They speak vanity every ONE | with his | neighbour: ‖ with flattering lips and WITH a | double heart | do they | speak.

3 The Lord shall cut off ALL | flattering | lips, ‖ and the TONGUE that | speaketh | proud | things:

4 Who have said, With our TONGUE will | we pre|vail; ‖ our lips are our OWN: | who is | Lord over | us?

5 For the oppression of the poor, for the sighing of the needy, now will I aRISE, | saith the | Lord; ‖ I will set him in safeTY from | him that | puffeth at | him.

6 The words of the LORD are | pure | words; ‖ as silver tried in a furnace of EARTH, | purified | seven | times.

12. *W. Russell.*

7 Thou shalt KEEP | them, O | Lord, ‖ thou shalt preserve them from THIS | gener|ation for | ever.

8 The wicked WALK on | every | side, ‖ WHEN the | vilest | men are-ex|alted.
                                                Glory be, etc.

PSALM XIII.

HOW long wilt thou forget ME, O | Lord? for | ever? ‖ how long wilt THOU | hide thy | face from | me?

2 How long shall I take counsel in my soul, having sorrow in MY | heart | daily? ‖ how long shall mine enemy BE ex|alted | over | me?

3 Consider and hear ME, O | Lord my | God : ‖ lighten mine eyes, lest I | sleep the | sleep of | death;

4 Lest mine enemy say, I HAVE pre|vailed a|gainst him ; ‖ and those that trouble ME re|joice when | I am | moved.

5 But I have trustED | in thy | mercy; ‖ my heart SHALL re|joice in | thy sal|vation.

6 I will SING | unto the | Lord, ‖ because he hath DEALT | bounti|fully with | me.
                                                  Glory be, etc.

PSALM XIV.

THE fool hath said in his HEART, There | is no | God. ‖ They are corrupt; they have done abominable works; THERE is | none that | doeth | good.

2 The Lord looked down from heaven upON the | children of | men, ‖ to see if there were any that did UNder|stand, and seek | God

13. Dr. Cooke.

3 They are ALL | gone a|side; || they are all together become filthy: there is NONE that | doeth good, | no, not | one.

4 Have all the workers of iniquiTY | no | knowledge? || who eat up my people as they eat bread, and CALL | not up|on the | Lord.

5 There were THEY in | great | fear: || for God is in the genER|ation | of the | righteous.

6 Ye have shamed the counSEL | of the | poor, || beCAUSE the | Lord | is his | refuge.

7 Oh that the salvation of Israel were COME | out of | Zion ! || when the Lord bringeth back the captivity of his people, Jacob shall reJOICE, and | Israel | shall be | glad.   GLORY BE, ETC.

PSALM XV.

LORD, who shall ABIDE | in thy | tabernacle? || who shall DWELL | in thy | holy | hill?

2 He that walketh uprightLY, and | worketh | righteousness, || and speakETH the | truth | in his | heart.

3 He that backbiteth not with his tongue, nor doeth eVIL | to his | neighbour, || nor taketh UP a re|proach a|gainst his | neighbour.

4 In whose eyes a vile person is contemned; but he honoureth THEM that | fear the | Lord. || He that sweareth to his OWN | hurt, and | changeth | not.

5 He that putteth not out his money to usury, nor taketh reWARD a|gainst the | innocent. || He that doeth THESE | things shall | never be | moved.   GLORY BE, ETC.

14.

H. Purcell.

PSALM XVI.

PRESERVE | me, O | God: ‖ for in THEE | do I | put my | trust.

2 O my soul, thou hast said unto the Lord, THOU | art my | Lord: ‖ my goodNESS ex|tendeth | not to | thee;

3 But to the saints that ARE | in the | earth, ‖ and to the excelLENT, in | whom is | all my-de|light.

4 Their sorrows shall be multiplied that hasten afTER an-| other | god: ‖ their drink-offerings of blood will I not offer, nor take up THEIR | names in|to my | lips.

5 The Lord is the portion of mine inheriTANCE and | of my | cup : ‖ THOU main|tainest | my | lot.

6 The lines are fallen unto ME in | pleasant | places; ‖ YEA, I | have a | goodly | heritage.

7 I will bless the Lord, who HATH | given me | counsel; ‖ my reins also instruct ME | in the | night-|seasons.

8 I have set the Lord alWAYS be|fore | me: ‖ because he is at my right HAND, | I shall | not be | moved.

9 Therefore my heart is glad, and MY | glory re|joiceth; ‖ my FLESH | also shall | rest in | hope:

10 For thou wilt not LEAVE my | soul in | hell; ‖ neither wilt thou suffer thine HOLY | One to | see cor|ruption.

11 Thou wilt show ME the | path of | life: ‖ in thy presence is fulness of joy; at thy right hand there ARE | pleasures for | ever|more.

GLORY BE, ETC.

15. *Battishill.*

PSALM XVII.

HEAR the | right, O | Lord, ‖ attend unto my cry, give ear unto my prayer, that goeth NOT | out of | feigned | lips.

2 Let my sentence come FORTH | from thy | presence; ‖ let thine eyes beHOLD the | things | that are | equal.

3 Thou hast proved mine heart; thou hast visited ME | in the | night; ‖ thou hast tried me, and shalt find nothing: I am purposed that MY | mouth shall | not trans|gress.

4 ConcernING the | works of | men, ‖ by the word of thy lips I have kept me FROM the | paths of | the de|stroyer.

5 Hold up my goINGS | in thy | paths, ‖ that MY | footsteps | slip | not.

6 I have called upon thee; for thou wilt HEAR | me, O | God: ‖ incline thine ear unTO | me, and | hear my | speech.

7 Show thy marvelLOUS | loving-|kindness, ‖ O thou that savest by thy right hand them which put their trust in THEE from | those that | rise up-a|gainst-them.

8 Keep me as the apPLE | of the | eye, ‖ hide me unDER the | shadow | of thy | wings,

9 From the wickED | that op|press-me, ‖ from my deadly eneMIES, who | compass | me a|bout.

10 They are enclosED in | their own | fat: ‖ WITH their | mouth they | speak | proudly.

11 They have now compassed US | in our | steps: ‖ they have set their EYES | bowing | down to the | earth;

12 Like as a lion that is greeDY | of his | prey, ‖ and as it were a young liON | lurking in | secret | places.

16.   *Dr. C. Gibbons.*

13 Arise, O Lord; disappoint HIM, | cast him | down: || deliver my soul FROM the | wicked, which | is thy | sword;

14 From men which are thy hand, O Lord, from men of the world, which have their portion in this life, and whose belly thou fillEST with | thy hid | treasure: || they are full of children, and leave the rest of THEIR | substance | to their | babes.

15 As for me, I will behold thy FACE in | righteous|ness: || I shall be satisFIED, when | I a|wake, with-thy | likeness.

GLORY BE, ETC.

PSALM XVIII.

I WILL | love | thee, || O | Lord, | my | strength.

2 The Lord is my rock, and my forTRESS, and | my de-|liverer; || my God, my strength, in whom I will trust; my buckler, and the horn of MY sal|vation, and | my high | tower.

3 I will call upon the Lord, who is worTHY | to be | praised:|| so shall I be | saved | from mine | enemies.

4 The sorrows of DEATH | compassed | me, || and the floods of ungodLY | men made | me a|fraid.

5 The sorrows of hell compassED | me a|bout; || the SNARES of | death pre|vented | me.

6 In my distress I called upon the Lord, and CRIED | unto my | God: || he heard my voice out of his temple, and my cry came before HIM, | even | into his | ears.

7 Then the EARTH | shook and | trembled; || the foundations also of the hills moved and were shakEN, be|cause | he was | wroth.

17. *John Weldon.*

8 There went up a SMOKE | out-of his | nostrils, ‖ and fire out of his mouth devourED: | coals were | kindled | by-it.

9 He bowed the heavens alSO, and | came | down: ‖ AND | darkness was | under his | feet.

10 And he rode upon a cherUB, | and did | fly; ‖ yea, he did FLY up|on the | wings of-the | wind.

11 He made darkNESS his | secret | place; ‖ his pavilion round about him were dark waTERS and | thick clouds | of the | skies.

12 At the brightness that was before HIM his | thick clouds | passed, ‖ HAIL-|stones and | coals of | fire.

13 The Lord also thundered in the heavens, and the HIGHEST | gave his | voice; ‖ HAIL-|stones and | coals of | fire.

14 Yea, he sent out his arROWS, and | scattered | them; ‖ and he shot out lightNINGS, | and dis|comfited | them.

15 Then the chanNELS of | waters were | seen, ‖ and the foundations of the world were discovered at thy rebuke, O Lord, at the blast OF the | breath of | thy | nostrils.

16 He SENT | from a|bove, ‖ he took me, he drew ME | out of | many | waters.

17 He delivered me from my strong enemy, and from THEM which | hated | me: ‖ for THEY | were too | strong for | me.

18 They prevented me in the DAY of | my ca|lamity: ‖ BUT the | Lord | was my | stay.

19 He brought me forth also inTO a | large | place; ‖ he delivered me, beCAUSE | he de|lighted in | me.

20 The Lord rewarded me according to MY | righteous|ness; ‖

18. *Battishill.*

according to the cleanness of my HANDS | hath he | recompensed | me.

21 For I have kept the WAYS | of the | Lord, ‖ and have not wickedLY de|parted | from my | God.

22 For all his judgMENTS | were be|fore-me, ‖ and I did not PUT a|way his | statutes | from-me.

23 I was also upRIGHT be|fore | him; ‖ and I KEPT my·| self from | mine in|iquity.

24 Therefore hath the Lord recompensed me according to MY | righteous|ness, ‖ according to the cleanNESS | of my | hands in-his | eyesight.

25 With the merciful thou wilt show thySELF | merci-| ful; ‖ with an upright man thou WILT | show thy|self up|right;

26 With the pure thou wilt SHOW | thyself | pure; ‖ and with the froward THOU | wilt show | thyself | froward.

27 For thou wilt SAVE the af|flicted | people; ‖ BUT | wilt bring | down high | looks.

28 For THOU wilt | light my | candle: ‖ the Lord my GOD | will en|lighten my | darkness.

29 For by thee I have RUN | through a | troop; ‖ and by my God have I | leaped | over a | wall.

30 As for GOD, his | way is | perfect: ‖ the word of the Lord is tried: he is a buckler to ALL | those that | trust in | him.

31 For who is GOD | save the | Lord? ‖ or WHO | is-a rock | save our | God?

19.

Rev. W. Tucker.

32 It is God that girdETH | me with | strength, ‖ AND | maketh | my way | perfect.

33 He maketh my FEET like | hinds' | feet, ‖ and setTETH | me-upon | my high | places.

34 He teachETH my | hands to | war, ‖ so that a bow of STEEL is | broken | by mine | arms.

35 Thou hast also given me the SHIELD of | thy sal|vation: ‖ and thy right hand hath holden me up, and THY | gentleness hath | made me | great.

36 Thou hast enlarged my STEPS | under | me, ‖ THAT | my feet | did not | slip.

37 I have pursued mine enemies, and oVER|taken | them; ‖ neither did I turn aGAIN | till they | were con|sumed.

38 I have wounded them, that they were NOT | able to | rise: ‖ THEY are | fallen | under my | feet.

39 For thou hast girded me with STRENGTH | unto the | battle: ‖ thou hast subdued under ME | those that | rose up-a-|gainst-me.

40 Thou hast also given me the NECKS | of mine | enemies; ‖ that I MIGHT de|stroy | them that | hate-me.

41 They cried, but THERE was | none to | save-them; ‖ even unto the LORD, | but he | answered them | not.

42 Then did I beat them small as the DUST be|fore the | wind: ‖ I did cast them OUT | as the | dirt in-the | streets.

43 Thou hast delivered me from the strivings of the people; and thou hast made me the HEAD | of the | heathen: ‖ a people whom I | have not | known shall | serve-me.

20. *Dr. W. Hayes.*

---

44 As soon as they hear of ME, they | shall o|bey-me: || the strangers SHALL sub|mit them|selves unto | me.

45 The stranGERS shall | fade a|way, || and be aFRAID | out of | their close | places.

46 The Lord liveth; and blessED | be my | rock; || and let the God of MY sal|vation | be ex|alted.

47 It is God THAT a|vengeth | me, || and subduETH the | people | under | me.

48 He delivereth me from mine enemies; yea, thou liftest me up above those that RISE | up a|gainst-me: || thou hast delivered ME | from the | violent | man.

49 Therefore will I give thanks unto thee, O LORD, a|mong the | heathen, || and SING | praises | unto thy | name.

50 Great deliverance giveth HE | to his | king; || and showeth mercy to his anointed, to David, and TO his | seed for | ever-|more. GLORY BE, ETC.

PSALM XIX.

THE heavens deCLARE the | glory of | God; || and the firma-MENT | showeth his | handy-|work.

2 Day unto DAY | uttereth | speech, || and NIGHT | unto night | showeth | knowledge.

3 There is NO | speech nor | language || WHERE their | voice | is not | heard.

4 Their line is gone OUT through | all the | earth, || and their WORDS | to the | end of-the | world.

5 In them hath he set a tabernaCLE | for the | sun; || which

21.

W. Hine.

is as a bridegroom coming out of his chamber, and rejoiceth as a STRONG | man to | run a | race.

6 His going forth is from the end of the heaven, and his circuit unTO the | ends of | it: || and there is nothing HID | from the | heat there|of.

7 The law of the Lord is perFECT, con|verting the | soul: || the testimony of the Lord is SURE, | making | wise the | simple.

8 The statutes of the Lord are RIGHT, re|joicing the | heart: || the commandment of the LORD is | pure, en|lightening the | eyes.

9 The fear of the Lord is CLEAN, en|during for | ever: || the judgments of the Lord are TRUE and | righteous | alto|gether.

10 More to be desired are they than gold, YEA, than | much fine | gold; || sweeter also than hoNEY, | and the | honey-|comb.

11 Moreover by them is THY | servant | warned: || and in keeping of THEM | there is | great re|ward.

12 Who can UNder|stand his | errors? || cleanse THOU | me from | secret | faults.

13 Keep back thy servant also from presumptuous sins; let them not have dominION | over | me: || then shall I be upright, and I shall be innoCENT | from the | great trans|gression.

14 Let the words of my mouth, and the meditation of my heart, be acceptaBLE | in thy | sight, || O LORD, my | strength, and | my re|deemer.

GLORY BE, ETC.

PSALM XX.

THE Lord hear thee IN the | day of | trouble; || the name of the GOD of | Jacob de|fend | thee.

22. *Dr. Crotch.*

2 Send thee help FROM the | sanctu|ary, || AND | strengthen thee | out of | Zion.

3 RememBER | all thy | offerings, || AND ac|cept thy | burnt-| sacrifice.

4 Grant thee accordING to | thine own | heart, || AND ful|fil | all thy | counsel.

5 We will rejoice in thy salvation, and in the name of our God we will SET | up our | banners: || the LORD ful|fil all | thy pe|titions.

6 Now know I that the Lord savETH | his a|nointed: || he will hear him from his holy heaven with the savING | strength of | his right | hand.

7 Some trust in chariOTS, and | some in | horses: || but we will rememBER the | name of-the | Lord our | God.

8 They are BROUGHT | down and | fallen: || but we ARE | risen, and | stand up|right.

9 SAVE, | ... | Lord: || let the KING | hear us | when we | call.

GLORY BE, ETC.

PSALM XXI.

23. *Dr. P. Hayes.*

4 He asked life of thee, and THOU | gavest it | him, ‖ even LENGTH of | days for | ever and | ever.

5 His glory is GREAT in | thy sal|vation: ‖ honour and majesTY | hast thou | laid up|on-him.

6 For thou hast made him MOST | blessed for | ever: ‖ thou hast made him exceeding GLAD | with thy | counte|nance.

7 For the king trustETH | in the | Lord; ‖ and through the mercy of the most HIGH | he shall | not be | moved.

8 Thine hand shall find OUT | all thine | enemies; ‖ thy right HAND shall | find out | those that | hate-thee.

9 Thou shalt make them as a fiery oven in the TIME | of thine | anger: ‖ the Lord shall swallow them up in his wrath, AND the | fire shall-de|vour | them.

10 Their fruit shalt thou deSTROY | from the | earth, ‖ and their seed FROM a|mong the | children of | men.

11 For they intendED | evil a|gainst-thee: ‖ they imagined a mischievous device, which they are NOT | able | to per|form.

12 Therefore shalt thou make THEM | turn their | back, ‖ when thou shalt make ready thine arrows upon thy STRINGS a-| gainst the | face of | them.

13 Be thou exalted, LORD, in | thine own | strength: ‖ so will WE | sing and | praise thy | power.   GLORY BE, ETC.

PSALM XXII.

MY God, my God, why hast THOU for|saken | me? ‖ why art thou so far from helping ME, and | from the | words of-my | roaring?

24. *Kelway.*

2 O my God, I cry in the day-time, but THOU | hearest | not; ‖ and in the NIGHT-|season, and | am not | silent.

3 BUT | thou art | holy, ‖ O thou that inhabitEST the | praises of | Isra|el.

4 Our faTHERS | trusted in | thee: ‖ they trusted, and THOU | didst de|liver | them.

5 They cried unto THEE, and | were de|livered: ‖ they trusted in THEE, | and were | not con|founded.

6 But I am a WORM, and | no | man; ‖ a reproach of men, AND de|spised | of the | people.

7 All they that see ME | laugh-me to | scorn : ‖ they shoot out the LIP, they | shake the | head, | saying,

8 He trusted on the Lord that he WOULD de|liver | him: ‖ let him deliver him, seeING | he de|lighted in | him.

9 But thou art he that took ME | out-of the | womb: ‖ thou didst make me hope when I WAS up|on my | mother's | breasts.

10 I was cast upon THEE | from the | womb: ‖ thou art my GOD | from my | mother's | belly.

11 Be not far from ME; for | trouble is | near; ‖ FOR | there is | none to | help.

12 Many BULLS have | compassed | me: ‖ strong bulls of BaSHAN | have be|set me | round.

13 They gaped upon ME | with their | mouths, ‖ as a raven-ING | and a | roaring | lion.

14 I am poured out like water, and all my BONES are | out of | joint: ‖ my heart is like wax; it is meltED | in the | midst of - my | bowels.

25.   *Dr. Aldrich.*

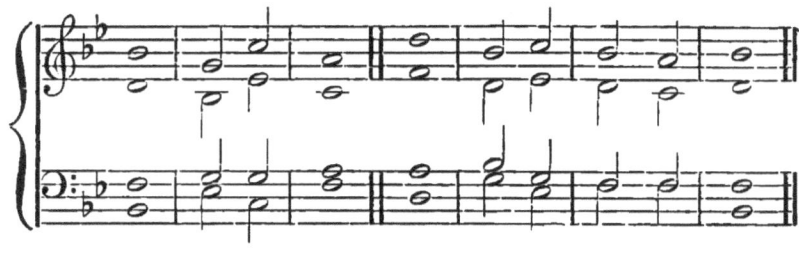

15 My strength is dried up like a potsherd; and my tongue cleavETH | to my | jaws; ‖ and thou hast brought ME | into the | dust of | death.

16 For dogs have compassed me: the assembly of the wicked HAVE in|closed | me: ‖ they pierCED my | hands | and my | feet.

17 I may TELL | all my | bones: ‖ THEY | look and | stare up|on - me.

18 They part my garMENTS a|mong | them, ‖ and CAST | lots up|on my | vesture.

19 But be not thou FAR from | me, O | Lord: ‖ O my STRENGTH, | haste | thee to | help - me.

20 Deliver my SOUL | from the | sword; ‖ my darling FROM the | power | of the | dog.

21 Save me FROM the | lion's | mouth: ‖ for thou hast heard me FROM the | horns | of the | unicorns.

22 I will declare thy NAME | unto my | brethren: ‖ in the midst of the congregaTION | will I | praise | thee.

23 Ye that fear the Lord, praise him; all ye the seed of JaCOB, | glorify | him; ‖ and fear him, ALL | ye the | seed of | Israel.

24 For he hath not despised nor abhorred the affliction of the afflicted, neither hath he HID his | face from | him; ‖ but when he CRIED | unto | him, he | heard.

25 My praise shall be of thee in the GREAT | congre|gation: ‖ I will pay my VOWS be|fore | them that | fear-him.

26 The meek shall eat and be satisfied: they shall PRAISE the | Lord that | seek-him: ‖ YOUR | heart shall | live for | ever.

27 All the ends of the world shall remember and TURN | unto

26.

the | Lord : ‖ and all the kindreds of the naTIONS shall | worship be|fore | thee.

28 For the kingDOM | is the | Lord's : ‖ and he IS the | governor a|mong the | nations.

29 All they that be fat upon EARTH shall | eat and | worship :‖ all they that go down to the dust shall bow before him: and none can KEEP a|live his | own | soul.

30 A SEED shall | serve | him; ‖ it shall be accounted to the LORD | for a | gener|ation.

31 They shall come, and shall declare his righteousness unto a peoPLE that | shall be | born, ‖ THAT | he hath | done | this.

GLORY BE, ETC.

PSALM XXIII.

THE LORD | is my | shepherd; ‖ I | shall | not | want.

2 He maketh me to lie DOWN in | green | pastures: ‖ he leadeth ME be|side the | still | waters.

3 HE re|storeth my | soul: ‖ he leadeth me in the paths of righteousNESS | for his | name's | sake.

4 Yea, though I walk through the valley of the shadow of death, I will | fear no | evil: ‖ for thou art with me; thy rod and THY staff they | comfort | me.

5 Thou preparest a table before me in the presENCE | of mine enemies: ‖ thou anointest my HEAD with | oil; my | cup runneth over.

6 Surely goodness and mercy shall follow me all the DAYS | of my | life: ‖ and I will dwell IN the | house of-the | Lord for | ever.

GLORY BE, ETC.

27. *Battishill.*

PSALM XXIV.

THE earth is the LORD'S, and the | fulness there|of; || the WORLD, and | they that | dwell there|in.

2 For he hath founded IT up|on the | seas, || and establishED | it up|on the | floods.

3 Who shall ascend into the HILL | of the | Lord? || and who shall STAND | in his | holy | place?

4 He that hath clean HANDS, and a | pure | heart; || who hath not lifted up his soul unto vaniTY, nor | sworn de|ceitful|ly.

5 He shall receive the blessING | from the | Lord, || and righteousness FROM the | God of | his sal|vation.

6 This is the generaTION of | them that | seek - him, || THAT | seek thy | face, O | Jacob.

7 Lift up your HEADS, | O ye | gates; || and be ye lift up, ye everlasting doors; and the KING of | glory | shall come | in.

8 Who IS this | King of | glory? || The Lord strong and MIGHTY, the | Lord | mighty in | battle.

9 Lift up your HEADS, | O ye | gates; || even lift them up, ye everlasting doors; and the KING of | glory | shall come | in.

10 Who IS this | King of | glory? || The Lord of HOSTS, | he is-the | King of | glory.   GLORY BE, ETC.

PSALM XXV.

UNTO | thee, O | Lord, || DO | I lift | up my | soul.

2 O my GOD, I | trust in | thee: || let me not be ashamed; let not mine eneMIES | triumph | over | me.

3 Yea, let none that wait on THEE | be a|shamed: || let them be ashamED which | transgress | without | cause.

4 Show me THY | ways, O | Lord; || TEACH | me | thy | paths.

5 Lead me IN thy | truth, and | teach - me : || for thou art the God of my salvation; on THEE | do I | wait all - the | day.

6 Remember, O Lord, thy tender mercies and THY | loving-| kindnesses; || for THEY | have been | ever of | old.

7 Remember not the sins of my YOUTH, nor | my trans-| gressions: || according to thy mercy remember thou me for THY | goodness' | sake, O | Lord.

8 Good and upRIGHT | is the | Lord: || therefore will he TEACH | sinners | in the | way.

9 The meek will HE | guide in | judgment; || and the MEEK | will he | teach his | way.

10 All the paths of the LORD are | mercy and | truth || unto such as keep his coveNANT | and his | testi|monies.

11 For thy NAME'S | sake, O | Lord, || pardon MINE in-| iquity; | for it - is | great.

12 What man is HE that | feareth the | Lord? || him shall he teach IN the | way that | he shall | choose:

13 His SOUL shall | dwell at | ease; || and his SEED | shall in|herit the | earth.

14 The secret of the Lord IS with | them that | fear - him; |' and HE will | show | them his | covenant.

15 Mine eyes are evER | toward the | Lord; || for he shall PLUCK my | feet out | of the | net.

16 Turn thee unto me, and HAVE | mercy up|on - me; || for I am | desolate | and af|flicted.

17 The troubles of my HEART | are en|larged: || O bring thou ME | out of | my dis|tresses.

18 Look upon mine afflicTION | and my | pain; || AND for-| give | all my | sins.

19 Consider mine eneMIES; for | they are | many; || and THEY | hate-me with | cruel | hatred.

20 O keep my soul, AND de|liver | me: || let me not be ashamed; for I | put my | trust in | thee.

21 Let integrity and uprightNESS pre|serve | me; || FOR | I | wait on | thee.

22 Redeem IsraEL, | O | God, || OUT of | all his | trou|bles.

GLORY BE, ETC.

PSALM XXVI.

JUDGE me, O Lord; for I have walkED in | mine in|tegrity: || I have trusted also in the LORD; | therefore I | shall not | slide.

2 Examine ME, O | Lord, and | prove - me; || TRY my | reins| and my | heart.

3 For thy loving-kindness IS be|fore mine | eyes; || and I have | walked | in thy | truth.

4 I have not SAT with | vain | persons, || neither will I | go in | with dis|semblers.

5 I have hated the congregaTION of | evil-|doers; || AND will not | sit with-the | wicked.

30.   *Langdon.*

6 I will WASH mine | hands in | innocency: ‖ so will I com-PASS thine | altar, | O | Lord;

7 That I may publish with the VOICE | of thanks|giving, ‖ and TELL of | all thy | wondrous | works.

8 Lord, I have loved the habitaTION | of thy | house, ‖ and the PLACE | where thine | honour | dwelleth.

9 Gather NOT my | soul with | sinners, ‖ NOR my | life with | bloody | men;

10 In WHOSE | hands is | mischief, ‖ and their RIGHT | hand is | full of | bribes.

11 But as for me, I will WALK in | mine in|tegrity: ‖ redeem me, AND be | merciful | unto | me.

12 My foot standeth IN an | even | place: ‖ in the congrega-TIONS | will I | bless the | Lord.   GLORY BE, ETC.

PSALM XXVII.

THE Lord is my light and my salvaTION; | whom shall I fear? ‖ the Lord is the strength of my life; of WHOM | shall I | be a|fraid?

2 When the wicked, even mine eneMIES | and my | foes, ‖ came upon me to eat UP my | flesh, they | stumbled and | fell.

3 Though an host should encamp against me, my HEART | shall not | fear: ‖ though war should rise against ME, in | this will | I be | confident.

4 One thing have I desired of the Lord, THAT will | I seek | after; ‖ that I may dwell in the house of the Lord all the days of

31.

my life, to behold the beauty of the Lord, and TO in|quire | in his | temple.

5 For in the time of trouble he shall hide ME in | his pa|vilion:‖ in the secret of his tabernacle shall he hide me; he shall set ME | up up|on a | rock.

6 And now shall mine head be lifted up above mine eneMIES | round a|bout-me:‖ therefore will I offer in his tabernacle sacrifices of joy; I will sing, yea, I will SING | praises | unto the | Lord.

7 Hear, O Lord, when I CRY | with my | voice:‖ have mercy alSO up|on-me, and | answer | me.

8 When thou SAIDST, | Seek ye-my | face; ‖ my heart said unto THEE, Thy | face, Lord, | will I | seek.

9 Hide not thy face far from me; put not thy serVANT a|way in | anger:‖ thou hast been my help; leave me not, neither forsake ME, O | God of | my sal|vation.

10 When my father and my moTHER for|sake | me, ‖ THEN the | Lord will | take me | up.

11 Teach ME thy | way, O | Lord, ‖ and lead me in a plain PATH, be|cause | of mine | enemies.

12 Deliver me not over unto the WILL | of mine | enemies:‖ for false witnesses are risen up against ME, and | such as | breathe out | cruelty.

13 I had fainted, unless I had believed to see the goodNESS | of the | Lord ‖ IN the | land | of the | living.

14 WAIT | on the | Lord: ‖ be of good courage, and he shall strengthen thine HEART: | wait, I | say, on-the | Lord.

GLORY BE, ETC.

32. *Dr. Alcock.*

PSALM XXVIII.

UNTO thee will I cry, O Lord my rock; be NOT | silent to | me: ‖ lest, if thou be silent to me, I become like THEM that | go down | into the | pit.

2 Hear the voice of my supplications, when I CRY | unto | thee, ‖ when I lift up my HANDS | toward thy | holy | oracle.

3 Draw me not away with the wicked, and with the workERS | of in|iquity, ‖ which speak peace to their neighBOURS, but | mischief is | in their | hearts.

4 Give them according to their deeds, and according to the wickedNESS of | their en|deavours: ‖ give them after the work of their hands; renDER | to them | their de|sert.

5 Because they regard not the works of the Lord, nor the operaTION | of his | hands, ‖ he shall destroy THEM, | and not | build them | up.

6 BlessED | be the | Lord, ‖ because he hath heard the VOICE | of my | suppli|cations.

7 The Lord is my strength and my shield; my heart trusted in HIM, and | I am | helped: ‖ therefore my heart greatly rejoiceth; and WITH my | song will - I | praise | him.

8 The LORD | is their | strength, ‖ and he is the savING | strength of | his a|nointed.

9 Save thy people, and BLESS | thine in|heritance: ‖ feed them alSO, and | lift them | up for | ever.

GLORY BE, ETC.

33.  *A. L. Peace.*

PSALM XXIX.

GIVE unto the LORD, | O ye | mighty, || give unTO the | Lord | glory and | strength.

2 Give unto the Lord the glory DUE | unto his | name: || worship the LORD | in the | beauty of | holiness.

3 The voice of the LORD is up|on the | waters: || the God of glory thundereth: the LORD | is-upon | many | waters.

4 The VOICE of the | Lord is | powerful; || the voice of the LORD is | full of | majes|ty.

5 The voice of the LORD | breaketh the | cedars; || yea, the LORD | breaketh the | cedars of | Lebanon.

6 He maketh them also to SKIP | like a | calf; || Lebanon and SiriON | like a | young | unicorn.

7 The VOICE | of the | Lord || DI|videth the | flames of | fire.

8 The voice of the Lord shakETH the | wilder|ness; || the Lord shakETH the | wilder|ness of | Kadesh.

9 The voice of the Lord maketh the hinds to calve, AND dis-| covereth the | forests; || and in his temple doth eveRY | one speak | of his | glory.

10 The Lord sitTETH up|on the | flood; || yea, the LORD | sitteth | King for | ever.

11 The Lord will give STRENGTH | unto his | people; || the LORD will | bless his | people with | peace.   GLORY BE, ETC.

PSALM XXX.

I WILL exTOL | thee, O | Lord; || for thou hast lifted me up, and hast not made my FOES | to re|joice over | me.

34.   *Dr. Croft.*

2 O Lord my God, I CRIED | unto | thee, ‖ AND | thou hast | healed | me.

3 O Lord, thou hast brought up my SOUL | from the | grave; ‖ thou hast kept me alive, that I should NOT | go down | to the | pit.

4 Sing unto the Lord, O ye | saints of | his, ‖ and give thanks at the rememBRANCE | of his | holi|ness.

5 For his anger endureth but a moment; IN his | favour is | life: ‖ weeping may endure for a night, but JOY | cometh | in the | morning.

6 And in MY pros|perity I | said, ‖ I SHALL | never | be | moved.

7 Lord, by thy favour thou hast made my mounTAIN to | stand | strong: ‖ thou didst HIDE thy | face, and | I was | troubled.

8 I CRIED to | thee, O | Lord; ‖ and unto the LORD | I made | suppli|cation.

9 What profit is there in my blood, when I go DOWN | to the | pit? ‖ shall the dust praise THEE? shall | it de|clare thy | truth?

10 Hear, O Lord, and HAVE | mercy up|on - me: ‖ LORD, | be | thou my | helper.

11 Thou hast turned for me my mournING | into | dancing: ‖ thou hast put off my sackCLOTH, and | girded | me with | gladness;

12 To the end that my glory may sing praise to THEE, and | not be | silent. ‖ O Lord my God, I will give THANKS | unto | thee for | ever.   GLORY BE, ETC.

35. *Travers.*

PSALM XXXI.

IN thee, O Lord, do I | put my | trust; || let me never be ashamed: deliver ME | in thy | righteous|ness.

2 Bow down thine ear to ME; de|liver me | speedily: || be thou my strong rock, for AN | house of - de|fence to | save - me.

3 For thou art my ROCK | and my | fortress; || therefore for thy name's SAKE | lead - me, and | guide | me.

4 Pull me out of the net that they have LAID | privily for | me: || FOR | thou | art my | strength.

5 Into thine hand I com|mit my | spirit: || thou hast redeemed ME, | O Lord | God of | truth.

6 I have hated them that reGARD | lying | vanities: || BUT I trust | in the | Lord.

7 I will be glad and reJOICE | in thy | mercy: || for thou hast considered my trouble; THOU hast | known my | soul in - ad-| versities;

8 And hast not shut me up into the HAND | of the | enemy: || thou hast set my FEET | in a | large | room.

9 Have mercy upon me, O Lord, for I | am in | trouble: || mine eye is consumed with GRIEF, | yea, my | soul and-my | belly.

10 For my life is spent with grief, AND my | years with | sighing: || my strength faileth because of mine iniquiTY, | and my | bones are-con|sumed.

11 I was a reproach among all mine enemies, but especially among my neighbours, and a FEAR to | mine ac|quaintance: || they that did SEE | me with|out fled | from-me.

36.   Turle.

12 I am forgotten as a dead MAN | out of | mind; ‖ I am | like a | broken | vessel.

13 For I have heard the slander of many: fear WAS on | every | side: ‖ while they took counsel together against me, they devisED to | take a|way my | life.

14 But I trustED in | thee, O | Lord: ‖ I | said, Thou | art my | God.

15 My TIMES are | in thy | hand: ‖ deliver me from the hand of mine enemies, AND from | them that | perse|cute-me.

16 Make thy face to SHINE up|on thy | servant: ‖ save ME | for thy | mercies' | sake.

17 Let me not be ashamed, O Lord; for I HAVE | called up|on-thee: ‖ let the wicked be ashamed, and let THEM be | silent | in the | grave.

18 Let the lying LIPS be | put to | silence; ‖ which speak grievous things proudly AND con|temptuously-a|gainst the | righteous.

19 Oh how great is thy goodness, which thou hast laid UP for | them that | fear-thee; ‖ which thou hast wrought for them that trust in THEE be|fore the | sons of | men!

20 Thou shalt hide them in the secret of thy presence FROM the | pride of | man: ‖ thou shalt keep them secretly in a pavilION | from the | strife of | tongues.

21 BlessED | be the | Lord; ‖ for he hath showed me his marvellous kindNESS | in a | strong | city.

22 For I said in my haste, I am cut off FROM be|fore thine | eyes: ‖ nevertheless thou heardest the voice of my supplicaTIONS | when I | cried unto | thee.

37. *Turner.*

23 O love the LORD, all | ye his | saints: || for the Lord pre‑serveth the faithful, and plentifulLY re|wardeth‑the | proud | doer.

24 Be of good courage, and HE shall | strengthen your | heart, || ALL | ye that | hope in‑the | Lord.   GLORY BE, ETC.

PSALM XXXII.

BLESSED is he whose transgresSION | is for|given, || WHOSE | sin | is | covered.

2 Blessed is the man unto whom the Lord imputETH | not in|iquity, || and in WHOSE | spirit there | is no | guile.

3 WHEN | I kept | silence, || my bones waxed old through MY | roaring | all‑the day | long.

4 For day and night thy HAND was | heavy up|on‑me: || my moisture is turnED | into the | drought of | summer.

5 I acknowledged my sin unto thee, and mine iniquiTY have | I not | hid. || I said, I will confess my transgressions unto the Lord; and thou forgavest THE in|iquity | of my | sin.

6 For this shall every one that is godly pray unto thee in a time when THOU | mayest be | found: || surely in the floods of great waters THEY shall | not come | nigh unto | him.

7 Thou art my hiding‑place; thou shalt preSERVE | me from | trouble; || thou shalt compass ME a|bout with | songs of‑de|liver‑ance.

8 I will instruct thee, and teach thee in the WAY which | thou shalt | go: || I will | guide thee | with mine | eye.

9 Be ye not as the horse, or as the mule, which have NO |

38. *Dr. Aldrich.*

under|standing; ‖ whose mouth must be held in with bit and briDLE, lest | they come | near unto | thee.

10 Many sorrows SHALL be | to the | wicked: ‖ but he that trusteth in the Lord, merCY shall | compass | him a|bout.

11 Be glad in the LORD, and re|joice, ye | righteous: ‖ and shout for JOY, all | ye that-are | upright in | heart.

GLORY BE, ETC.

PSALM XXXIII.

REJOICE in the LORD, | O ye | righteous; ‖ for PRAISE is | comely | for the | upright.

2 PRAISE the | Lord with | harp: ‖ sing unto him with the psaltery AND an | instrument | of ten | strings.

3 Sing unto HIM a | new | song; ‖ play skilfulLY | with a | loud | noise.

4 For the word OF the | Lord is | right; ‖ and ALL his | works are | done in | truth.

5 He loveth rightEOUS|ness and | judgment: ‖ the earth is full OF the | goodness | of the | Lord.

6 By the word of the Lord WERE the | heavens | made; ‖ and all the host of THEM | by the | breath of-his | mouth.

7 He gathereth the waters of the sea togethER | as an | heap: ‖ he layETH | up the | depth in | storehouses.

8 Let all the EARTH | fear the | Lord: ‖ let all the inhabitants of the WORLD | stand in | awe of | him:

9 For he SPAKE, and | it was | done; ‖ he commandED, | and it | stood | fast.

39. *Rev. W. H. Havergal.*

10 The Lord bringeth the counsel OF the | heathen to | nought: ‖ he maketh the devices OF the | people of | none ef|fect.

11 The counsel of the LORD | standeth for | ever, ‖ the thoughts OF his | heart to | all gener|ations.

12 Blessed is the nation whose GOD | is the | Lord; ‖ and the people whom he hath chosEN | for his | own in|heritance.

13 The LORD | looketh from | heaven; ‖ he beholdETH | all the | sons of | men.

14 From the place of HIS | habi|tation ‖ he looketh upon ALL the in|habitants | of the | earth.

15 He fashionETH their | hearts a|like; ‖ HE con|sidereth | all their | works.

16 There is no king saved by the multiTUDE | of an | host: ‖ a mighty man is NOT de|livered | by much | strength.

17 An horse is a VAIN | thing for | safety: ‖ neither shall he delivER | any by | his great | strength.

18 Behold, the eye of the Lord is upON | them that | fear-him, ‖ upON | them that | hope in-his | mercy;

19 To delivER their | soul from | death, ‖ and to KEEP | them a|live in | famine.

20 Our soul waitETH | for the | Lord: ‖ HE | is our | help and-our | shield.

21 For our heart SHALL re|joice in | him; ‖ because we have trustED | in his | holy | name.

22 Let thy mercy, O LORD, | be up|on-us, ‖ accordING | as we | hope in | thee. GLORY BE, ETC.

40. *Dr. Greene.*

PSALM XXXIV.

I WILL bless the LORD | at all | times: || his praise SHALL con|tinually | be in-my | mouth.

2 My soul shall make her BOAST | in the | Lord: || the humBLE shall | hear there|of, and-be | glad.

3 O magniFY the | Lord with | me, || and let US ex|alt his | name to|gether.

4 I sought the LORD, | and he | heard-me, || and deliverED | me from | all my | fears.

5 They looked unto HIM, | and were | lightened; || and THEIR | faces were | not a|shamed.

6 This poor man cried, AND the | Lord | heard-him, || and saved HIM | out of | all his | troubles.

7 The angEL | of the | Lord || encampeth round about them that fear HIM, | and de|livereth | them.

8 O taste and see THAT the | Lord is | good: || blessed IS the | man that | trusteth in | him.

9 O fear the LORD, | ye his | saints: || for there is NO | want to | them that | fear-him.

10 The young lions do LACK, and | suffer | hunger: || but they that seek the LORD shall | not want | any good | thing.

11 Come, ye children, hearkEN | unto | me; || I will TEACH | you the | fear of-the | Lord.

12 What man is he THAT de|sireth | life, || and loveth many DAYS, | that he | may see | good?

13 KEEP thy | tongue from | evil, || AND thy | lips from | speaking | guile.

41. *Dr. Nares.*

14 Depart from EVIL, | and do | good; ‖ SEEK | peace, | and pur|sue-it.

15 The eyes of the LORD are up|on the | righteous, ‖ and his EARS are | open | unto their | cry.

16 The face of the Lord is against THEM | that do | evil, ‖ to cut off the rememBRANCE | of them | from the | earth.

17 The righteous CRY, and the | Lord | heareth, ‖ and delivereth THEM | out of | all their | troubles.

18 The Lord is nigh unto them that are OF a | broken | heart; ‖ and saveth SUCH as | be of-a | contrite | spirit.

19 Many are the afflicTIONS | of the | righteous: ‖ but the Lord deliverETH | him out | of them | all.

20 He keepETH | all his | bones: ‖ NOT | one of | them is | broken.

21 EVIL shall | slay the | wicked: ‖ and they that HATE the | righteous | shall be | desolate.

22 The Lord redeemETH the | soul of-his | servants: ‖ and none of them that TRUST in | him | shall be | desolate.

GLORY BE, ETC.

PSALM XXXV.

PLEAD my cause, O Lord, with THEM that | strive with | me; ‖ fight aGAINST | them that | fight a|gainst-me.

2 Take HOLD of | shield and | buckler, ‖ AND | stand up | for mine | help.

3 Draw out also the spear, and stop the way against THEM that | persecute | me: ‖ say unto my SOUL, | I am | thy sal|vation.

42. *Dupuis.*

4 Let them be confounded and put to shame that SEEK | after my | soul: ‖ let them be turned back and brought to confuSION | that de|vise my | hurt.

5 Let them be as CHAFF be|fore the | wind: ‖ and let the anGEL | of the | Lord | chase-them.

6 Let their WAY be | dark and | slippery: ‖ and let the angel OF the | Lord | persecute | them.

7 For without cause have they hid for me their NET | in a | pit, ‖ which without cause they HAVE | digged | for my | soul.

8 Let destruction come upon HIM at | una|wares; ‖ and let his net that he hath hid catch himself: into that veRY de|struction | let him | fall.

9 And my soul shall be joyFUL | in the | Lord: ‖ it SHALL re|joice in | his sal|vation.

10 All my bones shall say, Lord, WHO is | like unto | thee, ‖ which deliverest the poor from him that is too strong for him, yea, the poor and the neeDY from | him that | spoileth | him?

11 False witnessES | did rise | up; ‖ they laid to my CHARGE | things that | I know | not.

12 They rewarded ME | evil for | good, ‖ TO the | spoiling | of my | soul.

13 But as for me, when they were SICK, my | clothing was | sackcloth: ‖ I humbled my soul with fasting; and my prayer returnED | into | mine own | bosom.

14 I behaved myself as though he had BEEN my | friend or |

43.

Tallis.

brother: ‖ I bowed down heavily, as ONE that | mourneth | for his | mother.

15 But in mine adversity they rejoiced, and gatherED them-|selves to|gether: ‖ yea, the abjects gathered themselves together against me, and I knew it not; THEY did | tear me,- and | ceased| not:

16 With hypocritiCAL | mockers in | feasts, ‖ they gnashED up|on me | with their | teeth.

17 Lord, how LONG wilt | thou look | on? ‖ rescue my soul from their destrucTIONS, my | darling | from the | lions.

18 I will give thee thanks in the GREAT | congre|gation: ‖ I will PRAISE | thee a|mong much | people.

19 Let not them that are mine enemies wrongfully reJOICE | over | me: ‖ neither let them wink with the EYE that | hate me-with|out a | cause.

20 FOR they | speak not | peace: ‖ but they devise deceitful matters against them that ARE | quiet | in the | land.

21 Yea, they opened their MOUTH | wide a|gainst-me, ‖ and said, AHA, a|ha! our | eye hath | seen-it.

22 This thou hast seen, O LORD: | keep not | silence: ‖ O LORD, | be not | far from | me.

23 Stir up thyself, and aWAKE | to my | judgment, ‖ even unTO my | cause, my | God and-my | Lord.

24 Judge me, O Lord my God, according TO thy | righteous-|ness; ‖ and LET them | not re|joice over | me.

25 Let them not say in their hearts, Ah, SO | would we | have-it: ‖ let them not SAY, | We have | swallowed him | up.

44. *E. J. Hopkins.*

26 Let them be ashamed and brought to confusion together that reJOICE | at mine | hurt: ‖ let them be clothed with shame and dishonour that MAGni|fy them|selves a|gainst-me.

27 Let them shout for joy, and be glad, that faVOUR my righteous | cause: ‖ yea, let them say continually, Let the Lord be magnified, which hath pleasure in the PROS|perity | of his | servant.

28 And my tongue shall speak of THY | righteous|ness ‖ and of THY | praise | all-the day | long.   GLORY BE, ETC.

PSALM XXXVI.

THE transgression of the wicked SAITH with|in my | heart, ‖ that there is no FEAR of | God be|fore his | eyes.

2 For he flattereth himSELF in | his own | eyes, ‖ until his iniquiTY be | found | to be | hateful.

3 The words of his mouth are iniquiTY | and de|ceit: ‖ he hath left off to BE | wise | and-to do | good.

4 He deviseth misCHIEF up|on his | bed; ‖ he setteth himself in a way that is not GOOD; | he ab|horreth not | evil.

5 Thy mercy, O LORD, is | in the | heavens; ‖ and thy faithfulNESS | reacheth | unto the | clouds.

6 Thy righteousness is like the great mountains; thy judgMENTS | are-a great | deep: ‖ O Lord, THOU pre|servest | man and | beast.

7 How excellent is thy lovING-|kindness, O | God! ‖ therefore the children of men put their trust unDER the | shadow | of thy | wings.

45.

Gregorian 1st Tone.

8 They shall be abundantly satisfied with the fatNESS | of thy | house; || and thou shalt make them DRINK of the | river | of thy | pleasures.

9 For with THEE is the | fountain of | life : || in THY | light shall | we see | light.

10 O continue thy loving-kindNESS unto | them that | know-thee; || and thy righteousNESS | to the | upright in | heart.

11 Let not the foot of PRIDE | come a|gainst-me, || and let not the HAND | of the | wicked re|move-me.

12 There are the workers OF in|iquity | fallen: || they are cast DOWN, and shall | not be | able to | rise.

GLORY BE, ETC.

PSALM XXXVII.

FRET not thyself beCAUSE of | evil-|doers, || neither be thou envious aGAINST the | workers | of in|iquity.

2 For they shall soon be cut DOWN | like the | grass, || and withER | as the | green | herb.

3 Trust in the LORD, | and do | good; || so shalt thou dwell in the LAND, and | verily thou | shalt be | fed.

4 Delight thyself alSO | in the | Lord; || and he shall give thee THE de|sires | of thine | heart.

5 Commit thy WAY | unto the | Lord: || trust also in HIM; and | he shall | bring-it to | pass:

6 And he shall bring forth thy righteousNESS | as the | light,|| and THY | judgment | as the | noon-day.

7 Rest in the Lord, and wait paTIENT|ly for | him: || fret not

46. *Gregorian 3rd Tone.*

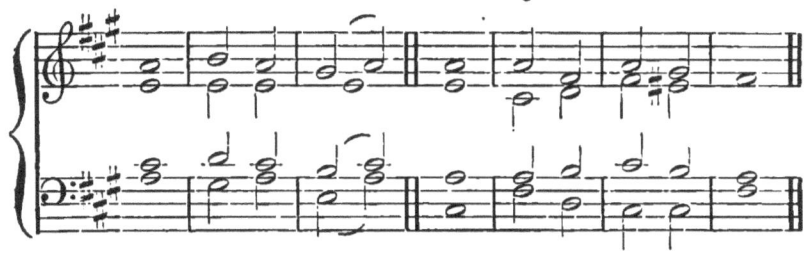

thyself because of him who prospereth in his way, because of the man who bringETH | wicked de|vices to | pass.

8 Cease from anger, AND for|sake | wrath : ‖ fret not thySELF in | any | wise-to do | evil.

9 For evil-doERS shall | be cut | off: ‖ but those that wait upon the LORD, | they shall-in|herit the | earth.

10 For yet a little while, and the wickED | shall not | be: ‖ yea, thou shalt diligently consider his PLACE, | and it | shall not | be.

11 But the MEEK shall in|herit the | earth; ‖ and shall delight themSELVES | in the-a|bundance of | peace.

12 The wicked plotTETH a|gainst the | just, ‖ and gnashETH up|on him | with his | teeth.

13 The LORD shall | laugh at | him : ‖ for he SEETH | that his | day is | coming.

14 The wicked have drawn out the SWORD, and have | bent their | bow, ‖ to cast down the poor and needy, and to slay such as BE of | upright | conver|sation.

15 Their sword shall enter inTO their | own | heart, ‖ AND their | bows | shall be | broken.

16 A litTLE that a | righteous man | hath ‖ is betTER than the | riches of | many | wicked.

17 For the arms of the wickED | shall be | broken : ‖ BUT the | Lord up|holdeth the | righteous.

18 The Lord knowETH the | days of-the | upright, ‖ and THEIR in|heritance | shall be-for | ever.

19 They shall not be ashamed IN the | evil | time : ‖ and in the DAYS of | famine they | shall be | satisfied.

47. *Gregorian 5th Tone.*

20 But the wicked shall perish, and the enemies of the Lord shall BE as the | fat of | lambs: ‖ they shall consume; into SMOKE shall | they con|sume a|way.

21 The wicked borroweth, and payETH | not a|gain: ‖ but the rightEOUS | showeth | mercy, and | giveth.

22 For such as be blessed of HIM shall in|herit the | earth; ‖ and they that be cursED of | him shall | be cut | off.

23 The steps of a good man are orderED | by the | Lord; ‖ and HE de|lighteth | in his | way.

24 Though he fall, he shall not be utterLY | cast | down: ‖ for the LORD up|holdeth him | with his | hand.

25 I have been YOUNG, and | now am | old; ‖ yet have I not seen the righteous forsakEN, nor his | seed | begging | bread.

26 He is evER | merciful, and | lendeth; ‖ AND | his | seed is | blessed.

27 Depart from EVIL, | and do | good; ‖ AND | dwell for | ever|more.

28 For the Lord loveth judgment, and forsaketh not his saints; THEY are pre|served for | ever: ‖ but the SEED of the | wicked shall | be cut | off.

29 The rightEOUS shall in|herit the | land, ‖ AND | dwell there|in for | ever.

30 The mouth of the rightEOUS | speaketh | wisdom, ‖ AND his | tongue | talketh of | judgment.

31 The law of his GOD is | in his | heart; ‖ NONE | of his | steps shall | slide.

48. *Gregorian 7th Tone.*

32 The wickED | watcheth the | righteous, ‖ AND | seeketh to | slay | him.

33 The Lord will not leave HIM | in his | hand, ‖ NOR con-| demn-him when | he is | judged.

34 Wait on the Lord, and keep his way, and he shall exalt thee TO in|herit the | land: ‖ when the wickED are | cut off, | thou shalt | see-it.

35 I have seen the wickED | in great | power, ‖ and spreading himSELF | like a | green bay-|tree.

36 Yet he passed away, and, LO, | he was | not; ‖ yea, I sought HIM, but | he could | not be | found.

37 Mark the perfect man, AND be|hold the | upright: ‖ for the END | of that | man is | peace.

38 But the transgressors shall BE de|stroyed to|gether: ‖ the end OF the | wicked shall | be cut | off.

39 But the salvation of the rightEOUS is | of the | Lord: ‖ he is their STRENGTH | in the | time of | trouble.

40 And the Lord shall help THEM, and de|liver | them: ‖ he shall deliver them from the wicked, and save THEM, be|cause they | trust in | him.   GLORY BE, ETC.

PSALM XXXVIII.

O LORD, rebuke me NOT | in thy | wrath; ‖ neither chasten ME | in thy | hot dis|pleasure.

2 For thine arrows STICK | fast in | me, ‖ AND | thy hand presseth me | sore.

3 There is no soundness in my flesh beCAUSE | of thine |

49.   *Gregorian 8th Tone.*

anger; ‖ neither is there any rest in MY | bones be|cause-of my | sin.

4 For mine iniquities are GONE | over mine | head: ‖ as an heavy burDEN they | are too | heavy for | me.

5 My wounds STINK, and | are cor|rupt, ‖ beCAUSE | of my | foolish|ness.

6 I am troubled; I am | bowed down | greatly; ‖ I GO | mourn-ing | all-the day | long.

7 For my loins are filled WITH a | loathsome dis|ease; ‖ and there is NO | soundness | in my | flesh.

8 I am feeBLE and | sore | broken: ‖ I have roared by reason of THE dis|quietness | of my | heart.

9 Lord, all my deSIRE | is be|fore-thee; ‖ and my groanING | is not | hid from | thee.

10 My heart panteth, my STRENGTH | faileth | me: ‖ as for the light of mine EYES, it | also is | gone from | me.

11 My lovers and my friends stand aLOOF | from my | sore; ‖ and MY | kinsmen | stand-afar | off.

12 They also that seek after my life LAY | snares for | me: ‖ and they that seek my hurt speak mischievous things, and imagine deCEITS | all the | day | long.

13 But I, as a deaf MAN, | heard | not; ‖ and I was as a dumb MAN that | openeth | not his | mouth.

14 Thus I was as a MAN that | heareth | not, ‖ and in WHOSE | mouth are | no re|proofs.

15 For in thee, O LORD, | do I | hope: ‖ THOU wilt | hear, O | Lord my | God.

50. *Gregorian 8th Tone.*

16 For I said, Hear me, lest otherwise they should reJOICE | over | me: || when my foot slippeth, they MAGni|fy them|selves a|gainst-me.

17 For I am | ready to | halt, || and my sorrow IS con|tinual|ly be|fore-me.

18 For I will deCLARE | mine in|iquity; || I will BE | sorry | for my | sin.

19 But mine enemies are liveLY, and | they are | strong; || and they that hate ME | wrongful|ly are | multiplied.

20 They also that render evil for good are MINE | adver-| saries; || because I folLOW the | thing that | good | is.

21 Forsake ME | not, O | Lord: || O my GOD, | be not | far from | me.

22 MAKE | haste to | help-me, || O | Lord | my sal|vation.

GLORY BE, ETC.

PSALM XXXIX.

I SAID, I will take heed to my ways, that I sin NOT | with my | tongue: || I will keep my mouth with a bridle, WHILE the | wicked | is be|fore-me.

2 I was | dumb with | silence; || I held my peace, even from GOOD; | and my | sorrow was | stirred.

3 My heart was hot within me; while I was musING the | fire | burned: || THEN | spake I | with my | tongue.

4 Lord, make me to know mine end, and the measure of my DAYS, | what it | is; || that I MAY | know how | frail I | am.

51. *Tonus Peregrinus.*

5 Behold, thou hast made my days as an hand-breadth, and mine age IS as | nothing be|fore-thee: || verily every man at his best STATE is | alto|gether | vanity.

6 Surely every man walketh in a vain show: surely they ARE dis|quieted in | vain: || he heapeth up riches, and knoweth NOT | who shall | gather | them.

7 And now, LORD, what | wait I | for? || MY | hope | is in | thee.

8 Deliver me from ALL | my trans|gressions: || make me not THE re|proach | of the | foolish.

9 I was dumb, I openED | not my | mouth; || BE|cause | thou | didst-it.

10 Remove thy STROKE a|way from | me: || I am consumED | by the | blow of-thine | hand.

11 When thou with rebukes dost correct man for iniquity, thou makest his beauty to consume aWAY | like a | moth: || sureLY | every | man is | vanity.

12 Hear my prayer, O Lord, and give ear unto my cry; hold not thy PEACE | at my | tears: || for I am a stranger with thee, and a sojournER, as | all my | fathers | were.

13 O spare me, that I MAY re|cover | strength, || before I GO | hence, and | be no | more.   GLORY BE, ETC.

PSALM XL.

I WAITED patientLY | for the | Lord; || and he inclined unTO | me, and | heard my | cry.

2 He brought me up also out of an horrible pit, out OF the |

miry | clay, ‖ and set my feet upon a ROCK, | and es|tablished my | goings.

3 And he hath put a new song in my mouth, even PRAISE | unto our | God: ‖ many shall see it, and FEAR, and | shall trust | in the | Lord.

4 Blessed is that man that makETH the | Lord his | trust, ‖ and respecteth not the proud, nor SUCH as | turn a|side to | lies.

5 Many, O Lord my God, are thy wonderful works which thou hast done, and thy THOUGHTS which | are to | us-ward; ‖ they cannot be reckoned up in order unto thee: if I would declare and speak of them, THEY are | more than | can be | numbered.

6 Sacrifice and offering thou didst not desire; mine EARS | hast thou | opened: ‖ burnt-offering and sin-offerING | hast thou | not re|quired.

7 Then said I, | Lo, I | come: ‖ in the volume of the BOOK | it is | written of | me,

8 I delight to do thy WILL, | O my | God: ‖ yea, thy LAW | is with|in my | heart.

9 I have preached righteousness in the GREAT | congre|gation: ‖ lo, I have not refrainED my | lips, O | Lord, thou | knowest.

10 I have not hid thy righteousness within my heart; I have declared thy faithfulNESS and | thy sal|vation: ‖ I have not concealed thy loving-kindness and thy truth FROM the | great | congre|gation.

11 Withhold not thou thy tender merCIES from | me, O | Lord: ‖ let thy loving-kindness and thy TRUTH con|tinual|ly pre|serve-me.

52.

12 For innumerable evils have compassED | me a|bout: || mine iniquities have taken hold upon me, so that I am not able to look up: they are more than the hairs of mine head; thereFORE my | heart | faileth | me.

13 Be pleased, O LORD, to de|liver | me: || O | Lord, make haste to | help-me.

14 Let them be ashamed and confounded together that seek afTER my | soul to-de|stroy-it; || let them be driven backward, and PUT to | shame, that | wish me | evil.

15 LET | them be | desolate || for a reward of their shame that SAY unto | me, A|ha, a|ha!

16 Let all those that seek thee reJOICE and be | glad in | thee: || let such as love thy salvation say continualLY, The | Lord be | magni|fied.

17 But I am poor and needy; yet the LORD | thinketh up-| on-me: || thou art my help and my deliverer; make NO | tarrying, | O my | God.   GLORY BE, ETC.

PSALM XLI.

BLESSED is HE that con|sidereth the | poor: || the Lord will delivER | him in | time of | trouble.

2 The Lord will preserve him, and keep him alive; and he shall be blessED up|on the | earth: || and thou wilt not deliver him unto the WILL | of his | ene|mies.

3 The Lord will strengthen him upon the BED of | languish-| ing: || thou wilt make ALL his | bed | in his | sickness.

4 I said, Lord, be merciFUL | unto | me: || heal my soul; for I HAVE | sinned a|gainst | thee.

(52. *Robinson.*

5 Mine enemies SPEAK | evil of | me, ‖ When shall HE | die, and | his name | perish?

6 And if he come to see me, he speakETH | vani|ty: ‖ his heart gathereth iniquity to itself; when he goETH a|broad, he | telleth | it.

7 All that hate me whisper togethER a|gainst | me: ‖ against ME do | they de|vise my | hurt.

8 An evil disease, say they, cleaveth FAST | unto | him: ‖ and now that he liETH, he | shall rise | up no | more.

9 Yea, mine own familiar friend, in whom I trusted, which did EAT | of my | bread, ‖ hath liftED | up his | heel a|gainst-me.

10 But thou, O Lord, be merciFUL | unto | me, ‖ and raise me up, that I | may re|quite | them.

11 By this I know that THOU | favourest | me, ‖ because mine enemy doth NOT | triumph | over | me.

12 And as for me, thou upholdest ME in | mine in|tegrity, ‖ and settest ME be|fore thy | face for | ever.

13 Blessed be the LORD | God of | Israel ‖ from everlasting. and to everlastING. | Amen, | and A|men.   GLORY BE, ETC.

PSALM XLII.

AS the hart panteth afTER the | water-|brooks, ‖ so panteth my SOUL | after | thee, O | God.

2 My soul thirsteth for God, FOR the | living | God: ‖ when shall I come AND ap|pear be|fore | God?

3 My tears have been my MEAT | day and | night, ‖ while they continually say unTO | me, Where | is thy | God?

53.

4 When I remember these things, I pour OUT my | soul in | me: || for I had gone with the multitude; I went with them to the house of God, with the voice of joy and praise, with a multi-TUDE | that kept | holy-|day.

5 Why art thou cast down, O my soul? and why art thou disquieted in ME? | hope thou-in | God; || for I shall yet praise him FOR the | help of-his | counte|nance.

6 O my God, my soul is CAST | down with|in-me: || therefore will I remember thee from the land of Jordan, and of the Hermon-ITES, | from the | hill | Mizar.

7 Deep calleth unto deep at the noise of THY | water-|spouts: || all thy waves and thy bilLOWS | are gone | over | me.

8 Yet the Lord will command his loving-kindNESS | in the day-time, || and in the night his song shall be with me, and my prayER | unto the | God of-my | life.

9 I will say unto God my rock, Why hast THOU for|gotten | me? || why go I mourning because of THE op|pression | of the | enemy?

10 As with a sword in my bones, mine eneMIES re|proach | me; || while they say daily unTO | me, Where | is thy | God?

11 Why art thou cast down, O my soul? and why art thou disquieted within ME? | hope thou-in | God; || for I shall yet praise him, who is the health of MY | countenance, | and my | God.   GLORY BE, ETC.

PSALM XLIII.

JUDGE me, O God, and plead my cause against AN un|godly | nation: || O deliver me from THE de|ceitful and | unjust | man.

2 For thou art the GOD | of my | strength: || why dost thou cast me off? why go I mourning because of THE op|pression | of the | enemy?

3 O send out thy LIGHT | and thy | truth: || let them lead me; let them bring me unto thy holy HILL, and | to thy | taber|nacles.

4 Then will I go unto the altar of God, unto God MY ex-| ceeding | joy: || yea, upon the harp will I PRAISE | thee, O | God, my | God.

5 Why art thou cast down, O my soul? and why art thou disquieted within ME? | hope in | God; || for I shall yet praise him, who is the health of MY | countenance, | and my | God.

GLORY BE, ETC.

PSALM XLIV.

WE have heard with our ears, O God, our faTHERS have | told | us, || what work thou didst in their DAYS, | in the | times of | old:

2 How thou didst drive out the heathen with thy HAND, and | plantedst | them; || how thou didst afFLICT the | people, and | cast them | out.

3 For they got not the land in possession by their own sword, neither did THEIR | own arm | save·them; || but thy right hand, and thine arm, and the light of thy countenance, because thou HADST a | favour | unto | them.

4 Thou ART my | King, O | God: || comMAND de|liveran|ces for | Jacob.

5 Through thee will we PUSH | down our | enemies: || through thy name will we tread them unDER that | rise up·a|gainst | us.

54.

6 For I will not TRUST | in my | bow, || neiTHER | shall my | sword save | me.

7 But thou hast saved US | from our | enemies, || and hast put THEM to | shame that | hated | us.

8 In God we BOAST | all-the day | long, || AND | praise thy | name for | ever.

9 But thou hast cast off, and PUT | us to | shame; || and goEST | not forth | with our | armies.

10 Thou makest us to turn BACK | from the | enemy; || and they which hate US | spoil | for them|selves.

11 Thou hast given us like SHEEP ap|pointed for | meat; || and hast scatterED | us a|mong the | heathen.

12 Thou sellEST thy | people for | nought, || and dost not in-CREASE | thy wealth | by their | price.

13 Thou makest us a rePROACH | to our | neighbours, || a scorn and a derision to THEM | that are | round a|bout-us.

14 Thou makest us a by-WORD a|mong the | heathen, || a shaking OF the | head a|mong the | people.

15 My confusion is continualLY be|fore | me, || and the shame of MY | face hath | covered | me,

16 For the voice of him that reproachETH | and blas|phemeth; || by reason OF the | enemy | and a|venger.

17 All THIS is | come up|on-us; || yet have we not forgotten thee, neither have we DEALT | falsely | in thy | covenant.

18 Our heart is NOT | turned | back, || neither have our STEPS de|clined | from thy | way,

(54.)   *Henley.*

19 Though thou hast sore broken us IN the | place of | dragons, ||
and covered US | with the | shadow of | death.

20 If we have forgotten the NAME | of our | God, || or stretched OUT our | hands to-a | strange | god;

21 Shall not GOD | search this | out? || for he knowETH the | secrets | of the | heart.

22 Yea, for thy sake are we killED | all-the day | long; || we are countED as | sheep | for the | slaughter.

23 Awake, why sleepEST | thou, O | Lord? || ARISE, | cast-us not | off for | ever.

24 Wherefore hidEST | thou thy | face, || and forgettest OUR af|fliction and | our op|pression?

25 For our soul is bowed DOWN | to the | dust; || our belLY | cleaveth | unto the | earth.

26 ARISE | for our | help, || and redeem US, | for thy | mercies' | sake.   GLORY BE, ETC.

PSALM XLV.

MY heart is inditing a good matter: I speak of the things which I have MADE | touching the | King; || my tongue is the PEN | of a | ready | writer.

2 Thou art fairer than the children of men; grace is pourED | into thy | lips: || therefore GOD hath | blessed | thee for | ever.

3 Gird thy sword upon thy THIGH, | O most | Mighty, || with THY | glory | and thy | majesty.

4 And in thy majesty ride prosperously, because of truth, and meekNESS, and | righteous|ness; || and thy right HAND shall | teach thee | terrible | things.

55.

5 Thine arrows are sharp in the heart of the KING'S | ene|mies; ‖ whereby the peoPLE | fall | under | thee.

6 Thy throne, O God, IS for | ever and | ever: ‖ the sceptre of thy kingDOM | is a | right | sceptre.

7 Thou lovest righteousness, and hatEST | wicked|ness: ‖ therefore God, thy God, hath anointed thee with the OIL of | gladness a|bove thy | fellows.

8 All thy garments smell of MYRRH, and | aloes, and | cassia, ‖ out of the ivory palaces, whereBY | they have | made thee | glad.

9 Kings' daughters were among THY | honourable | women: ‖ upon thy right hand did STAND the | queen in | gold of | Ophir.

10 Hearken, O daughter, and consider, AND in|cline thine | ear; ‖ forget also thine own peoPLE, | and thy | father's | house:

11 So shall the King greatLY de|sire thy | beauty: ‖ for he is thy LORD; and | worship | thou | him.

12 And the daughter of Tyre shall be THERE | with a | gift; ‖ even the rich among the peoPLE | shall en|treat thy | favour.

13 The King's daughter is ALL | glorious with|in: ‖ her cloth-ING | is of | wrought | gold.

14 She shall be brought unto the King in raiMENT of | needle-| work: ‖ the virgins her companions that follow HER | shall be | brought unto | thee.

15 With gladness and rejoicING shall | they be | brought: ‖ they shall enTER | into the | King's | palace.

16 Instead of thy faTHERS shall | be thy | children, ‖ whom thou mayest MAKE | princes in | all the | earth.

17 I will make thy name to be remembered in ALL | gener-| ations: ‖ therefore shall the people PRAISE | thee for | ever and | ever.　　　　　　　　　　　　　　Glory be, etc.

PSALM XLVI.

GOD is OUR | refuge and | strength, ‖ a veRY | present | help in | trouble:

2 Therefore will not we fear, though the EARTH | be re-| moved, ‖ and though the mountains be carRIED | into the | midst of-the | sea;

3 Though the waters thereof ROAR | and be | troubled, ‖ though the mountains SHAKE | with the | swelling there|of.

4 There is a river, the streams whereof shall make GLAD the | city of | God, ‖ the holy place of the tabernaCLES | of the | most | High.

5 God is in the midst of her; SHE shall | not be | moved: ‖ God shall HELP | her, and | that right | early.

6 The heathen RAGED; the | kingdoms were | moved: ‖ he utterED his | voice; the | earth | melted.

7 The LORD of | hosts is | with-us; ‖ the GOD of | Jacob | is our | refuge.

8 Come, behold the WORKS | of the | Lord, ‖ what desola-TIONS | he hath | made in-the | earth.

9 He maketh wars to cease unto the END | of the | earth; ‖ he breaketh the bow, and cutteth the spear in sunder; he burnETH the | chariot | in the | fire.

56.

10 Be still, and KNOW that | I am | God: ‖ I will be exalted among the heathen, I will BE ex|alted | in the | earth.

11 The Lord of HOSTS | is with | us: ‖ the GOD of | Jacob | is our | refuge.

GLORY BE, ETC.

PSALM XLVII.

O CLAP your HANDS, | all ye | people; ‖ shout unto GOD | with the | voice of | triumph.

2 For the LORD most | High is | terrible; ‖ he is a great KING | over | all the | earth.

3 He shall subdue the peoPLE | under | us, ‖ AND the | nations | under our | feet.

4 He shall choose OUR in|heritance | for-us, ‖ the excellenCY of | Jacob | whom he | loved.

5 God is gone UP | with a | shout, ‖ the LORD | with the | sound of-a | trumpet.

6 Sing praisES to | God, sing | praises: ‖ sing praisES | unto our | King, sing | praises.

7 For God is the KING of | all the | earth: ‖ sing YE | praises with | under|standing.

8 God reignETH | over the | heathen: ‖ God sitteth upON the | throne | of his | holiness.

9 The princes of the people are gathered together, even the people of the GOD of | Abra|ham: ‖ for the shields of the earth belong unto GOD; | he is | greatly ex|alted.

GLORY BE, ETC.

Norris.

PSALM XLVIII.

GREAT is the Lord, and greatly to be praised in the ciTY | of our | God, ‖ in the mounTAIN | of his | holi|ness.

2 Beautiful for situation, the joy of the whole EARTH, | is mount | Zion, ‖ on the sides of the north, the ciTY | of the | great | King.

3 GOD | is | known ‖ in HER | palaces | for a | refuge.

4 For, lo, the KINGS | were as|sembled, ‖ THEY | passed | by to|gether.

5 They saw IT, and | so they | marvelled; ‖ THEY were | troubled, and | hasted a|way.

6 Fear took HOLD up|on them | there, ‖ and PAIN, as | of a | woman in | travail.

7 Thou breakEST the | ships of | Tarshish ‖ WITH | an | east | wind.

8 As we have heard, so have we seen in the city of the Lord of hosts, in the ciTY | of our | God: ‖ GOD will es|tablish | it for | ever.

9 We have thought of thy lovING-|kindness, O | God, ‖ IN the | midst | of thy | temple.

10 According to thy name, O God, so is thy praise unto the ENDS | of the | earth: ‖ thy right HAND is | full of | righteous-|ness.

11 Let mount Zion rejoice, let the daughTERS of | Judah be | glad, ‖ BE|cause | of thy | judgments.

12 Walk about Zion, and GO | round a|bout-her: ‖ TELL | ... the | towers there|of.

57.

---

13 Mark ye well her bulwarks, consiDER her | pala|ces; || that ye may tell it TO the | gener|ation | following.
14 For this God is our GOD for | ever and | ever; || he will be our GUIDE | even | unto | death.   GLORY BE, ETC.

PSALM XLIX.

HEAR THIS, | all ye | people; || give ear, ALL ye in|habitants| of the | world:
2 BOTH | low and | high, || RICH | . . . and | poor, to|gether.
3 My MOUTH shall | speak of | wisdom; || and the meditation of my HEART shall | be of | under|standing.
4 I will incline mine EAR | to a | parable; || I will open my DARK | saying up|on the | harp.
5 Wherefore should I FEAR in the | days of | evil, || when the iniquity of my HEELS shall | compass | me a|bout?
6 They that TRUST | in their | wealth, || and boast them-SELVES in the | multitude | of their | riches;
7 None of them can by any MEANS re|deem his | brother, || nor GIVE to | God a | ransom for | him;
8 (For the redemption of THEIR | soul is | precious, || AND it | ceaseth | for | ever;)
9 That he should STILL | live for | ever, || AND | not | see cor|ruption.
10 For he seeth that wise men die, likewise the fool and the brutISH | person | perish, || AND | leave their | wealth to | others.
11 Their inward thought is, that their houses shall continue for

(57.)

ever, and their dwelling-places to ALL | gener|ations: || they call their LANDS | after | their own | names.

12 Nevertheless man being in honOUR a|bideth | not: || HE is | like the | beasts that | perish.

13 This their WAY | is their | folly; || yet THEIR pos|terity ap|prove their | sayings.

14 Like sheep they are laid in the grave; death shall feed on them; and the upright shall have dominion over THEM | in the | morning; || and their beauty shall conSUME in the | grave | from their | dwelling.

15 But God will redeem my soul from the powER | of the | grave: || for HE | shall re|ceive | me.

16 Be not thou afraid when ONE | is made | rich, || when the gloRY of | his house | is in|creased:

17 For when he dieth he shall carRY | nothing a|way; || his glory shall NOT de|scend | after | him.

18 Though while he LIVED he | blessed his | soul, || (and men will praise thee when THOU | doest well | to thy|self,)

19 He shall go to the generaTION | of his | fathers; || THEY shall | never | see | light.

20 Man that is in honour, and UNder|standeth | not, || IS | like the | beasts that | perish.   GLORY BE, ETC.

PSALM L.

THE mighty God, EVEN the | Lord, hath | spoken, || and called the earth, from the rising of the sun unTO the | going | down there|of.

E 67

58.

2 OUT ⌢of⌢ | Zion, ‖ the perfecTION of | beauty, | God hath | shined.

3 Our God shall COME, and shall | not keep | silence: ‖ a fire shall devour before him, and it shall be veRY tem|pestuous | round a|bout-him.

4 He shall call to the heavENS | from a|bove, ‖ and to the EARTH, that | he may | judge his | people.

5 Gather my saints togethER | unto | me; ‖ those that have made a coveNANT with | me by | sacri|fice.

6 And the heavens SHALL de|clare his | righteousness: ‖ FOR| God is | judge him|self.

7 Hear, O my peoPLE, and | I will | speak; ‖ O Israel, and I will testify against thee: I am | ⌢God,⌢ | even thy | God.

8 I will not reprove thee for thy sacrifiCES or | thy burnt-| offerings, ‖ to have BEEN con|tinual|ly be|fore-me.

9 I will take no bulLOCK | out-of thy | house, ‖ NOR | he-goats | out-of thy | folds:

10 For every BEAST of the | forest is | mine, ‖ and the catTLE up|on a | thousand | hills.

11 I know all the FOWLS | of the | mountains; ‖ and the wild BEASTS | of the | field are | mine.

12 If I were hunGRY, I | would not | tell-thee: ‖ for the world is MINE, | and the | fulness there|of.

13 Will I EAT the | flesh of | bulls, ‖ OR | drink the | blood of | goats?

14 OFFER unto | God thanks|giving; ‖ and pay thy VOWS | unto the | ⌢most⌢ | High:

Dr. Crotch.

15 And call upon ME in the | day of | trouble; || I will deliver THEE, and | thou shalt | glorify | me.

16 But unto the wicked God saith, What hast thou to DO to de|clare my | statutes, || or that thou shouldest TAKE my | covenant | in thy | mouth?

17 Seeing THOU | hatest in|struction, || and castEST my | words be|hind | thee.

18 When THOU | sawest a | thief, || then thou consentedst with him, and hast been partakER | with a|dulter|ers.

19 Thou givEST thy | mouth to | evil, || AND | thy tongue | frameth de|ceit.

20 Thou sittest and speakEST a|gainst thy | brother; || thou slanderEST | thine own | mother's | son.

21 These things hast thou done, and I kept silence; thou thoughtest that I was altogether such an ONE | as thy|self: || but I will reprove thee, and set THEM in | order be|fore thine | eyes.

22 Now consider this, YE that for|get | God, || lest I tear you in pieces, and THERE | be none | to de|liver.

23 Whoso offereth praise GLOri|fieth | me: || and to him that ordereth his conversation ARIGHT will I | show-the sal|vation of | God.   GLORY BE, ETC.

PSALM LI.

HAVE mercy upon me, O God, according to THY | loving-| kindness; || according unto the multitude of thy tender merCIES | blot out | my trans|gressions.

59.

2 Wash me thoroughLY from | mine in|iquity, ‖ AND | cleanse me | from my | sin.

3 For I acknowLEDGE | my trans|gressions, ‖ and MY | sin is | ever be|fore-me.

4 Against thee, thee only, have I sinned, and done this EVIL | in thy | sight: ‖ that thou mightest be justified when thou speakEST, and be | clear | when thou | judgest.

5 Behold, I was shapEN | in in|iquity; ‖ and in SIN | did my | mother con|ceive-me.

6 Behold, thou desirest TRUTH in the | inward | parts; ‖ and in the hidden part thou SHALT | make-me to | know | wisdom.

7 Purge me with hyssop, and I | shall be | clean; ‖ wash me, and I | shall be | whiter than | snow.

8 Make me to HEAR | joy and | gladness; ‖ that the bones which THOU hast | broken | may re|joice.

9 Hide thy FACE | from my | sins, ‖ AND | blot out | all mine-in|iquities.

10 Create in me a CLEAN | heart, O | God; ‖ AND re|new-a right | spirit with|in-me.

11 Cast me not AWAY | from thy | presence; ‖ and take NOT thy | Holy | Spirit | from-me.

12 Restore unto me the JOY of | thy sal|vation; ‖ and up-HOLD | me with | thy free | Spirit.

13 Then will I TEACH trans|gressors thy | ways; ‖ and sinners shall BE con|verted | unto | thee.

14 Deliver me from blood-guiltiness, O God, thou GOD of |

(59.)   *Lawes.*

my sal|vation; ‖ and my tongue shall sing ALOUD | of thy | righteous|ness.

15 O Lord, OPEN | thou my | lips, ‖ and my MOUTH | shall show | forth thy | praise.

16 For thou desirest not sacrifice, ELSE | would I | give-it: ‖ thou delightEST | not in | burnt-|offering.

17 The sacrifices of GOD are a | broken | spirit: ‖ a broken and a contrite heart, O GOD, | thou wilt | not des|pise.

18 Do good in thy good pleaSURE | unto | Zion; ‖ BUILD | thou the | walls of-Jer|usalem.

19 Then shalt thou be pleased with the sacrifices of righteousness, with burnt-offerING, and | whole burnt-|offering: ‖ then shall they ofFER | bullocks up|on thine | altar.

                                                     GLORY BE, ETC.

PSALM LII.

WHY boastest thou thyself in mischief, O | mighty | man? ‖ the goodness of GOD en|dureth con|tinual|ly.

2 Thy TONGUE de|viseth | mischiefs; ‖ like a sharp raZOR, | working de|ceitful|ly.

3 Thou lovest EVIL | more than | good, ‖ and lying rather THAN to | speak | righteous|ness.

4 Thou lovest ALL-de|vouring | words, ‖ O | thou de|ceitful | tongue.

5 God shall likewise deSTROY | thee for | ever: ‖ he shall take thee away, and pluck thee out of thy dwelling-place, and root thee out OF the | land | of the | living.

60.

6 The righteous alSO shall | see, and | fear, ‖ AND ⌈shall⌉ laugh at | him:

7 Lo, this is the man that made NOT | God his | strength; ‖ but trusted in the abundance of his riches, and strengthened himSELF | in his | wicked|ness.

8 But I am like a green olive-TREE in the | house of | God: ‖ I trust in the merCY of | God for | ever and | ever.

9 I will praise thee for ever, beCAUSE | thou hast | done-it: ‖ and I will wait on thy name; for IT is | good be|fore thy | saints.

GLORY BE, ETC.

PSALM LIII.

THE fool hath said in his HEART, There | is no | God. ‖ Corrupt are they, and have done abominable iniquity: THERE is | none that | doeth | good.

2 God looked down from heaven upON the | children of | men, ‖ to see if there were any that did UNder|stand, that | did seek | God.

3 Every one of them is gone back; they are altogethER be-| come | filthy: ‖ there is NONE that | doeth good, | no, not | one.

4 Have the workers of iniquity no knowledge? who eat up my peoPLE as | they eat | bread: ‖ THEY | have not | called-upon | God.

5 There were they in great fear, where no fear was; for God hath scattered the bones of him that encampETH a⌈gainst⌉ thee: ‖ thou hast put them to shame, because GOD | hath des|pised | them.

6 O that the salvation of Israel were COME | out of | Zion! ‖ When God bringeth back the captivity of his people, Jacob shall reJOICE, and | Israel | shall be | glad.   GLORY BE, ETC.

PSALM LIV.

SAVE me, O GOD, | by thy | name, ‖ AND | judge me | by thy | strength.

2 HEAR my | prayer, O | God; ‖ give EAR to the | words | of my | mouth.

3 For strangers are risen up against me, and oppressors SEEK | after my | soul: ‖ they HAVE | not set | God be|fore-them.

4 Behold, GOD | is mine | helper: ‖ the Lord is with THEM | that up|hold my | soul.

5 He shall reward EVIL | unto mine | enemies: ‖ CUT them | off in | thy | truth.

6 I will freely sacriFICE | unto | thee; ‖ I will praise thy NAME, O | Lord, for | it is | good.

7 For he hath delivered ME | out-of all | trouble; ‖ and mine eye hath SEEN his de|sire up|on mine | enemies.

                        GLORY BE, ETC.

PSALM LV.

GIVE ear to MY | prayer, O | God; ‖ and hide not thySELF | from my | suppli|cation.

2 Attend unto ME, and | hear | me: ‖ I mourn in MY com-| plaint, and | make a | noise;

3 Because of the voice of the enemy, because of the oppres-

61.

SION | of the | wicked: || for they cast iniquity upon ME, | and in | wrath they | hate-me.

4 My heart is sore painED with|in | me; || and the terRORS of | death are | fallen up|on-me.

5 Fearfulness and tremBLING are | come up|on-me, || and horROR hath | over|whelmed | me.

6 And I said, Oh that I had WINGS | like a | dove! || for then would I FLY a|way, and | be at | rest.

7 Lo, then would I wanDER | far | off, || AND re|main | in the | wilderness.

8 I would hastEN | my es|cape || FROM the | windy | storm and | tempest.

9 Destroy, O LORD, and di|vide their | tongues: || for I have seen vioLENCE and | strife | in the | city.

10 Day and night they go about it upON the | walls there|of; || mischief also and sorROW are | in the | midst of | it.

11 Wickedness is IN the | midst there|of; || deceit and GUILE de|part not | from her | streets.

12 For it was not an enemy that reproached me; THEN I | could have | borne-it: || neither was it he that hated me that did magnify himself against me; then I WOULD have | hid my|self | from-him:

13 But it was THOU, a | man mine | equal, || MY | guide, and | mine ac|quaintance.

14 We took SWEET | counsel to|gether, || and walked unTO the | house of | God in | company.

15 Let death seize upon them, and let them go down QUICK |

W. Russell.

into | hell: ‖ for wickedness is IN their | dwellings, | and a|mong-them.

16 As for me, I will | call-upon | God; ‖ AND the | Lord shall | save | me.

17 Evening, and morning, and at noon, will I PRAY, and | cry a|loud; ‖ AND | he shall | hear my | voice.

18 He hath delivered my soul in peace from the batTLE that | was a|gainst-me: ‖ FOR | there were | many | with-me.

19 God shall hear, and afflict them, even he THAT a|bideth of | old. ‖ Because they have no chanGES, | therefore they | fear not | God.

20 He hath put forth his hands against such as BE at | peace | with-him: ‖ HE | . . . hath | broken his | covenant.

21 The words of his mouth were smoother than butter, but WAR was | in his | heart: ‖ his words were softer than OIL, | yet were | they drawn | swords.

22 Cast thy burden upon the Lord, and HE shall sus|tain | thee: ‖ he shall never sufFER the | righteous | to be | moved.

23 But thou, O God, shalt bring them down into the PIT | of des|truction: ‖ bloody and deceitful men shall not live out half their DAYS; but | I will | trust in | thee.

GLORY BE, ETC.

PSALM LVI.

BE merciFUL unto | me, O | God; ‖ for man would swallow me up: he fightING | daily op|presseth | me.

2 Mine enemies would daiLY | swallow me | up: ‖ for they be many that fight AGAINST | me, O | thou most | High.

62.

3 What TIME I | am a|fraid, || I | will | trust in | thee.

4 In God I will praise his word: in God I HAVE | put my | trust; || I will not fear what FLESH | can do | unto | me.

5 Every DAY they | wrest my | words: || all their thoughts ARE a|gainst | me for | evil.

6 They gather themselves togethER, they | hide them|selves, || they mark my STEPS, | when they | wait for-my | soul.

7 Shall they esCAPE | by in|iquity? || in thine anger CAST | down the | people, O | God.

8 THOU | tellest my | wanderings: || put thou my tears into thy botTLE: are | they not | in thy | book?

9 When I cry unto thee, then shall mine eneMIES | turn | back: || THIS I | know; for | God is | for-me.

10 In GOD will I | praise his | word: || in the LORD | will I | praise his | word.

11 In GOD have I | put my | trust: || I will not be afraid what MAN | can do | unto | me.

12 Thy vows are upON | me, O | God: || I will renDER | praises | unto | thee.

13 For thou hast deliverED my | soul from | death: || wilt not thou deliver my feet from falling, that I may walk before GOD in the | light | of the | living?   GLORY BE, ETC.

PSALM LVII.

BE merciful unto me, O God; be merciful unto me; for my SOUL | trusteth in | thee: || yea, in the shadow of thy wings will I make my refuge, until THESE ca|lamities | be over-|past.

2 I will CRY unto | God most | high; ‖ unto GOD that per|formeth all | things for | me.

3 He shall send from heaven, and save me from the reproach of HIM that would | swallow me | up. ‖ God shall send forth HIS | mercy | and his | truth.

4 My SOUL is a|mong | lions: ‖ and I lie even among them that are set on fire, even the sons of men, whose teeth are spears and arROWS, and their | tongue a | sharp | sword.

5 Be thou exalted, O GOD, a|bove the | heavens; ‖ let thy gloRY | be-above | all the | earth.

6 They have prepared a net for my steps; my SOUL is | bowed | down: ‖ they have digged a pit before me, into the midst whereOF | they are | fallen them|selves.

7 My heart is fixed, O GOD, my | heart is | fixed; ‖ I will | sing and | give | praise.

8 Awake up, my glory; AWAKE, | psaltery and | harp: ‖ I my|self will-a|wake | early.

9 I will praise thee, O LORD, a|mong the | people: ‖ I will SING unto | thee a|mong the | nations:

10 For thy mercy is GREAT | unto the | heavens, ‖ and THY | truth un|to the | clouds.

11 Be thou exalted, O GOD, a|bove the | heavens; ‖ let thy gloRY | be-above | all the | earth.   GLORY BE, ETC.

PSALM LVIII.

D^O ye indeed speak righteousNESS, O | congre|gation? ‖ do ye judge uprightLY, | O ye | sons of | men?

63.

2 Yea, in heart ye WORK | wicked|ness; ‖ ye weigh the vioLENCE | of your | hands in-the | earth.

3 The wicked are estrangED | from the | womb: ‖ they go astray as soon as THEY be | born, | speaking | lies.

4 Their poison is like the poiSON | of a | serpent: ‖ they are like the DEAF | adder that | stoppeth her | ear;

5 Which will not hearkEN to the | voice of | charmers, ‖ charmING | never | so | wisely.

6 Break their teeth, O GOD, | in their | mouth: ‖ break out the great teeth of the YOUNG | lions, | O | Lord.

7 Let them melt away as waters which RUN con|tinual|ly: ‖ when he bendeth his bow to shoot his arrows, let THEM | be as | cut in | pieces.

8 As a snail which melteth, let every ONE of them | pass a|way: ‖ like the untimely birth of a woman, that THEY | may not | see the | sun.

9 Before your POTS can | feel the | thorns, ‖ he shall take them away as with a whirlWIND, both | living, and | in his | wrath.

10 The righteous shall rejoice when HE | seeth the | vengeance: ‖ he shall wash his FEET | in the | blood of-the | wicked.

11 So that a man shall say, Verily there is a reWARD | for the | righteous; ‖ verily he is a GOD that | judgeth | in the | earth. GLORY BE, ETC.

PSALM LIX.

DELIVER me from mine eneMIES, | O my | God: ‖ defend me from THEM that | rise up-a|gainst | me.

2 Deliver me from the workERS | of in|iquity, || and SAVE | me from | bloody | men.

3 For, lo, they lie in WAIT | for my | soul: || the mighty are gathered against me; not for my transgresSION, nor | for my | sin, O | Lord.

4 They run and prepare themSELVES with|out my | fault: || AWAKE to | help me, | and be|hold.

5 Thou therefore, O Lord God of hosts, the God of Israel, awake to viSIT | all the | heathen: || be not merciFUL to | any | wicked trans|gressors.

6 THEY re|turn at | evening: || they make a noise like a dog, and GO | round a|bout the | city.

7 Behold, they belch OUT | with their | mouth: || swords are in their LIPS: for | who, say | they, doth | hear?

8 But thou, O LORD, shalt | laugh at | them; || thou shalt have ALL the | heathen | in de|rision.

9 Because of his strength will I | wait-upon | thee: || FOR | God is | my de|fence.

10 The God of my mercy SHALL pre|vent | me: || God shall let me SEE my de|sire up|on mine | enemies.

11 Slay them NOT, lest my | people for|get: || scatter them by thy power; and bring THEM | down, O | Lord our | shield.

12 For the sin of their mouth, and the words of their lips, let them even be takEN | in their | pride; || and for cursING and | lying | which they | speak.

13 Consume them in wrath, consume them, THAT they | may

64.

not | be; || and let them know that God ruleth in JACOB unto the | ends | of the | earth.

14 And at evenING let | them re|turn; || and let them make a noise like a DOG, and go | round a|bout the | city.

15 Let them wander UP and | down for | meat, || and grudge if THEY | be not | satis|fied.

16 But I will sing of thy power; yea, I will sing aloud of thy merCY | in the | morning: || for thou hast been my defence and refUGE | in the | day-of my | trouble.

17 Unto thee, O my STRENGTH, | will I | sing: || for God is my deFENCE, and the | God | of my | mercy.

GLORY BE, ETC.

PSALM LX.

O GOD, thou hast cast us off, thou hast scattered us, thou HAST | been dis|pleased; || O TURN thy|self to | us a|gain.

2 Thou hast made the earth to tremble; thou HAST | broken | it: || heal the breachES | thereof; | for it | shaketh.

3 Thou hast showed thy peoPLE | hard | things; || thou hast made us to DRINK the | wine of-as|tonish|ment.

4 Thou hast given a banner to THEM that | fear | thee, || that it may be displayED be|cause | of the | truth.

5 That thy belovED may | be de|livered, || save with thy RIGHT | hand, and | hear | me.

6 God hath spoken in his holiNESS; I | will re|joice: || I will divide Shechem, and METE | out the | valley of | Succoth.

7 Gilead is mine, and Manasseh is mine; Ephraim also is the STRENGTH | of mine | head; || JUDAH | is my | law|giver;

(64.)
Dr. Woodward.

---

8 Moab is my washpot; over Edom will I CAST | out my | shoe: || Philistia, triUMPH | thou be|cause of | me.

9 Who will bring me inTO the | strong | city? || WHO will | lead me | into | Edom?

10 Wilt not thou, O God, which HADST | cast us | off? || and thou, O God, which didst NOT | go out | with our | armies?

11 Give US | help from | trouble: || for VAIN | is the | help of | man.

12 Through God we shall DO | valiant|ly: || for he it IS that | shall tread | down our | enemies.
                                                                    GLORY BE, ETC.

PSALM LXI.

HEAR my | cry, O | God; || AT|tend un|to my | prayer.

2 From the end of the earth will I cry unto thee, when my HEART is | over|whelmed: || lead ME to the | Rock that-is | higher than | I.

3 For thou hast BEEN a | shelter for | me, || and a STRONG | tower | from the | enemy.

4 I will abide in thy tabernaCLE | for | ever; || I will trust IN the | covert | of thy | wings.

5 For thou, O GOD, hast | heard my | vows: || thou hast given me the heritAGE of | those that | fear thy | name.

6 Thou wilt proLONG the | king's | life; || and his YEARS as | many | gener|ations.

7 He shall abide beFORE | God for | ever: || O prepare mercy and TRUTH, which | may pre|serve | him.

65.

8 So will I sing praise unto THY | name for | ever, ‖ that I MAY | daily per|form my | vows. GLORY BE, ETC.

PSALM LXII.

TRULY my soul waitETH up|on | God: ‖ from HIM | cometh | my sal|vation.

2 He only is my ROCK and | my sal|vation; ‖ he is my defence; I shall | not be | greatly | moved.

3 How long will ye imagine misCHIEF a|gainst a | man? ‖ ye shall be slain all of you: as a bowing wall shall ye BE, and | as a | tottering | fence.

4 They only consult to cast him DOWN | from his | excellency: ‖ they delight in lies: they bless with their MOUTH, | but they | curse | inwardly.

5 My soul, wait thou onLY up|on | God; ‖ for my EXpec|tation | is from | him.

6 He only is my ROCK and | my sal|vation; ‖ he is my deFENCE: ‖ I shall | not be | moved.

7 In God is my salvaTION | and my | glory: ‖ the rock of my strength, AND my | refuge, | is in | God.

8 Trust in him at all times; ye people, pour OUT your | heart be|fore-him: ‖ GOD | is a | refuge | for-us.

9 Surely men of low degree are vanity, and men of high deGREE | are a | lie: ‖ to be laid in the balance, they are ALto-| gether | lighter than | vanity.

10 Trust not in oppression, and become NOT | vain in | robbery: ‖ if riches increase, SET | not your | heart up|on-them.

(65.) *Mornington.*

11 GOD hath | spoken | once; ‖ twice have I heard this, that powER be|longeth | unto | God.

12 Also unto thee, O LORD, be|longeth | mercy; ‖ for thou renderest to every MAN ac|cording | to his | work.

Glory be, etc.

PSALM LXIII.

O GOD, thou art my God; earLY | will I | seek·thee: ‖ my soul thirsteth for thee, my flesh longeth for thee in a dry and thirsty LAND, | where no | water | is;

2 To see thy powER | and thy | glory, ‖ so as I have | seen thee | in the | sanctuary.

3 Because thy loving-kindNESS is | better than | life, ‖ MY | lips shall | praise | thee.

4 Thus will I bless THEE | while I | live: ‖ I will lift UP my | hands | in thy | name.

5 My soul shall be satisfied as WITH | marrow and | fatness;‖ and my mouth shall PRAISE | thee with | joyful | lips;

6 When I remember THEE up|on my | bed, ‖ and meditate on THEE | in the | night- | watches.

7 Because THOU hast | been my | help, ‖ therefore in the shadow of THY | wings will | I re|joice.

8 My soul followeth HARD | after | thee: ‖ thy RIGHT | hand up|holdeth | me.

9 But those that seek my SOUL, | to des|troy·it, ‖ shall go inTO the | lower | parts of·the | earth.

10 They shall FALL | by the | sword: ‖ THEY shall | be a | portion for | foxes.

66.

11 But the king shall rejoice in God; every one that swearETH by | him shall | glory: ‖ but the mouth of them that SPEAK | lies | shall be | stopped. GLORY BE, ETC.

PSALM LXIV.

HEAR my voice, O GOD, | in my | prayer: ‖ preSERVE my | life from | fear of-the | enemy.

2 Hide me from the secret counSEL | of the | wicked; ‖ from the insurrecTION of the | workers | of in|iquity:

3 Who whet their TONGUE | like a | sword, ‖ and bend their bows to shoot their arROWS, | even | bitter | words;

4 That they may shoot in seCRET | at the | perfect: ‖ suddenly do they SHOOT at | him, and | fear | not.

5 They encourage themSELVES in an | evil | matter: ‖ they commune of laying snares privily; they SAY, | Who shall | see | them?

6 They search out iniquities; they accomPLISH a | diligent | search: ‖ both the inward thought of every one of THEM, | and the | heart, is | deep.

7 But God shall shoot at THEM | with an | arrow: ‖ sudden-LY | shall | they be | wounded.

8 So they shall make their own tongue to FALL up|on them-|selves: ‖ ALL that | see-them shall | flee a|way.

9 And all men shall fear, and shall deCLARE the | work of | God: ‖ for they shall wiseLY con|sider | of his | doing.

10 The righteous shall be glad in the LORD, and shall | trust in | him: ‖ and ALL the | upright in | heart shall | glory.

GLORY BE, ETC.

PSALM LXV.

PRAISE waiteth for THEE, O | God, in | Zion: ‖ and unto THEE shall the | vow | be per|formed.

2 O THOU that | hearest | prayer, ‖ unTO | thee shall | all flesh | come.

3 IniquiTIES pre|vail a|gainst-me : ‖ as for our transgresSIONS, | thou shalt | purge them-a|way.

4 Blessed is the man whom thou choosest, and causest to approach unto thee, that HE may | dwell-in thy | courts: ‖ we shall be satisfied with the goodness of thy HOUSE, even | of thy | holy | temple.

5 By terrible things in righteousness wilt thou answer us, O GOD of | our sal|vation; ‖ who art the confidence of all the ends of the earth, and of them that are AFAR | off up|on the | sea:

6 Which by his strength setTETH | fast the | mountains; ‖ beING | gird|ed with | power:

7 Which stillETH the | noise of-the | seas, ‖ the noise of their WAVES, and the | tumult | of the | people.

8 They also that dwell in the uttermost parts are AFRAID | at thy | tokens: ‖ thou makest the outgoings of the mornING and | evening | to re|joice.

9 Thou visitest the earth, and waterest it; thou greatly enrichest it with the river of GOD, which is | full of | water; ‖ thou preparest them corn, when THOU hast | so pro|vided | for-it.

10 Thou waterest the ridges thereof abundantly; thou setTLEST the | furrows there|of; ‖ thou makest it soft with showers; THOU | blessest the | springing there|of:

67.

11 Thou crownest the YEAR | with thy | goodness; || AND | thy paths | drop | fatness.

12 They drop upon the pasTURES | of the | wilderness; || and the little HILLS re|joice on | every | side.

13 The pastures are clothed with flocks; the valleys also are coverED | over with | corn; || they SHOUT for | joy, they | also | sing.
GLORY BE, ETC.

PSALM LXVI.

MAKE a | joyful | noise || unTO | God, | all ye | lands:

2 Sing forth the honOUR | of his | name; || MAKE | his | praise | glorious.

3 Say unto God, How terrible art THOU | in thy | works! || through the greatness of thy power shall thine enemies subMIT them|selves | unto | thee.

4 All the earth shall worship thee, and shall SING | unto | thee; || THEY shall | sing | to thy | name.

5 Come and SEE the | works of | God: || he is terrible in his doING | toward the | children of | men.

6 He turned the sea into dry land: they went THROUGH the | flood on | foot: || THERE did | we re|joice in | him.

7 He ruleth by his power for ever; his EYES be|hold the | nations: || let NOT the re|bellious ex|alt them|selves.

8 O BLESS our | God, ye | people, || and make the VOICE of his | praise | to be | heard;

9 Which holdETH our | soul in | life, || and suffereth NOT our | feet | to be | moved.

Flintoft.

10 For thou, O GOD, hast | proved | us: ‖ thou hast TRIED | us, as | silver is | tried.

11 Thou broughtest US | into the | net; ‖ thou laidEST af-| fliction up|on our | loins.

12 Thou hast caused men to ride over our heads: we went through FIRE | and through | water; ‖ but thou broughtest us OUT | into a | wealthy | place.

13 I will go into thy HOUSE | with burnt-|offerings; ‖ I will | pay | thee my | vows,

14 WHICH my | lips have | uttered, ‖ and my mouth hath spokEN, | when I | was in | trouble.

15 I will offer unto thee burnt-sacrifices of fatLINGS, with the | incense of | rams; ‖ I will | offer | bullocks with | goats.

16 Come and hear, all YE that | fear | God, ‖ and I will declare what HE hath | done | for my | soul.

17 I cried unto HIM | with my | mouth, ‖ and HE was ex-| tolled | with my | tongue.

18 If I regard iniquiTY | in my | heart, ‖ the LORD | will not | hear | me:

19 But veriLY | God hath | heard-me; ‖ he hath attendED to the | voice | of my | prayer.

20 BlessED | be | God, ‖ which hath not turned away my PRAYER, | nor his | mercy from | me.   G<small>LORY</small> <small>BE</small>, <small>ETC</small>.

PSALM LXVII.

G<small>OD</small> be merciFUL unto | us, and | bless-us; ‖ and CAUSE his | face to | shine up|on-us.

68.

2 That thy way may be KNOWN up|on | earth, ‖ thy sav-ING | health a|mong all | nations.

3 Let the people PRAISE | thee, O | God; ‖ LET | all the | people | praise-thee.

4 O let the nations be GLAD, and | sing for | joy; ‖ for thou shalt judge the people righteously, and govERN the | nations-up-|on | earth.

5 Let the people PRAISE | thee, O | God; ‖ LET | all the | people | praise-thee.

6 Then shall the EARTH | yield her | increase; ‖ and God, even our OWN | God, shall | bless | us.

7 GOD shall | bless | us; ‖ and ALL the | ends of-the | earth shall | fear-him.   GLORY BE, ETC.

PSALM LXVIII.

LET God arise, let his eneMIES be | scatter|ed: ‖ let them alSO that | hate him | flee be|fore-him.

2 As smoke is driven AWAY, so | drive them-a|way: ‖ as wax melteth before the fire, so let the wicked perISH | at the | presence of | God.

3 But let the righteous be glad; let them reJOICE be|fore | God: ‖ yea, let THEM ex|ceeding|ly re|joice.

4 Sing unto God, sing praisES | to his | name: ‖ extol him that rideth upon the heavens by his name JAH, | and re|joice be|fore-him.

5 A father of the fatherless, and a JUDGE | of the | widows, ‖ is GOD in his | holy | habi|tation.

(68.) *Dupuis.*

6 God setteth the solitary in families: he bringeth out THOSE which are | bound with | chains: ‖ but the rebelliOUS | dwell in-a | dry | land.

7 O God, when thou wentest FORTH be|fore thy | people, ‖ when thou didst MARCH | through the | wilder|ness;

8 The earth shook, the heavens also DROPPED at the | presence of | God: ‖ even Sinai itself was moved at the presENCE of | God, the | God of | Israel.

9 Thou, O God, didst SEND a | plentiful | rain, ‖ whereby thou didst confirm thine inheritANCE | when | it was | weary.

10 Thy congregaTION hath | dwelt there|in: ‖ thou, O God, hast preparED of thy | goodness | for the | poor.

11 The LORD | gave the | word: ‖ great was the compaNY of | those that | published | it.

12 Kings of arMIES did | flee a|pace; ‖ and she that tarRIED at | home di|vided the | spoil.

13 Though ye have LIEN a|mong the | pots, ‖ yet shall ye be as the wings of a dove covered with silVER, and her | feathers with | yellow | gold.

14 When the AlmighTY | scattered kings | in-it, ‖ IT was | white as | snow in | Salmon.

15 The hill of GOD is as the | hill of | Bashan; ‖ an high HILL, | as the | hill of | Bashan.

16 Why leap YE, ye | high | hills? ‖ this is the hill which God desireth to dwell in; yea, the LORD will | dwell in | it for | ever.

17 The chariots of God are twenty thousand, EVEN | thousands

69.

of | angels: ‖ the Lord is among them, as in SINAI, | in the | holy | place.

18 Thou hast ascended on high, thou hast LED cap|tivity | captive: ‖ thou hast received gifts for men; yea, for the rebellious also, that the LORD | God might | dwell a|mong-them.

19 BlessED | be the | Lord, ‖ who daily loadeth us with benefits, EVEN the | God of | our sal|vation.

20 He that is our GOD is the | God-of sal|vation; ‖ and unto God the LORD be|long the | issues from | death.

21 But God shall WOUND the | head of-his | enemies, ‖ and the hairy scalp of such an ONE as | goeth on | still-in his | trespasses.

22 The Lord said, I will BRING a|gain from | Bashan, ‖ I will bring my people AGAIN | from the | depths of-the | sea;

23 That thy foot may be dipped in the BLOOD | of thine | enemies, ‖ and the tongue of THY | dogs | in the | same.

24 They have SEEN thy | goings, O | God; ‖ even the goings of my GOD, my | King, | in the | sanctuary.

25 The singers went before, the players on instruMENTS | followed | after; ‖ among them WERE the | damsels | playing with | timbrels.

26 Bless ye GOD in the | congre|gations, ‖ even the LORD, | from the | fountain of | Israel.

27 There is little BenjaMIN | with their | ruler, ‖ the princes of Judah and their council, the princes of ZebuLUN, | and the | princes of | Naphtali.

28 Thy GOD hath com|manded thy | strength: ‖ strengthen, O God, THAT which | thou hast | wrought for | us.

(69.)  *Battishill.*

---

29 Because of thy temPLE | at Jer|usalem || shall KINGS bring | presents | unto | thee.

30 Rebuke the company of spearmen, the multitude of the bulls, with the calves of the people, till every one submit himSELF with | pieces of | silver: || scatter thou the peoPLE | that de|light in | war.

31 Princes shall COME | out of | Egypt: || Ethiopia shall soon STRETCH | out her | hands unto | God.

32 Sing unto God, ye kingDOMS | of the | earth; || O SING | praises | unto the | Lord;

33 To him that rideth upon the heavens of heavENS, which | were of | old; || lo, he doth send out his VOICE, and | that a | mighty | voice.

34 Ascribe ye STRENGTH | unto | God: || his excellency is over IsraEL, and his | strength is | in the | clouds.

35 O God, thou art terrible out of THY | holy | places: || the God of Israel is he that giveth strength and powER unto his | people. | Blessed be | God.

GLORY BE, ETC.

PSALM LXIX.

SAVE | me, O | God; || for the waTERS are | come in | unto my | soul.

2 I sink in deep mire, WHERE there | is no | standing: || I am come into deep waters, where the FLOODS | over|flow | me.

3 I am weary of my cryING: my | throat is | dried: || mine eyes FAIL | while I | wait for-my | God.

4 They that hate me without a cause are MORE than the |

91

70.

hairs-of mine | head: || they that would destroy me, being mine enemies wrongfully, are mighty: then I restored THAT which | I took | not a|way.

5 O GOD, thou | knowest my | foolishness; || and my SINS | are not | hid from | thee.

6 Let not them that wait on thee, O Lord God of hosts, be ashamED | for my | sake: || let not those that seek thee be confounded for MY | sake, O | God of | Israel.

7 Because for thy sake I have | borne re|proach; || SHAME | hath | covered my | face.

8 I am become a stranGER | unto my | brethren, || and an aliEN | unto my | mother's | children.

9 For the zeal of thine HOUSE hath | eaten me | up; || and the reproaches of them that reproachED | thee are | fallen up|on-me.

10 When I wept, and chastenED my | soul with | fasting, || THAT | was to | my re|proach.

11 I made sackCLOTH | also my | garment; || and I be|came a | proverb | to-them.

12 They that sit in the GATE | speak a|gainst-me; || and I WAS the | song | of the | drunkards.

13 But as for me, my prayer is unto thee, O Lord, in AN ac-| ceptable | time: || O God, in the multitude of thy mercy hear ME, in the | truth of | thy sal|vation.

14 Deliver me out of the MIRE, and let | me not | sink: || let me be delivered from them that hate ME, and | out of-the | deep | waters.

15 Let not the water-flood overflow me, neither let the DEEP |

swallow me | up, || and let not the PIT | shut her | mouth up-| on-me.

16 Hear me, O Lord; for thy lovING-|kindness is | good: || turn unto me, according to the multiTUDE | of thy | tender | mercies.

17 And hide-not thy FACE | from thy | servant; || for I am in | trouble: | hear me | speedily.

18 Draw nigh unto my SOUL, | and re|deem-it: || deliver ME, be|cause | of mine | enemies.

19 Thou hast known my reproach, and my SHAME, and | my dis|honour: || mine adversarIES are | all be|fore | thee.

20 Reproach hath broken my heart; and I am | full of | heaviness: || and I looked for some to take pity, but there was none; and for comfortERS, | but I | found | none.

21 They gave me also GALL | for my | meat; || and in my THIRST they | gave me | vinegar to | drink.

22 Let their table beCOME a | snare be|fore-them: || and that which should have been for their welFARE, let | it be|come a | trap.

23 Let their eyes be darkenED, that they | see | not; || and make their LOINS con|tinual|ly to | shake.

24 Pour out thine indignaTION up|on | them, || and let thy wrathFUL | anger take | hold of | them.

25 Let their habitaTION be | deso|late; || and LET | none | dwell-in their | tents.

26 For they persecute HIM whom | thou hast | smitten; || and they talk to the GRIEF of | those whom | thou hast | wounded.

71.

27 Add iniquiTY unto | their in|iquity; || and let them not COME | into thy | righteous|ness.

28 Let them be blotted OUT of the | book of-the | living, || and NOT be | written | with the | righteous.

29 But I am | poor and | sorrowful: || let thy salvation, O GOD, | set me | up on | high.

30 I will praise the name of GOD | with a | song, || and will magniFY | him with | thanks|giving.

31 This alSO shall | please the | Lord || better than an ox or bulLOCK | that hath | horns and | hoofs.

32 The humble shall see THIS, | and be | glad; || and your HEART shall | live that | seek | God.

33 For the LORD | heareth the | poor, || and despisETH | not his | prison|ers.

34 Let the heaven and EARTH | praise | him, || the seas, and eveRY | thing that | moveth there|in:

35 For God will save Zion, and will BUILD the | cities of | Judah; || that they may dwell THERE, and | have it | in pos-| session.

36 The seed also of his servants SHALL in|herit | it; || and they that LOVE his | name shall | dwell there|in.

GLORY BE, ETC.

PSALM LXX.

MAKE haste, O GOD, to de|liver | me; || make HASTE to | help | me, O | Lord.

2 Let them be ashamed and confounded that SEEK | after my |

soul; ‖ let them be turned backward, and put to confuSION, | that de|sire my | hurt.

3 Let THEM be | turned | back ‖ for a reward of their SHAME that | say, A|ha, a|ha!

4 Let all those that seek thee reJOICE and be | glad in | thee: ‖ and let such as love thy salvation say continualLY, Let | God be | magni|fied.

5 But I am poor and needy: make haste unTO | me, O | God: ‖ thou art my help and my deliverER; O | Lord, | make no | tarrying. GLORY BE, ETC.

PSALM LXXI.

IN thee, O LORD, do I | put my | trust: ‖ let me nevER be | put | to con|fusion.

2 Deliver me in thy righteousness, and cause ME | to es|cape: ‖ incline thine EAR | unto | me, and | save-me.

3 Be thou my strong habitation, whereunto I MAY con-| tinually re|sort: ‖ thou hast given commandment to save me; for THOU art my | rock | and my | fortress.

4 Deliver me, O my God, out of the HAND | of the | wicked, ‖ out of the HAND of the un|righteous and | cruel | man.

5 For thou art my HOPE, | O Lord | God: ‖ THOU art my | trust | from my | youth.

6 By thee have I been holden UP | from the | womb: ‖ thou art he that took me out of my mother's bowels: my praise shall BE con|tinual|ly of | thee.

7 I am as a wonDER | unto | many: ‖ BUT | thou art | my strong | refuge.

72.

8 Let my mouth be fillED | with thy | praise ‖ and with THY | honour | all the | day.

9 Cast me not OFF in the | time-of old | age; ‖ forsake me NOT | when my | strength | faileth.

10 For mine eneMIES | speak a|gainst-me; ‖ and they that lay WAIT for my | soul take | counsel to|gether,

11 Saying, GOD hath for|saken | him : ‖ persecute and take him; FOR there is | none to-de|liver | him.

12 O God, be NOT | far from | me: ‖ O my GOD, | make haste | for my | help.

13 Let them be confounded and consumed that are adversar-IES | to my | soul; ‖ let them be covered with rePROACH and dis|honour that | seek my | hurt.

14 But I will | hope con|tinually, ‖ and will YET | praise thee | more and | more.

15 My mouth shall show forth thy righteousness and thy salva-TION | all the | day; ‖ for I KNOW | not the | numbers there|of.

16 I will go in the STRENGTH of the | Lord | God: ‖ I will make mention of thy righteousNESS, | even of | thine | only.

17 O God, thou hast taught ME | from my | youth; ‖ and hitherto have I de|clared thy | wondrous | works.

18 Now also when I am old and gray-headed, O GOD, for|sake me | not; ‖ until I have showed thy strength unto this generation, and thy power to eveRY | one that | is to | come.

19 Thy righteousness also, O God, is very high, who HAST | done great | things: ‖ O GOD, | who is | like unto | thee?

20 Thou, which hast showed me great and sore troubles, shalt

(72.)   *Dr. Aldrich.*

quickEN | me a|gain, ‖ and shalt bring me up AGAIN | from the | depths of-the | earth.

21 Thou SHALT in|crease my | greatness, ‖ and comFORT | me on | every | side.

22 I will also praise thee with the psaltery, even thy TRUTH, | O my | God: ‖ unto thee will I sing with the harp, O THOU | Holy | One of | Israel.

23 My lips shall greatly rejoice when I SING | unto | thee; ‖ and my SOUL, | which thou | hast re|deemed.

24 My tongue also shall talk of thy righteousNESS | all-the day | long: ‖ for they are confounded, for they are brought unTO | shame, that | seek my | hurt.   Glory be, etc.

PSALM LXXII.

GIVE the KING thy | judgments, O | God, ‖ and thy righteousNESS | unto the | king's | son.

2 He shall JUDGE thy | people with | righteousness, ‖ AND | thy | poor with | judgment.

3 The mountains shall bring PEACE | to the | people, ‖ AND the | little | hills, by | righteousness.

4 He shall JUDGE the | poor of-the | people, ‖ he shall save the children of the needy, and shall BREAK in | pieces | the op|pressor.

5 They shall fear thee as long as the SUN and | moon en-|dure, ‖ THROUGH|out all | gener|ations.

6 He shall come down like RAIN upon the | mown | grass; ‖ AS | showers that | water the | earth.

73.

7 In his days SHALL the | righteous | flourish; || and abundance of PEACE so | long as-the | moon en|dureth.

8 He shall have dominion alSO from | sea to | sea, || and from the rivER | unto the | ends of-the | earth.

9 They that dwell in the wilderNESS shall | bow be|fore-him; || and HIS | enemies shall | lick the | dust.

10 The kings of Tarshish and of the ISLES | shall bring | presents: || the kings of SheBA and | Seba shall | offer | gifts.

11 Yea, all kings shall FALL | down be|fore-him; || ALL | nations shall | serve | him.

12 For he shall deliver the NEEDY | when he | crieth; || the poor alSO, and | him that | hath no | helper.

13 He shall SPARE the | poor and | needy, || AND shall | save the | souls of-the | needy.

14 He shall redeem their SOUL from de|ceit and | violence: || and precious shall THEIR | blood be | in his | sight.

15 And he shall live, and to him shall be givEN of the | gold of | Sheba: || prayer also shall be made for him continualLY; and | daily shall | he be | praised.

16 There shall be an handful of corn in the EARTH upon the | top of-the | mountains; || the fruit thereof shall shake like Lebanon: and they of the ciTY shall | flourish like | grass of-the | earth.

17 His name SHALL en|dure for | ever: || his name shall be continued as long as the sun; and men shall be blessed in him: ALL | nations shall | call him | blessed.

18 Blessed be the Lord God, the GOD of | Isra|el, || who onLY | doeth | wondrous | things:

(73.) *Mornington.*

19 And blessed be his gloriOUS | name for | ever; || and let the whole earth be filled with his glory. | Amen, | and A|men.

GLORY BE, ETC.

PSALM LXXIII.

TRULY GOD is | good to | Israel, || even to SUCH as | are of-a | clean | heart.

2 But as for me, my FEET were | almost | gone, || MY | steps had | well nigh | slipped.

3 For I was enviOUS | at the | foolish, || when I SAW the pros|perity | of the | wicked:

4 For there are no BANDS | in their | death; || BUT | their | strength is | firm.

5 They are not in trouBLE as | other | men; || neither are THEY | plagued like | other | men:

6 Therefore pride compasseth them ABOUT | as a | chain; || violence coverETH | them | as a | garment.

7 Their eyes STAND | out with | fatness: || THEY have | more than | heart could | wish.

8 THEY | are cor|rupt, || and speak wickedly concernING op|pression: | they speak | loftily.

9 They set their MOUTH a|gainst the | heavens, || and their TONGUE | walketh | through the | earth.

10 Therefore his peoPLE re|turn | hither; || and waters of a full CUP | are wrung | out to | them.

11 And they SAY, | How-doth God | know? || and is there knowLEDGE | in the | most | High?

74.

12 Behold, THESE | are the-un|godly, ‖ who prosper in the WORLD; | they in|crease in | riches.

13 Verily I have cleansED my | heart in | vain, ‖ AND | washed my | hands in | innocency.

14 For all the day LONG have | I been | plagued, ‖ AND | chastened | every | morning.

15 If I SAY, | I-will speak | thus; ‖ behold, I should offend against the genER|ation | of thy | children.

16 When I THOUGHT to | know | this, ‖ IT | was too | painful | for-me,

17 Until I went into the sanctuaRY | of | God; ‖ THEN | understood | I their | end.

18 Surely thou didst set THEM in | slippery | places; ‖ thou castedst THEM | down | into de|struction.

19 How are they brought into desolaTION, as | in a | moment! ‖ THEY are | utterly con|sumed with | terrors.

20 As a DREAM when | one a|waketh; ‖ so, O Lord, when thou awakEST, thou | shalt des|pise their | image.

21 THUS my | heart was | grieved, ‖ and I was | pricked | in my | reins.

22 So foolISH was | I, and | ignorant: ‖ I was | as a | beast be|fore-thee.

23 Nevertheless I AM con|tinually with | thee: ‖ thou hast holdEN | me by | my right | hand.

24 Thou shalt guide ME | with thy | counsel, ‖ and afterWARD | re|ceive | me to | glory.

25 Whom have I in | heaven but | thee? ‖ and there is none upon earth that I de|sire be|sides | thee.

26 My flesh and MY | heart | faileth: || but God is the strength of my HEART, | and my | portion for | ever.

27 For, lo, they that are FAR from | thee shall | perish: || thou hast destroyed all THEM that | go a | whoring from | thee.

28 But it is good for me to DRAW | near to | God: || I have put my trust in the Lord God, that I MAY de|clare | all thy | works.   GLORY BE, ETC.

PSALM LXXIV.

O GOD, why hast thou CAST us | off for | ever? || why doth thine anger smoke AGAINST the | sheep | of thy | pasture?

2 Remember thy congregation, which thou HAST | purchased of | old; || the rod of thine inheritance, which thou hast redeemed; this mount ZION, | wherein | thou hast | dwelt.

3 Lift up thy feet unto the perpetuAL | deso|lations; || even all that the enemy hath DONE | wickedly | in the | sanctuary.

4 Thine enemies roar in the midst of THY | congre|gations; || they set UP their | ensigns | for | signs.

5 A | man was | famous || according as he had lifted up axES up|on the | thick | trees.

6 But now they break down the carvED | work there|of || AT | once with | axes and | hammers.

7 They have cast fire into THY | sanctu|ary; || they have defiled by casting down the dwelling-PLACE of | thy name | to the | ground.

8 They said in their hearts, Let us deSTROY | them to-| gether: || they have burnt up all the synagogues OF | God | in the | land.

75.

9 We SEE | not our | signs: ‖ there is no more any prophet; neither is there among US | any that | knoweth how | long.

10 O God, how long shall the adVER|sary re|proach? ‖ shall the eneMY blas|pheme thy | name for | ever?

11 Why withdrawest thou thy HAND, even | thy right | hand? ‖ PLUCK it | out of | thy | bosom.

12 For God is MY | King of | old, ‖ working salvaTION | in the | midst of-the | earth.

13 Thou didst divide the SEA | by thy | strength: ‖ thou brakest the HEADS of the | dragons | in the | waters.

14 Thou brakest the HEADS of le|viathan in | pieces, ‖ and gavest him to be meat to the peoPLE in|habiting the | wilder|ness.

15 Thou didst cleave the founTAIN | and the | flood: ‖ THOU | driedst up | mighty | rivers.

16 The day is thine, the NIGHT | also is | thine: ‖ thou HAST pre|pared the | light and-the | sun.

17 Thou hast set all the borDERS | of the | earth: ‖ THOU | hast made | summer and | winter.

18 Remember this, that the enemy HATH re|proached, O | Lord, ‖ and that the foolish peoPLE | have blas|phemed thy | name.

19 O deliver not the soul of thy turtle-dove unto the multi-TUDE | of the | wicked: ‖ forget not the congregaTION | of thy | poor for | ever.

20 Have reSPECT | unto the | covenant: ‖ for the dark places of the earth are FULL of the | habi|tations of | cruelty.

21 O let not the oppressED re|turn a|shamed: ‖ let the POOR and | needy | praise thy | name.

Adapted from Luther.

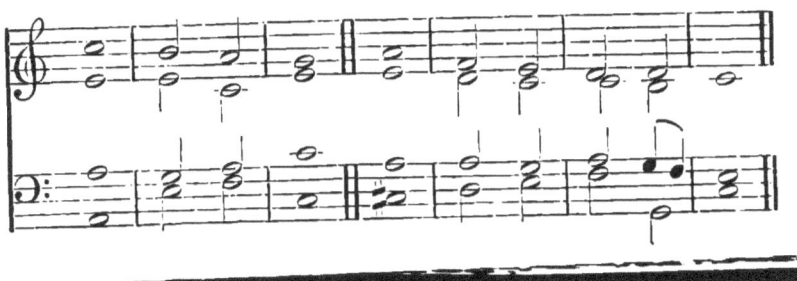

22 Arise, O God, PLEAD thine | own | cause: || remember how the foolISH | man re|proacheth thee | daily.

23 Forget not the VOICE | of thine | enemies: || the tumult of those that rise up AGAINST | thee in|creaseth con|tinually.

GLORY BE, ETC.

PSALM LXXV.

UNTO thee, O God, do we give thanks, unto THEE do | we give | thanks: || for that thy name is NEAR thy | wondrous | works de|clare.

2 When I shall reCEIVE the | congre|gation || I | will | judge up'rightly.

3 The earth and all the inhabitants thereOF | are dis|solved: || I BEAR | up the | pillars | of-it.

4 I said unto the FOOLS, | Deal not | foolishly; || and to the wickED, | Lift not | up the | horn:

5 Lift not UP your | horn on | high: || speak NOT | with a | stiff | neck.

6 For promotion cometh neiTHER | from the | east, || nor FROM the | west, nor | from the | south;

7 But GOD | is the | judge: || he putteth down ONE, and | setteth | up an|other.

8 For in the hand of the Lord there is a cup, and the wine is red; it is full of mixture; and he poureth OUT | of the | same: || but the dregs thereof, all the wicked of the EARTH shall | wring them | out, and | drink-them.

9 But I WILL de|clare for | ever; || I will sing praisES | to the | God of | Jacob.

76

10 All the horns of the wicked alSO will | I cut | off; ‖ but the HORNS of the | righteous shall | be ex|alted.

GLORY BE, ETC.

PSALM LXXVI.

IN JUDAH | is God | known: ‖ HIS | name is | great in | Israel.

2 In Salem alSO | is his | tabernacle, ‖ and HIS | dwelling-| place in | Zion.

3 There brake he the arROWS | of the | bow, ‖ the shield, AND the | sword, | and the | battle.

4 Thou art more gloriOUS and | excel|lent ‖ THAN the | moun|tains of | prey.

5 The stout-hearted are spoiled, THEY have | slept their | sleep;‖ and none of the MEN of | might have | found their | hands.

6 At thy reBUKE, O | God of | Jacob, ‖ both the chariot and horse are CAST | into a | dead | sleep.

7 Thou, even THOU, art | to be | feared: ‖ and who may stand in thy SIGHT | when once | thou art | angry?

8 Thou didst cause judgMENT to be | heard from | heaven; ‖ the EARTH | feared, | and was | still,

9 When GOD a|rose to | judgment, ‖ to SAVE | all the | meek of-the | earth.

10 Surely the wrath of MAN shall | praise | thee: ‖ the re-mainDER of | wrath shalt | thou re|strain.

11 Vow, and pay unTO the | Lord your | God: ‖ let all that be round about him bring preSENTS unto | him that | ought to-be | feared.

Soaper.

(76.)

12 He shall cut OFF the | spirit of | princes: || he is terriBLE | to the | kings of-the | earth.　　　　　Glory be, etc.

PSALM LXXVII.

I CRIED unto God with my voice, even unto GOD | with my | voice; || AND | he gave | ear unto | me.

2 In the day of my trouBLE I | sought the | Lord: || my sore ran in the night, and ceased not: my SOUL re|fused | to be | comforted.

3 I remembered GOD, | and was | troubled: || I complained, and MY | spirit was | over|whelmed.

4 Thou holdEST mine | eyes | waking: || I am so trouBLED | that I | cannot | speak.

5 I have considerED the | days of | old, || THE | years of | ancient | times.

6 I call to remembrance my SONG | in the | night: || I commune with mine own heart; and MY | spirit made | diligent | search.

7 Will the Lord CAST | off for | ever? || and WILL | he be | favourable no | more?

8 Is his mercy CLEAN | gone for | ever? || doth his proMISE | fail for | ever|more?

9 Hath God forgotTEN | to be | gracious? || hath he in anGER shut | up his | tender | mercies?

10 And I said, THIS is | my in|firmity: || but I will remember the years of the right HAND | of the | most | High.

11 I will remember the WORKS | of the | Lord; || surely I will re|member thy | wonders of | old.

77.

12 I will meditate alSO of | all thy | work, || AND | talk | of thy | doings.

13 Thy way, O GOD, is | in the | sanctuary: || who is so GREAT a | God as | our | God?

14 Thou art the GOD that | doest | wonders: || thou hast declarED thy | strength a|mong the | people.

15 Thou hast with thine ARM re|deemed thy | people, || THE | sons of | Jacob and | Joseph.

16 The waters saw thee, O GOD, the | waters | saw-thee; || they were AFRAID: the | depths | also were | troubled.

17 The clouds poured out water: the SKIES sent | out a | sound: || thine arROWS | also | went a|broad.

18 The voice of thy thunDER was | in the | heaven: || the lightnings lightened the WORLD: the | earth | trembled and | shook.

19 Thy way is in the sea, and thy PATH in the | great | waters, || and THY | footsteps | are not | known.

20 Thou leddest thy peoPLE | like a | flock || BY the | hand of | Moses and | Aaron.   GLORY BE, ETC.

PSALM LXXVIII.

GIVE ear, O my peoPLE, | to my | law: || incline your EARS to the | words | of my | mouth.

2 I will open my MOUTH | in a | parable; || I will | utter dark | sayings of | old;

3 Which WE have | heard and | known, || AND | our | fathers have | told-us.

(77.) *Adapted from* Handel.

4 We will not hide THEM | from their | children, ‖ showing to the generation to come the praises of the Lord, and his strength, and his wonderFUL | works that | he hath | done.

5 For he established a testimony in Jacob, and appointED a | law in | Israel, ‖ which he commanded our fathers, that they SHOULD | make them | known to-their | children:

6 That the generation to come might know them, even the chilDREN which | should be | born; ‖ who should arise AND de|clare them | to their | children:

7 That they might SET their | hope in | God, ‖ and not forget the works of GOD, but | keep | his com|mandments:

8 And might not be as their fathers, a stubborn and rebelli-OUS | gener|ation; ‖ a generation that set not their heart aright, and whose spirIT | was not | stedfast with | God.

9 The children of Ephraim, being armED, and | carrying | bows, ‖ turned BACK | in the | day of | battle.

10 They kept NOT the | covenant of | God, ‖ and refusED to | walk | in his | law;

11 AND for|gat his | works, ‖ and his wonDERS that | he had | showed | them.

12 Marvellous things did HE in the | sight of-their | fathers, ‖ in the land of EGYPT, | in the | field of | Zoan.

13 He divided the sea, and caused THEM to | pass | through; ‖ and he made the waTERS to | stand | as an | heap.

14 In the day-time also he led THEM | with a | cloud, ‖ and all the NIGHT | with a | light of | fire.

107

78.

15 He clave the rocks IN the | wilder|ness, ‖ and gave them DRINK as | out of-the | great | depths.

16 He brought streams alSO | out-of the | rock, ‖ and caused waTERS to | run | down like | rivers.

17 And they sinned yet MORE a|gainst | him, ‖ by provoking the most HIGH | in the | wilder|ness.

18 And they tempted GOD | in their | heart, ‖ by askING | meat | for their | lust.

19 Yea, they SPAKE a|gainst | God; ‖ they said, Can God furnish a taBLE | in the | wilder|ness?

20 Behold, he smote the rock, that the waters gushed out, and the STREAMS | over|flowed; ‖ can he give bread also? can HE pro|vide flesh | for his | people?

21 Therefore the Lord heard THIS, | and was | wroth; ‖ so a fire was kindled against Jacob, and anger alSO | came up-a|gainst | Israel;

22 Because they believED | not in | God, ‖ and trustED | not in | his sal|vation;

23 Though he had commanded the CLOUDS | from a|bove, ‖ AND | opened the | doors of | heaven,

24 And had rained down manna upON | them to | eat, ‖ and had given THEM | of the | corn of | heaven.

25 Man did EAT | angels' | food: ‖ HE | sent them | meat to-the | full.

26 He caused an east wind to BLOW | in the | heaven; ‖ and by his power he BROUGHT | in the | south | wind.

27 He rained flesh also upON | them as | dust, ‖ and feathered fowls LIKE | as the | sand of-the | sea;

Battishill.

28 And he let it fall in the MIDST | of their | camp, ‖ ROUND a|bout their | habi|tations.

29 So they did EAT, and | were well | filled: ‖ for he GAVE | them their | own de|sire;

30 They were not estrangED | from their | lust: ‖ but while their MEAT was | yet | in their | mouths,

31 The wrath of God came upon them, and SLEW the | fattest of | them, ‖ and smote DOWN the | chosen | men of | Israel.

32 For all THIS they | sinned | still, ‖ and believed NOT | for his | wondrous | works.

33 Therefore their days did HE con|sume in | vanity, ‖ AND | their | years in | trouble.

34 When he SLEW them, | then they | sought-him; ‖ and they returned and inquirED | early | after | God:

35 And they remembered that GOD | was their | Rock, ‖ AND the | high God | their Re|deemer.

36 Nevertheless they did flatter HIM | with their | mouth, ‖ and they LIED | unto him | with their | tongues.

37 For their HEART was | not right | with-him, ‖ neither were THEY | stedfast | in his | covenant.

38 But he, being full of compassion, forgave their iniquity, AND de|stroyed them | not; ‖ yea, many a time turned he his anger away, and did NOT | stir up | all his | wrath.

39 For he remembered that THEY | were but | flesh; ‖ a wind that passeth AWAY, and | cometh | not a|gain.

40 How oft did they provoke him IN the | wilder|ness, ‖ AND | grieve him | in the | desert!

79.

41 Yea, they turned BACK and | tempted | God, || and limit-ED the | Holy | One of | Israel.

42 They rememberED | not his | hand, || nor the day when HE de|livered them | from the | enemy.

43 How he had WROUGHT his | signs in | Egypt, || and his wonDERS | in the | field of | Zoan;

44 And had turned their rivERS | into | blood; || and their FLOODS, | that they | could not | drink.

45 He sent divers sorts of flies among them, WHICH de-| voured | them; || and FROGS, | which de|stroyed | them.

46 He gave also their inCREASE | unto the | caterpillar, || and THEIR | labour | unto the | locust.

47 He destroyED their | vines with | hail, || and THEIR | sycamore-|trees with | frost.

48 He gave up their cattle alSO | to the | hail, || and their FLOCKS | to hot | thunder|bolts.

49 He cast upon them the fierceness of his anger, wrath, and INdig|nation, and | trouble, || by sendING | evil | angels a|mong-them.

50 He made a WAY | to his | anger; || he spared not their soul from death, but gave their LIFE | over | to the | pestilence;

51 And smote all the FIRST-|born in | Egypt; || the chief of their STRENGTH in the | taber|nacles of | Ham:

52 But made his own people to GO | forth like | sheep, || and guided THEM in the | wilderness | like a | flock.

53 And he led them on safely, so that THEY | feared | not: but the SEA | over|whelmed their | enemies.

54 And he brought them to the border of his sanctuary, EVEN | to this | mountain, ‖ WHICH | his right | hand had | purchased.

55 He cast out the heathen alSO be|fore | them, ‖ and divided them an inheritance by line, and made the tribes of IsraEL to | dwell | in their | tents.

56 Yet they tempted and provokED the | most high | God, ‖ AND | kept | not his | testimonies:

57 But turned back, and dealt unfaithfulLY | like their | fathers: ‖ they were turned ASIDE | like a-de|ceitful | bow.

58 For they provoked him to anGER with | their high | places, ‖ and moved him to jealouSY | with their | graven | images.

59 When God heard THIS, | he was | wroth, ‖ AND | greatly ab|horred | Israel:

60 So that he forsook the taBER|nacle of | Shiloh, ‖ the tent which HE | placed a|mong | men;

61 And delivered his STRENGTH | into cap|tivity, ‖ and his gloRY | into the | enemy's | hand.

62 He gave his people over alSO | unto the | sword; ‖ and WAS | wroth with | his in|heritance.

63 The fire consumED | their young | men; ‖ and their maid-ENS | were not | given to | marriage.

64 Their priests FELL | by the | sword; ‖ and their widOWS | made no | lamen|tation.

65 Then the Lord awaked as ONE | out of | sleep, ‖ and like a mighty MAN that | shouteth by | reason of | wine:

66 And he smote his eneMIES in the | hinder | parts; ‖ he put them TO a per|petu|al re|proach.

80.

67 Moreover he refused the taBER|nacle of | Joseph, || and CHOSE | not the | tribe of | Ephraim:

68 But CHOSE the | tribe of | Judah, || the MOUNT | Zion | which he | loved.

69 And he built his sanctuaRY like | high | palaces, || like the earth which he HATH es|tablish|ed for | ever.

70 He chose DAVID | also his | servant, || AND | took him | from the | sheep-folds:

71 From following the EWES | great with | young || he brought him to feed Jacob his peoPLE, and | Israel | his in|heritance.

72 So he fed them according to the integriTY | of his | heart, || and guided them BY the | skilfulness | of his | hands.

GLORY BE, ETC.

PSALM LXXIX.

O GOD, the heathen are come inTO | thine in|heritance; || thy holy temple have they defiled; they have LAID Jer|usa|lem on | heaps.

2 The dead bodies of thy servants have they given to be meat unto the FOWLS | of the | heaven, || the flesh of thy SAINTS | unto the | beasts of-the | earth.

3 Their blood have they shed like water round ABOUT Jer|u-sa|lem; || AND | there was | none to | bury-them.

4 We are become a rePROACH | to our | neighbours, || a scorn and derision to THEM | that are | round a|bout-us.

5 How long, Lord? wilt THOU be | angry for | ever? || shall THY | jealousy | burn like | fire?

Dr. P. Hayes.

6 Pour out thy wrath upon the heaTHEN that | have not | known-thee, || and upon the kingdoms that have NOT | called up|on thy | name.

7 For they HAVE de|voured | Jacob, || and LAID | waste his | dwelling-|place.

8 O remember not against US | former in|iquities: || let thy tender mercies speedily prevent us; FOR | we are | brought very | low.

9 Help us, O God of our salvation, for the gloRY | of thy | name; || and deliver us, and purge away our SINS, | for thy | name's | sake.

10 Wherefore should the heathen say, WHERE | is their | God? || let him be known among the heathen in our sight by the revenging of the blood of THY | servants | which is | shed.

11 Let the sighing of the prisonER | come be|fore-thee: || according to the greatness of thy power preserve thou THOSE that | are ap|pointed to | die:

12 And render unto our neighbours sevenfold into their bo-SOM | their re|proach, || wherewith they HAVE re|proached | thee, O | Lord.

13 So we thy people, and sheep of thy pasture, will give THEE | thanks for | ever; || we will show forth thy PRAISE | to all | gener|ations.   GLORY BE, ETC.

PSALM LXXX.

GIVE ear, O Shepherd of Israel, thou that leadest JOSEPH | like a | flock; || thou that dwellest beTWEEN the | cheru-bims, | shine | forth.

81.

2 Before Ephraim, and BenjaMIN, | and Ma|nasseh, ‖ stir up thy STRENGTH, and | come and | save | us.

3 Turn US a|gain, O | God, ‖ and cause thy face to SHINE; | and we | shall be | saved.

4 O LORD | God of | hosts, ‖ how long wilt thou be angry AGAINST the | prayer | of thy | people?

5 Thou feedest them WITH the | bread of | tears; ‖ and givest them TEARS to | drink in | great | measure.

6 Thou makest us a STRIFE | unto our | neighbours; ‖ and our eneMIES | laugh a|mong them|selves.

7 Turn as AGAIN, O | God of | hosts, ‖ and cause thy face to SHINE; | and we | shall be | saved.

8 Thou hast brought a VINE | out of | Egypt: ‖ thou hast CAST | out the | heathen, and | planted-it.

9 Thou preparEDST | room be|fore-it, ‖ and didst cause it to take deep ROOT, | and it | filled the | land.

10 The hills were covered WITH the | shadow | of-it: ‖ and the boughs thereOF were | like the | goodly | cedars.

11 She sent out her BOUGHS | unto the | sea, ‖ and HER | branches | unto the | river.

12 Why hast thou then brokEN | down her | hedges, ‖ so that all they which PASS | by the | way do | pluck-her?

13 The BOAR out of the | wood doth | waste-it, ‖ and the wild BEAST of the | field | doth de|vour-it.

14 Return, we beseech THEE, O | God of | hosts: ‖ look down from heaven, AND be|hold, and | visit this | vine;

15 And the vineyard which thy RIGHT | hand hath |

Higgins.

planted, || and the branch that THOU | madest strong | for thy-| self.

16 It is burnt with FIRE, it | is cut | down: || they perish AT the re|buke | of thy | countenance.

17 Let thy hand be upon the MAN of | thy right | hand, || upon the son of man whom THOU | madest strong | for thy-| self.

18 So will we NOT go | back from | thee: || quicken us, and WE will | call up|on thy | name.

19 Turn us again, O LORD | God of | hosts, || cause thy face to SHINE; | and we | shall be | saved.   GLORY BE, ETC.

PSALM LXXXI.

SING aloud unTO | God our | strength: || make a joyful NOISE | unto the | God of | Jacob.

2 Take a psalm, and BRING | hither the | timbrel, || the plea-SANT | harp | with the | psaltery.

3 Blow up the trumPET in the | new-|moon, || in the time appointED, | on our | solemn | feast-day.

4 For this was a statUTE for | Isra|el, || and a LAW | of the | God of | Jacob.

5 This he ordained in Joseph for a testimony, when he went out THROUGH the | land of | Egypt: || where I heard a language | that I | understood | not.

6 I removed his shoulDER | from the | burden: || his hands WERE de|livered | from the | pots.

7 Thou calledst in trouble, and I de|livered | thee; || I answered

82.

thee in the secret place of thunder: I proved THEE | at the | waters of | Meribah.

8 Hear, O my people, and I will testiFY | unto | thee; ‖ O Israel, if THOU wilt | hearken | unto | me;

9 There shall no strange GOD | be in | thee; ‖ neither shalt THOU | worship | any strange | god.

10 I am the Lord thy God, which brought thee OUT of the | land of | Egypt: ‖ open thy MOUTH | wide, and | I will | fill-it.

11 But my people would not hearkEN | to my | voice; ‖ AND | Israel would | none of | me.

12 So I gave them up unTO their | own hearts' | lust; ‖ and they walkED | in their | own | counsels.

13 Oh that my people had hearkenED | unto | me, ‖ and IsraEL had | walked | in my | ways!

14 I should soon HAVE sub|dued their | enemies, ‖ and turnED my | hand a|gainst their | adversaries.

15 The haters of the Lord should have submitted themSELVES | unto | him: ‖ but their TIME should | have en|dured for | ever.

16 He should have fed them also with the finEST | of the | wheat: ‖ and with honey out of the ROCK should | I have | satisfied | thee.   GLORY BE, ETC.

PSALM LXXXII.

GOD standeth in the congregaTION | of the | mighty; ‖ HE | judgeth a|mong the | gods.

2 How long will YE | judge un|justly, ‖ and acCEPT the | persons | of the | wicked?

3 DEFEND the | poor and | fatherless: ‖ do jusTICE | to the-af|flicted and | needy.

4 DelivER the | poor and | needy: ‖ RID them | out of-the | hand of-the | wicked.

5 They know not, neither will they understand; they WALK | on in | darkness: ‖ all the foundaTIONS of the | earth are | out of | course.

6 I have SAID, | Ye are | gods; ‖ and all of you are chil-DREN | of the | most | High:

7 But YE shall | die like | men, ‖ AND | fall like | one-of the | princes.

8 Arise, O GOD, | judge the | earth: ‖ for THOU | shalt in-|herit all | nations. GLORY BE, ETC.

PSALM LXXXIII.

KEEP not THOU | silence, O | God: ‖ hold not thy PEACE, and | be not | still, O | God.

2 For, lo, thine eneMIES | make a | tumult; ‖ and they that hate THEE have | lifted | up the | head.

3 They have taken crafty counSEL a|gainst thy | people, ‖ and consultED a|gainst thy | hidden | ones.

4 They have said, Come, and let us cut them OFF from | being a | nation; ‖ that the name of Israel MAY be | no more | in re-|membrance.

5 For they have consulted togethER with | one con|sent; ‖ THEY | are con|federate a|gainst-thee:

83.

6 The tabernacles of EDOM, | and the | Ishmaelites; ‖ of MOAB, | and the | Hagar|enes;

7 Gebal, and AMMON, and | Ama|lek; ‖ the PhilisTINES, | with the-in|habitants of | Tyre;

8 Assur alSO is | joined with | them: ‖ THEY have | holpen the | children of | Lot.

9 Do unto them as unTO the | Midian|ites; ‖ as to Sisera, as to JABIN | at the | brook of | Kison;

10 WHICH | perished at | En-dor: ‖ THEY be|came as | dung for-the | earth.

11 Make their nobles like OREB, | and like | Zeeb; ‖ yea, all their prinCES as | Zebah, | and as | Zalmunna:

12 Who said, Let us TAKE | to our|selves ‖ THE | houses of | God in-pos|session.

13 O my God, make THEM | like a | wheel; ‖ AS the | stubble be|fore the | wind.

14 As the FIRE | burneth a | wood, ‖ and as the FLAME | setteth the | mountains on | fire;

15 So persecute THEM | with thy | tempest, ‖ and make THEM a|fraid | with thy | storm.

16 FILL their | faces with | shame; ‖ that THEY may | seek thy | name, O | Lord.

17 Let them be confoundED and | troubled for | ever; ‖ yea, let THEM be | put to | shame, and | perish:

18 That men may know that thou, whose name ALONE | is Je|hovah, ‖ art the most HIGH | over | all the | earth.

GLORY BE, ETC.

Attwood.

PSALM LXXXIV.

HOW amiable ARE thy | taber|nacles, ‖ O | Lord | of | hosts!

2 My soul longeth, yea, even fainteth, for the COURTS | of the | Lord: ‖ my heart and my flesh crieth OUT | for the | living | God.

3 Yea, the sparrow hath found an house, and the swallow a nest for herself, where SHE may | lay her | young, ‖ even thine altars, O LORD of | hosts, my | King, and-my | God.

4 Blessed are they that DWELL | in thy | house: ‖ THEY will | be still | praising | thee.

5 Blessed is the man whose STRENGTH | is in | thee; ‖ in whose HEART | are the | ways of | them;

6 Who passing through the valley of BACA | make-it a | well: ‖ the RAIN | also | filleth the | pools.

7 They GO from | strength to | strength; ‖ every one of them in ZION ap|peareth be|fore | God.

8 O Lord God of HOSTS, | hear my | prayer: ‖ GIVE | ear, O | God of | Jacob.

9 BEHOLD, O | God our | shield, ‖ and look upON the | face of | thine a|nointed.

10 For a day in thy courts is betTER | than a | thousand: ‖ I had rather be a door-keeper in the house of my God, than to DWELL | in the | tents of | wickedness.

11 For the Lord God is a sun and shield: the Lord will GIVE | grace and | glory: ‖ no good thing will he withHOLD from | them that | walk up|rightly.

12 O | Lord of | hosts, ‖ blessed IS the | man that | trusteth in | thee.   GLORY BE, ETC.

84.

PSALM LXXXV.

LORD, thou hast been favouraBLE | unto thy | land: ‖ thou hast brought BACK the cap|tivi|ty of | Jacob.

2 Thou hast forgiven the iniquiTY | of thy | people: ‖ THOU hast | covered | all their | sin.

3 Thou hast taken AWAY | all thy | wrath: ‖ thou hast turned thySELF from the | fierceness | of thine | anger.

4 Turn us, O GOD of | our sal|vation, ‖ and cause thine anGER | toward | us to | cease.

5 Wilt thou be anGRY with | us for | ever? ‖ wilt thou draw out thine anGER | to all | gener|ations?

6 Wilt thou not reVIVE | us a|gain, ‖ that thy peoPLE | may re|joice in | thee?

7 Show US thy | mercy, O | Lord, ‖ AND | grant us | thy sal|vation.

8 I will hear what God the Lord will speak: for he will speak peace unto his peoPLE, and | to his | saints: ‖ but let them NOT | turn a|gain to | folly.

9 Surely his salvation is NIGH | them that | fear-him; ‖ that gloRY may | dwell | in our | land.

10 Mercy and TRUTH are | met to|gether; ‖ righteousNESS and | peace have | kissed each | other.

11 Truth shall SPRING | out of-the | earth; ‖ and righteousNESS | shall look | down from | heaven.

12 Yea, the Lord shall give THAT | which is | good; ‖ and OUR | land shall | yield her | increase.

13 RighteousNESS shall | go be|fore-him; ‖ and shall set US | in the | way of-his | steps.   GLORY BE. ETC.

R. Cooke.

PSALM LXXXVI.

BOW down thine ear, O LORD, | hear | me: || FOR | I am | poor and | needy.

2 Preserve my SOUL; for | I am | holy: || O thou my God, SAVE thy | servant that | trusteth in | thee.

3 Be merciful unTO | me, O | Lord: || FOR I | cry unto | thee | daily.

4 Rejoice the SOUL | of thy | servant: || for unto thee, O LORD, do | I lift | up my | soul.

5 For thou, Lord, art good, and reaDY | to for|give; || and plenteous in mercy unto ALL | them that | call-upon | thee.

6 Give ear, O LORD, | unto my | prayer; || and attend to the VOICE | of my | suppli|cations.

7 In the day of my trouble I will | call-upon | thee: || FOR | thou wilt | answer | me.

8 Among the gods there is none like unTO | thee, O | Lord; || neither are there ANY | works like | unto thy | works.

9 All nations whom thou hast made shall come and worship beFORE | thee, O | Lord; || and SHALL | glori|fy thy | name.

10 For thou art great, and doEST | wondrous | things: || THOU | art | God a|lone.

11 Teach me thy way, O Lord; I will WALK | in thy | truth: || UNITE my | heart to | fear thy | name.

12 I will praise thee, O Lord my GOD, with | all my | heart; || and I will gloriFY thy | name for | ever|more.

13 For great is thy merCY | toward | me; || and thou hast delivered my SOUL | from the | lowest | hell.

85.

14 O God, the proud are risen against me, and the assemblies of violent men have SOUGHT | after my | soul, ‖ AND have | not set | thee be|fore-them.

15 BUT | thou, O | Lord, ‖ art a God full of compassion, and gracious, long-sufferING, and | plenteous in | mercy and | truth.

16 O turn unto ME, and have | mercy up|on-me; ‖ give thy strength unto thy serVANT, and | save the | son-of thine | handmaid.

17 Show me a token for good; that they which hate me may see IT, and | be a|shamed: ‖ because thou, Lord, hast holpEN | me, and | comforted | me.   G<small>LORY BE</small>, <small>ETC</small>.

PSALM LXXXVII.

HIS foundation is IN the | holy | mountains. ‖ The Lord loveth the gates of Zion MORE than | all the | dwellings of | Jacob.

2 GloriOUS | things are | spoken ‖ OF | thee, O | city of | God.

3 I will make mention of Rahab and BabyLON to | them that | know-me: ‖ behold Philistia, and Tyre, with Ethiopia; THIS | man was | born | there.

4 And of Zion it shall be said, This and that MAN was | born in | her; ‖ and the Highest himSELF | shall es|tablish | her.

5 The Lord shall count, when he writETH | up the | people, ‖ THAT | this man | was born | there.

6 As well the singers as the players on instruMENTS | shall be | there: ‖ ALL my | springs | are in | thee.   G<small>LORY BE</small>, <small>ETC</small>.

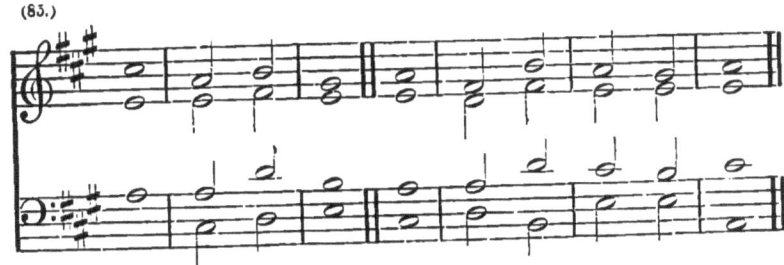

W. Marsh.

(85.)

PSALM LXXXVIII.

O LORD GOD of | my sal|vation, || I have CRIED | day and | night be|fore-thee.

2 Let my PRAYER | come be|fore-thee: || inCLINE thine | ear un|to my | cry;

3 For my SOUL is | full of | troubles; || and my life drawETH | nigh un|to the | grave.

4 I am counted with them that go DOWN | into the | pit: || I am AS a | man that | hath no | strength:

5 Free among the dead, like the slain that lie in the grave, whom THOU re|memberest no | more: || and THEY are | cut off | from thy | hand.

6 Thou hast laid ME in the | lowest | pit, || IN | darkness, | in the | deeps.

7 Thy wrath liETH | hard up|on-me, || and thou hast afflict-ED | me with | all thy | waves.

8 Thou hast put away mine acquaintance far from me; thou hast made me an abominaTION | unto | them: || I am shut UP, | and I | cannot come | forth.

9 Mine eye mourneth by reaSON | of af|fliction: || Lord, I have called daily upon thee; I have stretchED | out my | hands unto | thee.

10 Wilt thou show wonDERS | to the | dead? || shall the DEAD a|rise and | praise | thee?

11 Shall thy loving-kindness be declarED | in the | grave? || or THY | faithfulness | in des|truction?

12 Shall thy wonders be KNOWN | in the | dark? || and thy righteousNESS | in the | land of-for|getfulness?

123

86.

13 But unto thee have I | cried, O | Lord; || and in the morn-ING | shall my | prayer pre|vent-thee.

14 Lord, why castest THOU | off my | soul? || why hidEST | thou thy | face from | me?

15 I am afflicted and ready to DIE from | my youth | up: || while I sufFER thy | terrors I | am dis|tracted.

16 Thy fierce WRATH | goeth | over-me; || THY | terrors have | cut me | off.

17 They came round about ME | daily like | water; || they compassED | me a|bout to|gether.

18 Lover and friend hast thou PUT | far from | me, || and MINE ac|quaintance | into | darkness.   GLORY BE, ETC.

PSALM LXXXIX.

I WILL sing of the merCIES of the | Lord for | ever: || with my mouth will I make known thy faithfulNESS | to all | gener|ations.

2 For I have said, Mercy shall be BUILT | up for | ever: || thy faithfulness shalt thou estabLISH | in the | very | heavens.

3 I have made a coveNANT | with my | chosen, || I have SWORN | unto | David my | servant,

4 Thy seed will I es|tablish for | ever, || and build up thy THRONE | to all | gener|ations.

5 And the heavens shall PRAISE thy | wonders, O | Lord: || thy faithfulness also in the CONgre|gation | of the | saints.

6 For who in the heaven can be comparED | unto the | Lord? || who among the sons of the mighty CAN be | likened | unto the | Lord?

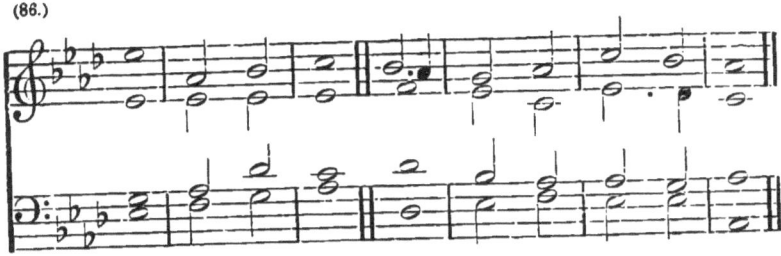

7 God is greatly to be feared in the assemBLY | of the | saints, || and to be had in reverence of ALL | them that | are a|bout-him.

8 O Lord God of hosts, who is a strong LORD like | unto | thee? || or to THY | faithfulness | round a|bout-thee?

9 Thou rulest the ragING | of the | sea: || when the waves thereOF a|rise, thou | stillest | them.

10 Thou hast broken Rahab in pieces, as ONE | that is | slain; | thou hast scattered thine eneMIES | with thy | strong | arm.

11 The heavens are thine, the EARTH | also is | thine: || as for the world, and the fulness thereOF, | thou hast | founded | them.

12 The north and the south thou HAST cre|ated | them: || Tabor and HerMON | shall re|joice in-thy | name.

13 Thou HAST a | mighty | arm: || strong is thy HAND, and | high is | thy right | hand.

14 Justice and judgment are the habitaTION | of thy | throne; || mercy and TRUTH shall | go be|fore thy | face.

15 Blessed is the people that KNOW the | joyful | sound: || they shall walk, O Lord, in the LIGHT | of thy | counte-| nance.

16 In thy name shall they reJOICE | all the | day; || and in thy righteousNESS | shall they | be ex|alted.

17 For thou art the gloRY | of their | strength; || and in thy faVOUR our | horn shall | be ex|alted.

18 For the LORD is | our de|fence; || and the Holy ONE of | Israel | is our | King.

87.

19 Then thou spakest in vision to THY | Holy | One, ‖ and saidst, I have laid help upon one that is mighty; I have exalted ONE | chosen | out of-the | people.

20 I have FOUND | David my | servant; ‖ with my holy OIL have | I a|nointed | him:

21 With whom my HAND shall | be es|tablished; ‖ mine ARM | also shall | strengthen | him.

22 The enemy shall NOT ex|act up|on-him; ‖ nor the SON of | wicked|ness af|flict-him.

23 And I will beat down his FOES be|fore his | face, ‖ and PLAGUE | them that | hate | him.

24 But my faithfulness and my merCY shall | be with | him; ‖ and in my name SHALL his | horn | be ex|alted.

25 I will set his hand alSO | in the | sea, ‖ and HIS | right hand | in the | rivers.

26 He shall CRY | unto | me, ‖ Thou art my Father, my GOD, and the | Rock of | my sal|vation.

27 Also I will MAKE | him my | first-born, ‖ highER | than the | kings of-the | earth.

28 My mercy will I keep for HIM for | ever|more, ‖ and my coveNANT | shall stand | fast with | him.

29 His seed also will I MAKE to en|dure for | ever, ‖ and his THRONE | as the | days of | heaven.

30 If his chilDREN for|sake my | law, ‖ AND | walk not | in my | judgments;

31 If THEY | break my | statutes, ‖ AND | keep not | my com|mandments;

(87.) Dr. Woodward.

32 Then will I visit their transgresSION | with the | rod, |⁞ and THEIR in|iqui|ty with | stripes.

33 Nevertheless my loving-kindness will I not utterLY | take from | him, ‖ nor sufFER my | faithful|ness to | fail.

34 My coveNANT will | I not | break, ‖ nor alter the THING that | is gone | out-of my | lips.

35 Once have I SWORN | by my | holiness ‖ that I | will not | lie unto | David.

36 His seed SHALL en|dure for | ever, ‖ and his THRONE | as the | sun be|fore-me.

37 It shall be established for evER | as the | moon, ‖ and AS a | faithful | witness in | heaven.

38 But thou hast cast OFF | and ab|horred; ‖ thou hast BEEN | wroth with | thine a|nointed.

39 Thou hast made void the coveNANT | of thy | servant; |⁞ thou hast profaned his CROWN, by | casting it | to the | ground.

40 Thou hast broken DOWN | all his | hedges; ‖ thou hast BROUGHT | his strong | holds to | ruin.

41 All that pass by the WAY | spoil | him: ‖ he IS a re-| proach | to his | neighbours.

42 Thou hast set up the right HAND | of his | adversaries; ‖ thou hast made ALL his | enemies | to re|joice.

43 Thou hast also turnED the | edge of-his | sword, ‖ and hast not MADE | him to | stand in-the | battle.

44 Thou hast MADE his | glory to | cease, ‖ and CAST his | throne down | to the | ground.

88.

45 The days of his YOUTH | hast thou | shortened; ‖ THOU hast | covered | him with | shame.

46 How long, Lord? wilt thou HIDE thy|self for | ever? ‖ SHALL thy | wrath | burn like | fire?

47 Remember how SHORT | my time | is: ‖ wherefore hast THOU | made all | men in | vain?

48 What man is he that livETH, and shall | not see | death? ‖ shall he deliver his SOUL | from the | hand of-the | grave?

49 Lord, where are thy forMER | loving-|kindnesses, ‖ which thou swarest unTO | David | in thy | truth?

50 Remember, Lord, the rePROACH | of thy | servants; ‖ how I do bear in my bosom the rePROACH of | all the | mighty | people;

51 Wherewith thine eneMIES have re|proached, O | Lord; ‖ wherewith they have reproachED the | footsteps of | thine a|nointed.

52 Blessed be the LORD for | ever|more. ‖ A|men, and | A|men.

PSALM XC.

LORD, thou hast BEEN our | dwelling-|place ‖ IN | all | gener|ations.

2 Before the mountains were brought forth, or ever thou hadst formed the EARTH | and the | world, ‖ even from everlasting to evER|lasting, | thou art | God.

3 Thou turnest MAN | to de|struction; ‖ and sayEST, Re|turn, ye | children of | men.

4 For a thousand years in thy sight are but as yesterDAY when | it is | past, ‖ AND | as a | watch in-the | night.

Dupuis.

(68.)

5 Thou carriest them away as with a FLOOD; they | are as-a : sleep: || in the morning they are LIKE | grass which | groweth | up.

6 In the morning it flourishETH, and | groweth | up; || in the evenING it | is cut | down, and | withereth.

7 For we are consumED | by thine | anger, || AND | by thy | wrath are-we | troubled.

8 Thou hast set our iniquiTIES be|fore | thee, || our secret SINS | in the | light of-thy | countenance.

9 For all our days are passed AWAY | in thy | wrath: || we spend our YEARS | as a | tale that-is | told.

10 The days of our years are threeSCORE | years and | ten; || and if by reason of strength they be fourscore years, yet is their strength labour and sorrow: for it is soon cut OFF, | and we | fly a|way.

11 Who knoweth the powER | of thine | anger? || even according to THY | fear, so | is thy | wrath.

12 So teach US to | number our | days, || that we MAY ap|ply our | hearts unto | wisdom.

13 RETURN, O | Lord, how | long? || and let it rePENT | thee con|cerning thy | servants.

14 O satisfy us earLY | with thy | mercy; || that we may re-JOICE and be | glad | all our | days.

15 Make us glad according to the days wherein thou HAST af|flicted | us, || and the YEARS where|in we | have seen | evil.

16 Let thy work apPEAR | unto thy | servants, || and THY | glory | unto their | children.

89.

17 And let the beauty of the Lord our GOD | be up|on-us : ‖ and establish thou the work of our hands upon us; yea, the work of OUR | hands es|tablish thou | it.

GLORY BE, ETC.

PSALM XCI.

HE that dwelleth in the secret PLACE of the | most | High ‖ shall abide unDER the | shadow | of the-Al|mighty.

2 I will say of the Lord, He is my refUGE | and my | fortress: ‖ MY | God; in | him will-I | trust.

3 Surely he shall deliver thee from the SNARE | of the | fowler, ‖ AND | from the | noisome | pestilence.

4 He shall cover thee with his feathers, and under his WINGS | shalt thou | trust : ‖ his TRUTH shall | be thy | shield and | buckler.

5 Thou shalt not be AFRAID for the | terror by | night; ‖ nor FOR the | arrow that | flieth by | day;

6 Nor for the pestiLENCE that | walketh in | darkness; ‖ nor for the destrucTION that | wasteth at | noon-|day.

7 A thousand shall fall at thy side, and ten thouSAND at | thy right | hand; ‖ BUT it | shall not | come nigh | thee.

8 Only with thine EYES shalt | thou be|hold, ‖ and SEE the re|ward | of the | wicked.

9 Because thou hast made the LORD which | is my | refuge, ‖ even the MOST | High, thy | habi|tation;

10 There shall NO | evil be|fall-thee, ‖ neither shall ANY | plague come | nigh thy | dwelling.

(89.)

11 For he shall give his angels CHARGE | over | thee, ‖ TO | keep thee-in | all thy | ways.

12 They shall bear thee UP | in their | hands, ‖ lest thou DASH thy | foot a|gainst a | stone.

13 Thou shalt tread upON the | lion and | adder: ‖ the young lion and the dragon shalt THOU | trample | under | feet.

14 Because he hath set his love upon me, therefore will I de|liver | him: ‖ I will set him on high, beCAUSE | he hath | known my | name.

15 He shall call upon me, and I will | answer | him: ‖ I will be with him in trouble; I will delivER | him, and | honour | him.

16 With long life will I | satisfy | him, ‖ AND | show him | my sal|vation. GLORY BE, ETC.

PSALM XCII.

IT is a good thing to give THANKS | unto the | Lord, ‖ and to sing praises unto THY | name, | O most | High:

2 To show forth thy loving-kindNESS | in the | morning, ‖ and THY | faithfulness | every | night,

3 Upon an instrument of ten STRINGS, and up|on the | psaltery; ‖ upon the HARP | with a | solemn | sound.

4 For thou, Lord, hast made me GLAD | through thy | work: ‖ I will triumph IN the | works | of thy | hands.

5 O Lord, how GREAT | are thy | works! ‖ and THY | thoughts are | very | deep.

6 A brutish MAN | knoweth | not; ‖ neither DOTH a | fool under|stand | this.

90.

7 When the wicked spring as the grass, and when all the workERS of in|iquity do | flourish; || it is that THEY shall | be de|stroyed for | ever:

8 BUT | thou, | Lord, || art MOST | high for | ever|more.

9 For, lo, thine enemies, O Lord, for, lo, thine eneMIES | shall | perish; || all the workERS of in|iquity | shall be | scattered.

10 But my horn shalt thou exALT like the | horn of-an | unicorn : || I shall BE a|nointed | with fresh | oil.

11 Mine eye also shall see my deSIRE | on mine | enemies; || and mine ears shall hear my desire of the wickED that | rise up-a|gainst | me.

12 The righteous shall flourISH | like the | palm-tree; || he shall GROW | like a | cedar in | Lebanon.

13 Those that be plantED in the | house of-the | Lord || shall flourISH | in the | courts of-our | God.

14 They shall still bring forth FRUIT in | old | age; || THEY | shall be | fat and | flourishing;

15 To SHOW that the | Lord is | upright; || he is my rock, and there is NO un|righteous|ness in | him.   GLORY BE, ETC.

PSALM XCIII.

THE Lord reigneth, he is clothed with majesty; the Lord is clothed with strength, wherewith he HATH | girded him|self: || the world also is stablishED, | that it | cannot be | moved.

2 Thy THRONE is es|tablished of | old : || THOU | art from | ever|lasting.

(90.) *Adapted from* Beethoven.

3 The floods have lifted up, O Lord, the floods have liftED | up their | voice ; ‖ THE | floods lift | up their | waves.

4 The Lord on high is mightier than the NOISE of | many | waters, ‖ YEA, than the | mighty | waves of· the | sea.

5 Thy testimonIES are | very | sure : ‖ holiness becomETH thine | house, O | Lord, for | ever.   GLORY BE, ETC.

PSALM XCIV.

O LORD God, to WHOM | vengeance be|longeth ; ‖ O God, to whom venGEANCE be|longeth, | show thy|self.

2 Lift up thyself, thou JUDGE | of the | earth : ‖ renDER a re|ward | to the | proud.

3 Lord, how LONG | shall the | wicked, ‖ how LONG | shall the | wicked | triumph ?

4 How long shall they utTER and | speak hard | things ? ‖ and all the workERS of in|iquity | boast them|selves ?

5 They break in pieCES thy | people, O | Lord, ‖ AND af|flict thine | heri|tage :

6 They slay the widOW | and the | stranger, ‖ AND | murder the | father|less :

7 Yet they say, The LORD | shall not | see, ‖ neither shall the GOD of | Jacob re|gard | it.

8 Understand, ye brutISH a|mong the | people ; ‖ and, ye FOOLS, | when will | ye be | wise ?

9 He that planted the EAR, shall | he not | hear ? ‖ he that formED the | eye, shall | he not | see ?

10 He that chastiseth the heathen, shall NOT | he cor|rect ? ‖ he that teacheth MAN | knowledge, shall | not he | know ?

91.

11 The Lord knowETH the | thoughts of | man, ‖ THAT ⊦ they are | vani|ty.

12 Blessed is the man whom THOU | chastenest, O | Lord, ‖ and teachest HIM | out of | thy | law;

13 That thou mayest give him rest from the DAYS | of ad|versity, ‖ until the PIT be | digged | for the | wicked.

14 For the Lord will not CAST | off his | people, ‖ neither will he forSAKE | his in|heri|tance :

15 But judgment shall return unTO | righteous|ness; ‖ and ALL the | upright in | heart shall | follow-it.

16 Who will rise up for me AGAINST the | evil-|doers? ‖ or who will stand up for me AGAINST the | workers | of in|iquity?

17 Unless the LORD had | been my | help, ‖ my SOUL had | almost | dwelt in | silence.

18 When I SAID, | My foot | slippeth; ‖ thy merCY, O | Lord, | held me | up.

19 In the multiTUDE of my | thoughts with|in-me ‖ THY | comforts de|light my | soul.

20 Shall the throne of iniquity have fellowSHIP | with | thee, ‖ which framETH | mischief | by a | law?

21 They gather themselves together against the SOUL | of the | righteous, ‖ AND con|demn the | innocent | blood.

22 But the LORD is | my de|fence; ‖ and my GOD | is the | rock-of my | refuge.

23 And he shall bring upon them their own iniquity, and shall cut them OFF in | their own | wickedness; ‖ yea, the LORD our | God shall | cut them | off.   Glory be, etc.

Dupuis.

PSALM XCV.

O COME, let us SING | unto the | Lord; || let us make a joyful NOISE to the | Rock of | our sal|vation.

2 Let us come before his presENCE | with thanks|giving, || and make a joyful NOISE | unto | him with | psalms.

3 For the LORD is a | great | God, || and a GREAT | King a|bove all | gods.

4 In his hand are the deep plaCES | of the | earth : || the STRENGTH of the | hills is | his | also.

5 The sea is HIS, | and he | made-it; || and his HANDS | formed the | dry | land.

6 O come, let us worSHIP and | bow | down: || let us KNEEL be|fore the | Lord our | maker.

7 For HE | is our | God; || and we are the people of his pasTURE, | and the | sheep of-his | hand.

8 To-day, if ye will hear his voice, hardEN | not your | heart, || as in the provocation, and as in the DAY of temp|tation | in the | wilderness;

9 When your faTHERS | tempted | me, || provED | me, and | saw my | work.

10 Forty years long was I grieved with THIS | gener|ation, || and said, It is a people that do err in their heart, and THEY | have not | known my | ways:

11 Unto whom I SWARE | in my | wrath, || that they should NOT | enter | into my | rest.

GLORY BE, ETC.

92.

PSALM XCVI.

O SING unto the LORD a | new | song: || sing unTO the | Lord, | all the | earth.

2 Sing unto the LORD, | bless his | name; || show forth HIS sal|vation from | day to | day.

3 Declare his gloRY a|mong the | heathen, || HIS | wonders a|mong all | people.

4 For the Lord is great, and greatLY | to be | praised: || he is to BE | feared a|bove all | gods.

5 For all the GODS of the | nations are | idols: || BUT the | Lord | made the | heavens.

6 Honour and majesTY | are be|fore-him; || STRENGTH and | beauty are | in his | sanctuary.

7 Give unto the Lord, O ye kinDREDS | of the | people, || give unTO the | Lord | glory and | strength.

8 Give unto the Lord the glory DUE | unto his | name: || bring an offerING, and | come in|to his | courts.

9 O worship the LORD in the | beauty of | holiness; || FEAR be|fore him, | all the | earth.

10 Say among the heathen that the Lord reigneth: the world also shall be established that IT shall | not be | moved: || HE shall | judge the | people | righteously.

11 Let the heavens rejoice, and LET the | earth be | glad; || let the sea ROAR, | and the | fulness there|of.

12 Let the field be joyful, and ALL that | is there|in; || then shall all the trees of the WOOD re|joice be|fore the | Lord:

(92.)   *Dr. Crotch.*

13 For he cometh, for he comETH to | judge the | earth : || he shall judge the world with righteousNESS, and the | people | with his | truth.   GLORY BE, ETC.

PSALM XCVII.

THE Lord reignETH; let the | earth re|joice; || let the multi- TUDE of | isles be | glad there|of.

2 Clouds and darkNESS are | round a|bout-him : || righteousness and judgment are the haBI|tation | of his | throne.

3 A FIRE | goeth be|fore-him, || and burneth UP his | enemies | round a|bout.

4 His lightNINGS en|lightened the | world; || THE | earth | saw, and | trembled.

5 The hills melted like wax at the presENCE | of the | Lord, || at the presence of the LORD | of the | whole | earth.

6 The heavens deCLARE his | righteous|ness, || and ALL the | people | see his | glory.

7 Confounded be all they that serve graven images, that BOAST them|selves of | idols: || worSHIP | him, | all ye | gods.

8 Zion HEARD, | and was | glad; || and the daughters of Judah rejoiced beCAUSE of thy | judgments, | O | Lord.

9 For thou, Lord, art high ABOVE | all the | earth; || thou art exaltED | far a|bove all | gods.

10 Ye that love the LORD, | hate | evil : || he preserveth the souls of his saints; he delivereth THEM | out of-the | hand of-the | wicked.

93.

11 Light is SOWN | for the | righteous, ‖ and gladNESS | for the | upright in | heart.

12 REJOICE in the | Lord, ye | righteous; ‖ and give thanks AT the re|membrance | of his | holiness.   GLORY BE, ETC.

PSALM XCVIII.

O SING unto the Lord a new song; for he hath DONE | marvellous | things: ‖ his right hand and his holy ARM hath | gotten | him the | victory.

2 The Lord hath made KNOWN | his sal|vation: ‖ his righteousness hath he openly showED | in the | sight of-the | heathen.

3 He hath remembered his mercy and his truth toWARD the | house of | Israel: ‖ all the ends of the earth have SEEN the sal|vation | of our | God.

4 Make a joyful noise unto the LORD, | all the | earth: ‖ make a loud NOISE, and re|joice, and | sing | praise.

5 Sing unto the LORD | with the | harp; ‖ with the HARP, | and the | voice of-a | psalm.

6 With trumPETS and | sound of | cornet ‖ make a joyful NOISE be|fore the | Lord, the | King.

7 Let the sea ROAR, and the | fulness there|of; ‖ the WORLD, and | they that | dwell there|in.

8 Let the FLOODS | clap their | hands; ‖ let the hills be joyFUL to|gether be|fore the | Lord;

9 For he comETH to | judge the | earth: ‖ with righteousness shall he judge the WORLD, | and the | people with | equity.

GLORY BE, ETC.

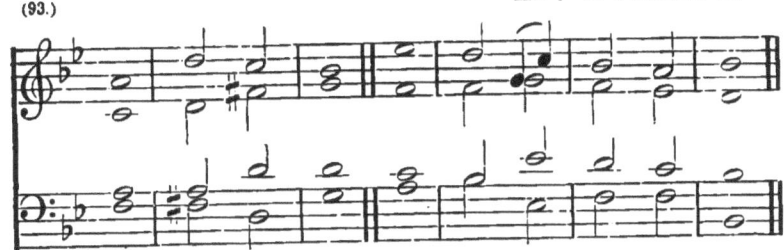
(93.) Dr. Woodward.

PSALM XCIX.

THE Lord reignETH; let the | people | tremble: ‖ he sitteth between the cheruBIMS; | let the | earth be | moved.

2 The LORD is | great in | Zion; ‖ and HE is | high a|bove all | people.

3 Let them praise thy GREAT and | terrible | name; ‖ FOR | it ⁀ is | holy.

4 The king's strength alSO | loveth | judgment: ‖ thou dost establish equity; thou executest judgMENT and | righteous|ness in | Jacob.

5 Exalt YE the | Lord our | God, ‖ and worship AT his | footstool; for | he is | holy.

6 Moses and Aaron among his priests, and Samuel among them that CALL up|on his | name; ‖ they called upon the LORD, | and he | answered | them.

7 He spake unto them IN the | cloudy | pillar: ‖ they kept his testimonIES, and the | ordinance | that he | gave-them.

8 Thou answeredst THEM, O | Lord our | God: ‖ thou wast a God that forgavest them, though thou tookEST | vengeance | of their-in|ventions.

9 Exalt the Lord our God, and worship AT his | holy | hill: ‖ FOR the | Lord our | God is | holy. GLORY BE, ETC.

PSALM C.

MAKE a joyful noise unto the LORD, | all ye | lands. ‖ Serve the Lord with gladness; COME be|fore his | presence with | singing.

2 Know ye that the Lord he is God: it is he that hath made

94.

us, and NOT | we our|selves: ‖ we are his peoPLE, | and the | sheep of-his | pasture.

3 Enter into his gates with thanksgiving, and inTO his | courts with | praise : ‖ be thankFUL unto | him, and | bless his | name.

4 FOR the | Lord is | good; ‖ his mercy is everlasting; and his TRUTH en|dureth to | all gener|ations.   GLORY BE, ETC.

PSALM CI.

I WILL SING of | mercy and | judgment : ‖ unto THEE, O | Lord, | will I | sing.

2 I will behave myself wisely in a perfect way. O when wilt thou COME | unto | me ? ‖ I will walk within my HOUSE | with a | perfect | heart.

3 I will set no wicked THING be|fore mine | eyes : ‖ I hate the work of them that turn ASIDE ; it | shall not | cleave to | me.

4 A froward HEART shall de|part from | me ; ‖ I will NOT | know a | wicked | person.

5 Whoso privily slandereth his neighbour, HIM will | I cut | off : ‖ him that hath an high look, and a PROUD | heart, will | not I | suffer.

6 Mine eyes shall be upon the faithful of the land, that THEY may | dwell with | me : ‖ he that walketh in a perfect WAY, | he shall | serve | me.

7 He that worketh deceit shall not DWELL with|in my | house : ‖ he that telleth lies shall NOT | tarry | in my | sight.

8 I will early destroy all the wickED | of the | land ; ‖ that I may cut off all wicked doers FROM the | city | of the | Lord.
   GLORY BE, ETC.

PSALM CII.

HEAR my | prayer, O | Lord, || and LET my | cry come | unto | thee.

2 Hide not thy face from me in the day when I am in trouble; incline thine EAR | unto | me: || in the DAY when I | call, | answer me | speedily.

3 For my DAYS are con|súmed like | smoke, || AND my | bones are | burnt as-an | hearth.

4 My heart is smitTEN, and | withered like | grass; || so that I for|get to | eat my | bread.

5 By reason of the VOICE | of my | groaning || MY | bones cleave | to my | skin.

6 I am like a peliCAN of the | wilder|ness: || I am | like an | owl of-the | desert.

7 I WATCH, and | am as-a | sparrow || A|lone up|on the | house-top.

8 Mine enemies reproach ME | all the | day; || and they that are mad against ME are | sworn a|gainst | me.

9 For I have eatEN | ashes like | bread, || AND | mingled my | drink with | weeping,

10 Because of thine indignaTION | and thy | wrath: || for thou hast lifted ME | up, and | cast me | down.

11 My days are like a shadOW | that de|clineth; || AND | I am | withered like | grass.

12 But thou, O Lord, SHALT en|dure for | ever; || and thy rememBRANCE | unto | all gener|ations.

95.

13 Thou shalt arise, and have merCY up|on | Zion : ‖ for the time to favour HER, | yea, the | set time, - is | come.

14 For thy servants take pleaSURE | in her | stones, ‖ AND | favour the | dust there|of.

15 So the heathen shall FEAR the | name of-the | Lord, ‖ and ALL the | kings of-the | earth thy | glory.

16 When the LORD shall | build up | Zion, ‖ he SHALL ap|pear | in his | glory.

17 He will regard the PRAYER | of the | destitute, ‖ AND | not des|pise their | prayer.

18 This shall be written for the genER|ation to | come : ‖ and the people which shall BE cre|ated shall | praise the | Lord.

19 For he hath looked down from the HEIGHT | of his | sanctuary ; ‖ from heavEN did the | Lord be|hold the | earth ;

20 To hear the groanING | of the | prisoner ; ‖ to loose THOSE that | are ap|pointed to | death ;

21 To declare the NAME of the | Lord in | Zion, ‖ and HIS | praise | in Jer|usalem :

22 When the peoPLE are | gathered to|gether, ‖ AND the | kingdoms, to | serve the | Lord.

23 He weakened my STRENGTH | in the | way ; ‖ HE | shortened | my | days.

24 I said, O my God, take me not AWAY in the | midst-of my | days : ‖ thy years ARE through|out all | gener|ations.

25 Of old hast thou laid the foundaTION | of the | earth ; ‖ and the heavENS | are the | work of-thy | hands.

(95.)   *Rev. W. H. Havergal.*

---

26 They shall perish, but thou shalt endure; yea, all of them shall wax OLD | like a | garment: ‖ as a vesture shalt thou change THEM, | and they | shall be | changed:

27 But THOU | art the | same, ‖ and THY | years shall | have no | end.

28 The children of thy serVANTS | shall con|tinue, ‖ and their SEED shall | be es|tablished be|fore-thee.   Glory be, etc.

PSALM CIII.

BLESS the LORD, | O my | soul; ‖ and all that is within ME, | bless his | holy | name.

2 Bless the LORD, | O my | soul, ‖ AND for|get not | all his | benefits :

3 Who forgivETH | all thine-in|iquities; ‖ WHO | healeth | all thy-dis|eases;

4 Who redeemeth thy LIFE | from de|struction; ‖ who crowneth thee with lovING-|kindness and | tender | mercies.

5 Who satisfieth thy MOUTH | with good | things; ‖ so that thy YOUTH is re|newed | like the | eagle's.

6 The Lord executETH | righteousness and | judgment ‖ FOR | all that | are op|pressed.

7 He made known his WAYS | unto | Moses, ‖ his ACTS | unto the | children of | Israel.

8 The LORD is | merciful and | gracious, ‖ SLOW to | anger, and | plenteous in | mercy.

9 He will NOT | always | chide; ‖ neither will HE | keep his | anger for | ever.

96.

10 He hath not dealt with US | after our | sins; ‖ nor rewarded US ac|cording to | our in|iquities.

11 For as the heaven is HIGH a|bove the | earth, ‖ so great is his merCY | toward | them that | fear-him.

12 As far as the EAST is | from the | west, ‖ so far hath he removED | our trans|gressions | from-us.

13 Like as a faTHER | pitieth his | children, ‖ so the LORD | pitieth | them that | fear-him.

14 For HE | knoweth our | frame; ‖ HE re|membereth that | we are | dust.

15 As for man, his DAYS | are as | grass; ‖ as a flowER of the | field, | so he | flourisheth.

16 For the wind passeth over IT, and | it is | gone; ‖ and the PLACE there|of shall | know-it no | more.

17 But the mercy of the Lord is from everlasting to everlasting upON | them that | fear-him, ‖ and his righteousNESS | unto | children's | children;

18 To SUCH as | keep his | covenant, ‖ and to those that rememBER | his com|mandments to | do-them.

19 The Lord hath prepared his THRONE | in the | heavens; ‖ and his kingDOM | ruleth | over | all.

20 Bless the Lord, ye his angels, that excel in strength, that DO | his com|mandments, ‖ hearkening unTO the | voice | of his | word.

21 Bless ye the LORD, all | ye his | hosts; ‖ ye minisTERS of | his, that | do his | pleasure.

22 Bless the Lord, all his works in all plaCES of | his do-|minion: ‖ BLESS the | Lord, | O my | soul.   GLORY BE, ETC.

PSALM CIV.

BLESS the LORD, | O my | soul. ‖ O Lord my God, thou art very great; THOU art | clothed with | honour and | majesty:

2 Who coverest thyself with LIGHT as | with a | garment; ‖ who stretchest OUT the | heavens | like a | curtain;

3 Who layeth the beams of his chamBERS | in the | waters; ‖ who maketh the clouds his chariot; who walkETH up|on the | wings of-the | wind;

4 Who makETH his | angels | spirits, ‖ HIS | ministers a | flaming | fire;

5 Who laid the foundaTIONS | of the | earth, ‖ that it should NOT | be re|moved for | ever.

6 Thou coveredst it with the DEEP as | with a | garment: ‖ the waTERS | stood a|bove the | mountains.

7 At THY re|buke they | fled; ‖ at the voice of THY | thunder they | hasted a|way.

8 They go UP | by the | mountains; ‖ they go down by the valleys unto the PLACE which | thou hast | founded | for-them.

9 Thou hast set a bound that THEY may | not pass | over; ‖ that they turn NOT a|gain to | cover the | earth.

10 He sendeth the SPRINGS | into the | valleys, ‖ WHICH | run a|mong the | hills.

11 They give drink to every BEAST | of the | field: ‖ the WILD | asses | quench their | thirst.

97.

12 By them shall the fowls of the heaven have THEIR | habi|tation, ‖ WHICH | sing a|mong the | branches.

13 He watereth the HILLS | from his | chambers; ‖ the earth is satisfiED | with the | fruit of-thy | works.

14 He causeth the grass to grow for the cattle, and HERB for the | service of | man; ‖ that he may bring FORTH | food out | of the | earth,

15 And wine that maketh GLAD the | heart of | man, ‖ and oil to make his face to shine, and BREAD which | strengtheneth | man's | heart.

16 The trees of the LORD are | full of | sap; ‖ the ceDARS of | Lebanon, which | he hath | planted;

17 Where the BIRDS | make their | nests: ‖ as for the STORK, the | fir-trees | are her | house.

18 The high hills are a refUGE for the | wild | goats, ‖ AND the | rocks | for the | conies.

19 He appointED the | moon for | seasons; ‖ the SUN | knoweth his | going | down.

20 Thou makest darkNESS, and | it is | night; ‖ wherein all the BEASTS of the | forest | do creep | forth.

21 The young lions ROAR | after their | prey, ‖ AND | seek their | meat from | God.

22 The sun ariseth, they gathER them|selves to|gether, ‖ AND | lay them | down in-their | dens.

23 Man goeth FORTH | unto his | work ‖ and to HIS | labour un|til the | evening.

24 O Lord, how manifold are thy works! in wisdom hast

A. Bennett.

THOU | made them | all : ‖ THE | earth is | full-of thy | riches:

25 So is this GREAT and | wide | sea, ‖ wherein are things creeping innumeraBLE, both | small and | great | beasts.

26 THERE | go the | ships : ‖ there is that leviathan, whom THOU hast | made to | play there|in.

27 These WAIT | all upon | thee; ‖ that thou mayest give THEM their | meat in | due | season.

28 That thou givEST | them they | gather : ‖ thou openest thine HAND, | they are | filled with | good.

29 Thou hidest thy FACE, | they are | troubled : ‖ thou takest away their breath, they DIE, | and re|turn to-their | dust.

30 Thou sendest forth thy spirIT, they | are cre|ated: ‖ and THOU re|newest the | face of-the | earth.

31 The glory of the LORD shall en|dure for | ever; ‖ the LORD | shall re|joice in-his | works.

32 He looketh on the EARTH, | and it | trembleth; ‖ HE | toucheth the | hills, and-they | smoke.

33 I will sing unto the LORD as | long as-I | live; ‖ I will sing praise to my GOD | while I | have my | being.

34 My meditation of HIM | shall be | sweet; ‖ I | will be | glad in-the | Lord.

35 Let the sinners be consumed out of the earth, and let the wickED | be no | more. ‖ Bless thou the Lord, O my SOUL. | Praise | ye the | Lord.

GLORY BE, ETC.

98.

PSALM CV.

O GIVE thanks unto the Lord; CALL up|on his | name; ‖ make KNOWN his | deeds a|mong the | people.

2 Sing unto him, sing PSALMS | unto | him; ‖ talk YE of | all his | wondrous | works.

3 Glory YE in his | holy | name: ‖ let the heart of THEM re|joice that | seek the | Lord.

4 Seek the LORD, | and his | strength; ‖ SEEK his | face | ever|more.

5 Remember his marvellous WORKS that | he hath | done; ‖ his wonDERS, and the | judgments | of his | mouth,

6 O ye SEED of | Abraham his | servant, ‖ YE | children of | Jacob his | chosen.

7 HE is the | Lord our | God: ‖ his judgMENTS | are in | all the | earth.

8 He hath rememberED his | covenant for | ever, ‖ the word which he commandED to a | thousand | gener|ations:

9 Which coveNANT he | made with | Abraham, ‖ and HIS | oath | unto | Isaac;

10 And confirmed the same unto JACOB | for a | law, ‖ and to IsraEL for an | ever|lasting | covenant;

11 Saying, Unto thee will I GIVE the | land of | Canaan, ‖ THE | lot of | your in|heritance:

12 When they were but a FEW | men in | number; ‖ yea, veRY | few, and | strangers | in-it.

13 When they went from one naTION | to an|other, ‖ from one kingDOM | to an|other | people,

Goodenough.

14 He suffered no MAN to | do them | wrong; || yea, he reprovED | kings | for their | sakes;

15 Saying, Touch NOT | mine a|nointed, || AND | do my | prophets no | harm.

16 Moreover, he called for a faMINE up|on the | land: || he BRAKE the | whole | staff of | bread.

17 He sent a man before THEM, | even | Joseph, || WHO was | sold | for a | servant;

18 Whose FEET they | hurt with | fetters: || HE | was | laid in | iron;

19 Until the TIME that | his word | came: || the WORD of the | Lord | tried | him.

20 The king SENT and | loosed | him; || even the rulER of the | people, and | let-him go | free.

21 He made HIM | lord of-his | house, || AND | ruler of | all his | substance;

22 To bind his prinCES | at his | pleasure, || AND | teach his | senators | wisdom.

23 Israel also CAME | into | Egypt, || and Jacob sojournED | in the | land of | Ham:

24 And he increasED his | people | greatly, || and made THEM | stronger | than their | enemies.

25 He turned their HEART to | hate his | people, || to DEAL | subtilely | with his | servants.

26 He SENT | Moses his | servant, || AND | Aaron | whom he-had | chosen.

27 They showED his | signs a|mong-them, || and wonDERS | in the | land of | Ham.

99.

28 He sent darkNESS, and | made it | dark; || and they rebelLED | not a|gainst his | word.

29 He turned their waTERS | into | blood, || AND | slew | their | fish.

30 Their land brought forth FROGS | in a|bundance || IN the | chambers | of their | kings.

31 He spake, and there came diVERS | sorts of | flies, || AND | lice in | all their | coasts.

32 He gave THEM | hail for | rain, || and flamING | fire | in their | land.

33 He smote their vines alSO, | and their | fig-trees; || AND | brake the | trees of-their | coasts.

34 He SPAKE, and the | locusts | came, || and caterpilLARS, and | that with|out | number,

35 And did eat up all the HERBS | in their | land, || and devourED the | fruit | of their | ground.

36 He smote also all the first-BORN | in their | land, || THE | chief of | all their | strength.

37 He brought them forth alSO with | silver and | gold: || and there was not one feeBLE | person a|mong their | tribes.

38 Egypt was GLAD when | they de|parted: || FOR the | fear of-them | fell up|on-them.

39 He spread a CLOUD | for a | covering; || and FIRE to give | light | in the | night.

40 The people askED, and | he brought | quails, || and satisfied THEM | with the | bread of | heaven.

Rev. T. Gregory.

41 He opened the rock, and the waTERS | gushed | out; || they ran in the DRY | places | like a | river.

42 For he rememberED his | holy | promise, || AND | Abra-| ham his | servant.

43 And he brought FORTH his | people with | joy, || and HIS | chosen | with | gladness;

44 And gave THEM the | lands of-the | heathen: || and they inheritED the | labour | of the | people;

45 That they might observe his statUTES, and | keep his | laws. || PRAISE | ... | ye the | Lord.

GLORY BE, ETC.

PSALM CVI.

PRAISE ye the Lord. O give thanks unto the LORD; for | he is | good: || FOR his | mercy en|dureth for | ever.

2 Who can utter the MIGHTY | acts of-the | Lord? || WHO can | show forth | all his | praise?

3 Blessed are THEY that | keep | judgment, || and he that doETH | righteousness | at all | times.

4 Remember me, O Lord, with the favour that thou bearEST | unto thy | people: || O visIT | me with | thy sal|vation;

5 That I may see the good of thy chosen, that I may rejoice in the gladNESS | of thy | nation, || that I MAY | glory with | thine in|heritance.

6 We have sinNED | with our | fathers; || we have committed iniquiTY; | we have | done | wickedly.

7 Our fathers understood not thy wonders in Egypt; they

100.

remembered not the multiTUDE | of thy | mercies; || but provoked him at the SEA, | even at-the | Red | sea.

8 Nevertheless he saved THEM for | his name's | sake, || that he might make his MIGHTY | power | to be | known.

9 He rebuked the Red sea also, and IT was | dried | up: || so he led them THROUGH the | depths, as | through the | wilderness.

10 And he saved them from the hand of HIM that | hated | them, || and redeemed THEM | from the | hand of-the | enemy.

11 And the waTERS | covered their | enemies; || THERE | was not | one-of them | left.

12 Then believED | they his | words; || THEY | sang | his | praise.

13 They SOON for|gat his | works; || THEY | waited | not for-his | counsel;

14 But lusted exceedingLY | in the | wilderness, || AND | tempted | God in-the | desert.

15 And he gave THEM | their re|quest; || but SENT | leanness | into their | soul.

16 They envied Moses alSO | in the | camp, || AND | Aaron the | saint of-the | Lord.

17 The earth openED and | swallowed up | Dathan, || and coverED the | company | of A|biram.

18 And a fire was kindlED | in their | company; || THE | flame burnt | up the | wicked.

19 They MADE a | calf in | Horeb, || AND | worshipped the | molten | image.

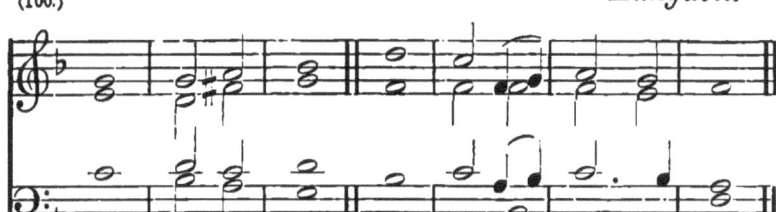

(100.)

20 THUS they | changed their | glory || into the similiTUDE of an | ox that | eateth | grass.

21 They forGAT | God their | saviour, || which HAD | done great | things in | Egypt;

22 Wondrous WORKS in the | land of | Ham, || and terrible THINGS | by the | Red | sea.

23 Therefore he said that HE | would de|stroy-them, || had not Moses his chosen stood before him in the breach, to turn away his WRATH, | lest he | should de|stroy-them.

24 Yea, they despisED the | pleasant | land; || THEY be-|lieved | not his | word;

25 But murmurED | in their | tents, || and hearkened NOT | unto the | voice of-the | Lord:

26 Therefore he lifted UP his | hand a|gainst-them, || to OVER|throw them | in the | wilderness:

27 To overthrow their seed alSO a|mong the | nations, || AND to | scatter them | in the | lands.

28 They joined themselves alSO | unto Baal-|peor, || and ATE the | sacrifices | of the | dead.

29 Thus they provoked him to anGER with | their in|ventions; || AND the | plague brake | in up|on-them.

30 Then stood up PhineHAS, and | executed | judgment; || AND | so the | plague was | stayed:

31 And that was countED unto | him for | righteousness || unto ALL gener|ations for | ever|more.

32 They angered him alSO at the | waters of | strife, || so that it went ILL with | Moses | for their | sakes:

101.

33 Because THEY pro|voked his | spirit, || so that he SPAKE unad|visedly | with his | lips.

34 They did NOT de|stroy the | nations, || concerning WHOM the | Lord com|manded | them;

35 But were minglED a|mong the | heathen, || AND | learned | their | works.

36 And THEY | served their | idols; || WHICH | were a | snare unto | them.

37 YEA, they | sacri|ficed || their SONS and their | daughters | unto | devils,

38 And shed innocent blood, even the blood of their sons and of their daughters, whom they sacrificed unTO the | idols of | Canaan: || and the LAND | was pol|luted with | blood.

39 Thus were they defilED with | their own | works, || and went a whorING | with their | own in|ventions:

40 Therefore was the wrath of the Lord kindlED a|gainst his | people, || insomuch that HE ab|horred his | own in|heritance.

41 And he gave them into the HAND | of the | heathen; || and they that hated THEM | ruled | over | them.

42 Their enemies alSO op|pressed | them, || and they were brought inTO sub|jection | under their | hand.

43 Many times did HE de|liver | them: || but they provoked him with their counsel, and were BROUGHT | low for | their in|iquity.

44 Nevertheless he regardED | their af|fliction || WHEN | he | heard their | cry:

45 And he rememberED for | them his | covenant, || and repented accordING to the | multitude | of his | mercies.

46 He made them alSO | to be | pitied ‖ of ALL | those that | carried them | captives.

47 Save us, O Lord our God, and gather us FROM a|mong the | heathen, ‖ to give thanks unto thy holy NAME, and to | triumph | in thy | praise.

48 Blessed be the Lord God of Israel from everlastING to | ever|lasting : ‖ and let all the people say, AMEN. | Praise | ye the | Lord.

PSALM CVII.

O GIVE thanks unto the LORD; for | he is | good : ‖ FOR his | mercy en|dureth for | ever.

2 Let the redeemED of the | Lord say | so, ‖ whom he hath redeemED | from the | hand of-the | enemy;

3 And gathered THEM | out of-the | lands, ‖ from the east, and from the WEST, from the | north, and | from the | south.

4 They wandered in the wilderNESS in a | solitary | way; ‖ THEY | found no | city to | dwell-in.

5 HunGRY | and | thirsty, ‖ THEIR | soul | fainted | in-them.

6 Then they cried unto the LORD | in their | trouble, ‖ and he delivered THEM | out of | their dis|tresses.

7 And he led them FORTH by the | right | way, ‖ that they might GO to a | city of | habi|tation.

8 Oh that men would praise the LORD | for his | goodness, ‖ and for his wonderful WORKS | to the | children of | men!

9 For he satisfiETH the | longing | soul, ‖ and fillETH the | hungry | soul with | goodness.

102.

10 Such as sit in darkness, and IN the | shadow of | death, ‖ being BOUND | in af|fliction and | iron;

11 Because they rebelled AGAINST the | words of | God, ‖ and contemned the counSEL | of the | most | High.

12 Therefore he brought DOWN their | heart with | labour: ‖ they fell DOWN, and | there was | none to | help.

13 Then they cried unto the LORD | in their | trouble, ‖ and he savED them | out of | their dis|tresses.

14 He brought them out of darkNESS and the | shadow of | death, ‖ AND | brake their | bands in | sunder.

15 Oh that men would praise the LORD | for his | goodness, ‖ and for his wonderful WORKS | to the | children of | men!

16 For he hath brokEN the | gates of | brass, ‖ and CUT the | bars of | iron in | sunder.

17 Fools beCAUSE of | their trans|gression, ‖ and because of THEIR in|iquities, | are af|flicted.

18 Their soul abhorreth ALL | manner of | meat; ‖ and they draw NEAR | unto the | gates of | death.

19 Then they cry unto the LORD | in their | trouble, ‖ and he saveth THEM | out of | their dis|tresses.

20 He sent his WORD, and | healed | them, ‖ and deliverED | them from | their de|structions.

21 Oh that men would praise the LORD | for his | goodness, ‖ and for his wonderful WORKS | to the | children of | men!

22 And let them sacrifice the sacrifiCES | of thanks|giving, ‖ and deCLARE his | works | with re|joicing.

A. L. Peace.

23 They that go DOWN to the | sea in | ships, || that DO | business | in great | waters;

24 These SEE the | works of-the | Lord, || and HIS | wonders | in the | deep.

25 For he commandeth, and raisETH the | stormy | wind, || which liftETH | up the | waves there|of.

26 They mount up to the heaven, they go down AGAIN | to the | depths; || their SOUL is | melted be|cause of | trouble.

27 They REEL | to and | fro, || and stagger like a drunken MAN, and | are at | their wit's | end.

28 Then they cry unto the LORD | in their | trouble, || and he bringeth THEM | out of | their dis|tresses.

29 He makETH the | storm a | calm, || SO that the | waves there|of are | still.

30 Then are they glad, beCAUSE | they be | quiet; || so he bringeth them unTO | their de|sired | haven.

31 Oh that men would praise the LORD | for his | goodness, || and for his wonderful WORKS | to the | children of | men!

32 Let them exalt him also in the congregaTION | of the | people, || and praise him IN the as|sembly | of the | elders.

33 He turneth rivERS | into a | wilderness, || AND the | water-springs | into dry | ground;

34 A fruitful LAND | into | barrenness, || for the wickedNESS of | them that | dwell there|in.

35 He turneth the wilderness inTO a | standing | water, || AND | dry ground | into | water-springs:

157

103.

36 And there he makETH the | hungry to | dwell, || that they may prePARE a | city for | habi|tation;

37 And sow the FIELDS, | and plant | vineyards, || WHICH may | yield | fruits of | increase.

38 He blesseth them also, so that THEY are | multiplied | greatly, || and suffereth NOT their | cattle | to de|crease.

39 AGAIN, | they are | minished, || and brought LOW through op|pression, af|fliction, and | sorrow.

40 He pourETH con|tempt-upon | princes, || and causeth them to wander in the wilderNESS, | where there | is no | way.

41 Yet setteth he the poor on HIGH | from af|fliction, || and maketh HIM | families | like a | flock.

42 The righteous shall see IT, | and re|joice; || and ALL in-|iquity shall | stop her | mouth.

43 Whoso is wise, and WILL ob|serve these | things, || even they shall understand the lovING-|kindness | of the | Lord.

GLORY BE, ETC.

PSALM CVIII.

O GOD, my | heart is | fixed; || I will sing and give PRAISE, | even | with my | glory.

2 AWAKE, | psaltery and | harp; || I mySELF | will a|wake | early.

3 I will praise thee, O LORD, a|mong the | people; || and I will sing praises unTO | thee a|mong the | nations.

4 For thy mercy is GREAT a|bove the | heavens; || and thy TRUTH | reacheth | unto the | clouds.

(103.) A. L. Peace.

5 Be thou exalted, O GOD, a|bove the | heavens, ‖ and thy gloRY a|bove | all the | earth;

6 That thy belovED may | be de|livered: ‖ save with thy RIGHT | hand, and | answer | me.

7 God hath spokEN | in his | holiness; ‖ I will rejoice, I will divide Shechem, and METE | out the | valley of | Succoth.

8 Gilead is MINE; Ma|nasseh is | mine; ‖ Ephraim also is the strength of mine HEAD; | Judah | is my | lawgiver.

9 Moab is my wash-pot; over Edom will I CAST | out my | shoe; ‖ OVER Phil|istia | will I | triumph.

10 Who will bring me inTO the | strong | city? ‖ WHO will | lead me | into | Edom?

11 Wilt not thou, O GOD, who hast | cast us | off? ‖ and wilt not thou, O GOD, | go forth | with our | hosts?

12 Give US | help from | trouble; ‖ for VAIN | is the | help of | man.

13 Through GOD we | shall do | valiantly : ‖ for he it IS that | shall tread | down our | enemies.

GLORY BE, ETC.

PSALM CIX.

HOLD | not thy | peace, ‖ O | God | of my | praise;

2 For the mouth of the wicked, and the mouth of the deceitFUL, are | opened a|gainst-me; ‖ they have spoken against ME | with a | lying | tongue.

3 They compassed me about alSO with | words of | hatred; ‖ and fought AGAINST | me with|out a | cause.

104.

4 For my LOVE they | are my | adversaries: || but I | give myself | unto | prayer.

5 And they have rewarded ME | evil for | good, || AND | hatred | for my | love.

6 Set thou a wicked MAN | over | him; || and let SATAN | stand at | his right | hand.

7 When he shall be judged, let HIM | be con|demned; || and LET his | prayer be|come | sin.

8 LET his | days be | few; || and LET an|other | take his | office.

9 LET his | children be | fatherless, || AND | his | wife a | widow.

10 Let his children be continualLY | vagabonds, and | beg; || let them seek their bread alSO | out of-their | desolate | places.

11 Let the extortioner CATCH | all that-he | hath; || and LET the | stranger | spoil his | labour.

12 Let there be none to extend merCY | unto | him; || neither let there be ANY to | favour his | fatherless | children.

13 Let his posteriTY | be cut | off; || and in the generation following LET their | name be | blotted | out.

14 Let the iniquity of his fathers be rememberED | with the | Lord; || and let not the SIN of his | mother be | blotted | out.

15 Let them be beFORE the | Lord con|tinually, || that he may cut off the memoRY | of them | from the | earth:

16 Because that he remembered not to show mercy, but persecuted the POOR and | needy | man, || that he might EVEN | slay the | broken in | heart.

(104.)   *Dr. Smith.*

17 As he loved cursing, so let it COME | unto | him; ‖ as he delighted not in blessING, | so let-it | be far | from-him.

18 As he clothed himself with cursing LIKE as | with his | garment, ‖ so let it come into his bowels like waTER, and | like oil | into his | bones.

19 Let it be unto him as the garMENT which | covereth | him, ‖ and for a girdle whereWITH | he is | girded con|tinually.

20 Let this be the reward of mine adversarIES | from the | Lord, ‖ and of them that SPEAK | evil a|gainst my | soul.

21 But do thou for me, O God the LORD, for | thy name's | sake: ‖ because thy merCY is | good, de|liver thou | me.

22 For I am | poor and | needy, ‖ AND my | heart is | wounded with|in-me.

23 I am gone like the shadOW when | it de|clineth; ‖ I am tossED | up and | down as-the | locust.

24 My KNEES are | weak through | fasting; ‖ AND my | flesh | faileth of | fatness.

25 I became also a rePROACH | unto | them: ‖ when they looked upON | me they | shaked their | heads.

26 Help ME, O | Lord my | God: ‖ O save ME ac|cording | to thy | mercy:

27 That they may KNOW that | this-is thy | hand; ‖ THAT | thou, | Lord, hast | done-it.

28 Let them CURSE, but | bless | thou: ‖ when they arise, let them be ashamED; but | let thy | servant re|joice.

29 Let mine adversarIES be | clothed with | shame, ‖ and let them cover themselves with their OWN con|fusion, as | with a | mantle.

105.

30 I will greatly praise the LORD | with my | mouth; ‖ yea, I will PRAISE | him a|mong the | multitude.

31 For he shall stand at the RIGHT | hand of-the | poor, ‖ to save HIM from | those that-con|demn his | soul.

GLORY BE, ETC.

PSALM CX.

THE Lord SAID | unto my | Lord, ‖ Sit thou at my right hand, until I | make thine | enemies thy | footstool.

2 The Lord shall send the rod of thy STRENGTH | out of | ZION: ‖ rule THOU | in the | midst-of thine | enemies.

3 Thy people shall be willing in the day of thy power, in the beauties of holiNESS from the | womb of-the | morning: ‖ THOU | hast the | dew of-thy | youth.

4 The Lord hath SWORN, and will | not re|pent, ‖ Thou art a priest for ever afTER the | order | of Mel|chizedek.

5 The LORD at | thy right | hand ‖ shall strike THROUGH | kings in-the | day-of his | wrath.

6 He shall judge among the heathen, he shall fill the plaCES | with-the dead | bodies; ‖ he shall wound the HEADS | over | many | countries.

7 He shall drink of the BROOK | in the | way: ‖ thereFORE shall | he lift | up the | head.   GLORY BE, ETC.

PSALM CXI.

PRAISE | ye the | Lord. ‖ I will praise the Lord with my whole heart, in the assembly of the upRIGHT, and | in the | congre|gation.

Cambridge Chant.

(105.)

2 The WORKS of the | Lord are | great, ‖ sought out of all THEM | that have | pleasure there|in.

3 His work is honouraBLE and | glori|ous; ‖ and his righteous-NESS en|dureth | for | ever.

4 He hath made his wonderful WORKS to | be re|membered: ‖ the LORD is | gracious, and | full-of com|passion.

5 He hath given MEAT unto | them that | fear-him: ‖ he will evER be | mindful | of his | covenant.

6 He hath showed his peoPLE the | power of-his | works, ‖ that he may give THEM the | heritage | of the | heathen.

7 The works of his HANDS are | verity and | judgment; ‖ ALL | his com|mandments are | sure.

8 They stand FAST for | ever and | ever, ‖ AND are | done in | truth and | uprightness.

9 He sent redemption unto his people; he hath commandED his | covenant for | ever: ‖ hoLY and | reverend | is his | name.

10 The fear of the Lord IS the be|ginning of | wisdom: ‖ a good understanding have all they that do his commandMENTS: his | praise en|dureth for | ever.   GLORY BE, ETC

PSALM CXII.

PRAISE | ye the | Lord. ‖ Blessed is the man that feareth the Lord, that delightETH | greatly in | his com|mandments.

2 His seed shall be MIGHTY | upon | earth : ‖ the genera-TION of the | upright | shall be | blessed.

3 Wealth and richES shall | be-in his | house ; ‖ and his righteousNESS en|dureth | for | ever.

106.

4 Unto the upright there ariseth LIGHT | in the | darkness: ‖ he is graCIOUS, and | full of-com|passion, and | righteous.

5 A good man showETH | favour, and | lendeth: ‖ he will GUIDE his af|fairs | with dis|cretion.

6 Surely he shall NOT be | moved for | ever: ‖ the righteous shall BE in | ever|lasting re|membrance.

7 He shall not be AFRAID of | evil | tidings: ‖ his heart is fixED, | trusting | in the | Lord.

8 His heart is established, he shall NOT | be a|fraid, ‖ until he see HIS de|sire up|on his | enemies.

9 He hath dispersed; he hath givEN | to the | poor; ‖ his righteousness endureth for ever; his HORN shall | be ex|alted with | honour.

10 The wicked shall see it, and be grieved; he shall gnash with his TEETH, and | melt a|way: ‖ the deSIRE | of the | wicked shall | perish.   GLORY BE, ETC.

PSALM CXIII.

PRAISE | ye the | Lord. ‖ Praise, O ye servants of the LORD, | praise the | name of-the | Lord.

2 Blessed be the NAME | of the | Lord ‖ from this time FORTH | and for | ever|more.

3 From the rising of the sun, unto the goING | down of-the | same, ‖ the LORD'S | name is | to be | praised.

4 The Lord is HIGH a|bove all | nations, ‖ and HIS | glory a|bove the | heavens.

5 Who is like unTO the | Lord our | God, ‖ WHO | dwelleth | on | high;

Adapted from Spohr.

6 WHO | humbleth him|self ‖ to behold the things that ARE in | heaven, and | in the | earth!

7 He raiseth up the POOR | out-of the | dust, ‖ and liftETH the | needy | out-of the | dunghill;

8 That he may SET | him with | princes, ‖ even WITH the | princes | of his | people.

9 He maketh the barren woMAN | to keep | house, ‖ and to be a joyful mother of chilDREN. | Praise | ye the | Lord.

GLORY BE, ETC.

PSALM CXIV.

WHEN IsraEL went | out of | Egypt, ‖ the house of JACOB from a | people of | strange | language,

2 JUDAH | was his | sanctuary, ‖ AND | Israel | his do-| minion.

3 The SEA | saw-it, and | fled; ‖ JorDAN | was | driven | back.

4 The mounTAINS | skipped like | rams, ‖ AND the | little | hills like | lambs.

5 What ailed thee, O thou SEA, | that thou | fleddest? ‖ thou JorDAN, that | thou wast | driven | back?

6 Ye mountains, that YE | skipped like | rams; ‖ and YE | little | hills, like | lambs?

7 Tremble, thou earth, at the presENCE | of the | Lord, ‖ at the presENCE | of the | God of | Jacob;

8 Which turned the rock inTO a | standing | water, ‖ the FLINT | into a | fountain of | waters. GLORY BE, ETC.

107.

PSALM CXV.

NOT unto us, O LORD, | not unto | us, ‖ but unto thy name give glory, for thy merCY, and | for thy | truth's | sake.

2 Wherefore SHOULD the | heathen | say, ‖ WHERE | is | now their | God?

3 But our GOD is | in the | heavens; ‖ he hath done WHATso|ever | he hath | pleased.

4 Their IDOLS are | silver and | gold, ‖ THE | work of | men's | hands.

5 They have MOUTHS, but they | speak | not; ‖ eyes have THEY, | but they | see | not;

6 They have EARS, but they | hear | not; ‖ noses have THEY, | but they | smell | not;

7 They have HANDS, but they | handle | not; ‖ feet have they, but they walk not; neiTHER | speak they | through their | throat.

8 They that make THEM are | like unto | them; ‖ so is eveRY | one that | trusteth in | them.

9 O Israel, trust THOU | in the | Lord: ‖ HE | is their | help and-their | shield.

10 O house of AARON, | trust in-the | Lord: ‖ HE | is their | help and-their | shield.

11 Ye that fear the LORD, | trust in-the | Lord: ‖ HE | is their | help and-their | shield.

12 The Lord hath BEEN | mindful of | us: ‖ he will bless us; he will bless the house of Israel; HE will | bless the | house of | Aaron.

(107.) *Barrow.*

13 He will bless THEM that | fear the | Lord, ‖ BOTH | small | and | great.

14 The Lord shall increase YOU | more and | more, ‖ YOU | and your | chil|dren.

15 Ye are blessED | of the | Lord, ‖ WHICH | made | heaven and | earth.

16 The heaven, even the heavENS, | are the | Lord's: ‖ but the earth hath he givEN | to the | children of | men.

17 The dead PRAISE | not the | Lord, ‖ neither ANY that | go down | into | silence.

18 But we will bless the Lord from this time FORTH and for | ever|more. ‖ PRAISE | ... | the | Lord.

GLORY BE, ETC.

PSALM CXVI.

I | love the | Lord, ‖ because he hath heard my VOICE | and my | suppli|cations.

2 Because he hath inclined his EAR | unto | me, ‖ therefore will I call upON | him as | long as-I | live.

3 The sorrows of death compassed me, and the pains of HELL gat | hold up|on-me: ‖ I | found | trouble and | sorrow.

4 Then called I upON the | name of-the | Lord; ‖ O Lord, I beSEECH | thee, de|liver my | soul.

5 Gracious IS the | Lord, and | righteous; ‖ YEA, our | God is | merci|ful.

6 The LORD pre|serveth the | simple: ‖ I was brought LOW, | and he | helped | me.

108.

7 Return unto thy REST, | O my | soul; ‖ for the Lord hath DEALT | bounti|fully with | thee.

8 For thou hast deliverED my | soul from | death, ‖ mine eyes from TEARS, | and my | feet from | falling.

9 I will WALK be|fore the | Lord ‖ IN the | land | of the | living.

10 I believed, thereFORE | have I | spoken: ‖ I | was | greatly af|flicted;

11 I SAID | in my | haste, ‖ ALL | men | are | liars.

12 What shall I renDER | unto the | Lord ‖ for ALL his | benefits | toward | me?

13 I will take the CUP | of sal|vation, ‖ and CALL up|on the | name of-the | Lord.

14 I will pay my VOWS | unto the | Lord ‖ NOW in the | presence of | all his | people.

15 PreCIOUS in the | sight of-the | Lord ‖ IS the | death | of his | saints.

16 O Lord, truLY | I-am thy | servant; ‖ I am thy servant, and the son of thine handMAID: | thou hast | loosed my | bonds.

17 I will offer to thee the sacriFICE | of thanks|giving, ‖ and will CALL up|on the | name of-the | Lord.

18 I will pay my VOWS | unto the | Lord ‖ NOW in the | presence of | all his | people,

19 In the COURTS of the | Lord's | house, ‖ in the midst of thee, O JerusaLEM. | Praise | ye the | Lord.

GLORY BE, ETC.

(108.)   Dr. Worgan.

PSALM CXVII.

O PRAISE the LORD, | all ye | nations: || PRAISE | him, | all ye | people.

2 For his merciful kindness is GREAT | toward | us: || and the truth of the Lord endureth for evER. | Praise | ye the | Lord.

Glory be, etc.

PSALM CXVIII.

O GIVE thanks unto the LORD; for | he is | good: || be-CAUSE his | mercy en|dureth for | ever.

2 Let IsraEL | now | say, || that HIS | mercy en|dureth for | ever.

3 Let the house of AARON | now | say, || that HIS | mercy en|dureth for | ever.

4 Let them now that FEAR the | Lord | say, || that HIS | mercy en|dureth for | ever.

5 I called upon the LORD | in dis|tress: || the Lord answered me, and set ME | in a | large | place.

6 The Lord is on my SIDE; I | will not | fear: || WHAT can | man do | unto | me?

7 The Lord taketh my PART with | them that | help-me; || therefore shall I see my desire upON | them that | hate | me.

8 It is betTER to | trust in-the | Lord || than to PUT | confi|dence in | man.

9 It is betTER to | trust in-the | Lord || than to PUT | confi|dence in | princes.

10 All nations compassED | me a|bout: || but in the NAME of the | Lord will | I de|stroy-them.

109.

11 They compassed me about; yea, they compassED | me a|bout: || but in the NAME of the | Lord I | will de|stroy-them.

12 They compassed me about like bees; they are quenchED as the | fire of | thorns: || for in the NAME of the | Lord I | will de|stroy-them.

13 Thou hast thrust sore at ME that | I might | fall; || BUT the | Lord | helped | me.

14 The LORD is my | strength and | song, || and IS be|come | my sal|vation.

15 The voice of rejoicing and salvation is in the tabernaCLES | of the | righteous : || the right HAND of the | Lord | doeth | valiantly.

16 The right hand of the LORD | is ex|alted; || the right HAND of the | Lord | doeth | valiantly.

17 I shall NOT | die, but | live, || AND de|clare the | works of-the | Lord.

18 The LORD hath | chastened me | sore; || but he hath not given ME | over | unto | death.

19 Open to ME the | gates of | righteousness: || I will go into THEM, and | I will | praise the | Lord:

20 THIS | gate of-the | Lord, || inTO | which the | righteous shall | enter.

21 I will | praise | thee; || for thou hast heard ME, and | art be|come my-sal|vation.

22 The STONE which the | builders re|fused || is beCOME the | head-stone | of the | corner.

(109.)   *Dr. Pring.*

23 THIS is the | Lord's | doing: ‖ IT is | marvellous | in our | eyes.

24 This is the DAY which the | Lord hath | made; ‖ we will reJOICE | and be | glad in | it.

25 Save NOW, I be|seech-thee, O | Lord: ‖ O Lord, I beseech THEE, ⌈ send ⌉ now pros|perity.

26 Blessed be he that comETH in the | name of-the | Lord: ‖ we have blessed you out OF the | ⌈house⌉ of the | Lord.

27 God is the Lord, which HATH | showed us | light: ‖ bind the sacrifice with cords, EVEN | unto the | horns of-the | altar.

28 Thou art my GOD, and | I will | praise-thee: ‖ thou art MY | God, I | will ex|alt-thee.

29 O give thanks unto the LORD; for | he is | good : ‖ for HIS | mercy en|dureth for | ever.   GLORY BE, ETC.

PSALM CXIX.
ALEPH.

BLESSED are the undefilED | in the | way, ‖ who WALK | in the | law of-the | Lord.

2 Blessed are THEY that | keep his | testimonies, ‖ and that seek HIM | with the | ⌈whole⌉ heart.

3 They alSO do | no in|iquity: ‖ THEY | ⌈walk⌉ | in his | ways.

4 Thou HAST com|manded | us ‖ TO | keep thy | precepts | diligently.

5 OH | that my | ways ‖ WERE di|rected to | keep thy | statutes!

6 Then shall I NOT | be a|shamed, ‖ when I have reSPECT unto | ⌈all⌉ | thy com|mandments.

110.

7 I will praise thee WITH up|rightness of | heart, || when I shall HAVE | learned thy | righteous | judgments.

8 I will | keep thy | statutes: || O for|sake me | not | utterly.

BETH.

9 Wherewithal shall a young MAN | cleanse his | way? || by taking heed thereTO ac|cording | to thy | word.

10 With my whole HEART | have I | sought-thee: || O let me NOT | wander from | thy com|mandments.

11 Thy word have I HID | in mine | heart, || that I | might not | sin a|gainst-thee.

12 BlessED art | thou, O | Lord: || TEACH | me | thy | statutes.

13 With my LIPS have | I de|clared || ALL the | judgments | of thy | mouth.

14 I have rejoicED in the | way-of thy | testimonies, || AS | much as | in all | riches.

15 I will mediTATE | in thy | precepts, || and HAVE re|spect un|to thy | ways.

16 I will delight mySELF | in thy | statutes: || I will | not for|get thy | word.

GIMEL.

17 Deal bountifulLY | with thy | servant, || that I may | live, and | keep thy | word.

18 OPEN | thou mine | eyes, || that I may behold wonDROUS | things out | of thy | law.

19 I am a stranGER | in the | earth: || hide NOT | thy com- | mandments | from-me.

20 My soul breaketh for the longING | that it | hath || unto THY | judgments | at all | times.

21 Thou hast rebuked the PROUD | that are | cursed, || which DO | err from | thy com|mandments.

22 Remove from me rePROACH | and con|tempt; || FOR | I have | kept thy | testimonies.

23 Princes also did SIT and | speak a|gainst-me: || but thy serVANT did | meditate | in thy | statutes.

24 Thy testimonies alSO are | my de|light, || AND | my | counsel|lors.

DALETH.

25 My soul cleavETH | unto the | dust: || quicken thou ME ac|cording | to thy | word.

26 I HAVE de|clared my | ways, || and thou heardest ME; | teach | me thy | statutes.

27 Make me to underSTAND the | way-of thy | precepts: || so shall I TALK | of thy | wondrous | works.

28 My SOUL | melteth for | heaviness: || strengthen thou ME ac|cording | unto thy | word.

29 Remove from ME the | way of | lying; || and GRANT | me thy | law | graciously.

30 I have choSEN the | way of | truth: || thy judgMENTS | have I | laid be|fore-me.

31 I have STUCK | unto thy | testimonies: || O LORD, | put me | not to | shame.

111.

32 I will run the WAY of | thy com|mandments, || when THOU | shalt en|large my | heart.

HE.

33 Teach me, O LORD, the | way-of thy | statutes; || and I shall | keep it | unto the | end.

34 Give me understanding, and I shall | keep thy | law; || yea, I shall observe IT | with my | whole | heart.

35 Make me to go in the PATH of | thy com|mandments; || FOR there|in do | I de|light.

36 Incline my HEART | unto thy | testimonies, || AND | not to | covetous|ness.

37 Turn away mine EYES from be|holding | vanity; || AND | quicken thou | me in-thy | way.

38 Stablish thy WORD | unto thy | servant, || who IS de-| voted | to thy | fear.

39 Turn away my rePROACH | which I | fear: || FOR | thy | judgments are | good.

40 Behold, I have longED | after thy | precepts: || quicken ME | in thy | righteous|ness.

VAU.

41 Let thy mercies come also unTO | me, O | Lord, || even thy salvaTION, ac|cording | to thy | word.

42 So shall I have wherewith to answer HIM that re|proach-eth | me: || for I | trust | in thy | word.

43 And take not the word of truth utterLY | out of-my | mouth: || for I HAVE | hoped | in thy | judgments.

(111.)   J. Turle.

44 So shall I | keep thy | law ‖ continualLY for | ever ⁀and | ever.

45 And I will | walk at | liberty : ‖ FOR | ⁀I | seek thy | precepts.

46 I will speak of thy testimonies alSO be|⁀fore | kings, ‖ AND | will not | be a|shamed.

47 And I WILL de|light my|self ‖ in THY com|mandments, which | I have | loved.

48 My hands also will I lift up unto thy commandMENTS, which | I have | loved ; ‖ and I will | meditate | in thy | statutes.

ZAIN.

49 Remember the WORD | unto thy | servant, ‖ upon which thou HAST | caused | me to | hope.

50 This is my comFORT in | my af|fliction : ‖ for THY | word hath | quickened | me.

51 The proud have had me greatLY ⊦ in de|rision ; ‖ yet have I NOT de|clined | from thy | law.

52 I remembered thy judgMENTS of | old, O | Lord, ‖ and HAVE | comfort|ed my|self.

53 Horror hath takEN | hold up|on-me ‖ because of the wickED | that for|sake thy | law.

54 Thy statUTES have | been my | songs ‖ IN the | ⁀house | of my | pilgrimage.

55 I have remembered thy name, O LORD, | in the | night, ‖ AND | ⁀have | kept thy | law.

56 THIS | ⁀I | had, ‖ BE|cause I | kept thy | precepts.

112.

CHETH.

57 Thou art MY | portion, O | Lord: ‖ I have SAID that | I would | keep thy | words.

58 I entreated thy faVOUR with my | whole | heart: ‖ be merciful unto ME ac|cording | to thy | word.

59 I THOUGHT | on my | ways, ‖ and turnED my | feet | unto thy | testimonies.

60 I | made | haste, ‖ and delayed NOT to | keep | thy com-| mandments.

61 The bands of the wickED have | robbed | me: ‖ but I have | not for|gotten thy | law.

62 At midnight I will rise to give THANKS | unto | thee ‖ beCAUSE | of thy | righteous | judgments.

63 I am a companion of ALL | them that | fear-thee, ‖ AND of | them that | keep thy | precepts.

64 The earth, O LORD, is | full-of thy | mercy: ‖ TEACH | me | thy | statutes.

TETH.

65 Thou hast dealt well with THY | servant, O | Lord, ‖ AC|cording | unto thy | word.

66 Teach me GOOD | judgment and | knowledge: ‖ for I HAVE be|lieved | thy com|mandments.

67 Before I was afflictED I | went a|stray: ‖ but NOW | have I | kept thy | word.

68 Thou art GOOD, and | doest | good: ‖ TEACH | me | thy | statutes.

J. Turle.

69 The proud have forgED a | lie a|gainst-me: || but I will keep thy preCEPTS | with my | whole | heart.

70 Their HEART is as | fat as | grease: || but I de|light | in thy | law.

71 It is good for me that I have | been af|flicted, || THAT | I might | learn thy | statutes.

72 The LAW | of thy | mouth || is better unto ME than | thousands of | gold and | silver.

JOD.

73 Thy hands have made ME, and | fashioned | me: || give me understanding, that I may | learn | thy com|mandments.

74 They that fear thee will be GLAD | when they | see-me; || because I HAVE | hoped | in thy | word.

75 I know, O Lord, that THY | judgments are | right, || and that thou in faithfulNESS | hast af|flicted | me.

76 Let, I pray thee, thy merciful kindNESS be | for my | comfort, || according to THY | word un|to thy | servant.

77 Let thy tender mercies come unto ME, that | I may | live: || for THY | law is | my de|light.

78 Let the proud be ashamed; for they dealt perversely with ME with|out a | cause: || but I will | meditate | in thy | precepts.

79 Let those that fear THEE | turn unto | me, || and THOSE | that have | known thy | testimonies.

80 Let my heart be SOUND | in thy | statutes, || THAT | I be | not a|shamed.

113.

CAPH.

81 My soul faintETH for | thy sal|vation: || BUT I | hope | in thy | word.

82 Mine eyes FAIL | for thy | word, || saying, WHEN | wilt thou | comfort | me?

83 For I am become like a botTLE | in the | smoke; || yet do I | not for|get thy | statutes.

84 How many are the DAYS | of thy | servant? || when wilt thou execute judgMENT on | them that | persecute | me?

85 The proud have digGED | pits for | me, || WHICH | are not | after thy | law.

86 All THY com|mandments are | faithful: || they persecute ME | wrongfully; | help thou | me.

87 They had almost consumED | me upon | earth: || but I for-|sook | not thy | precepts.

88 Quicken me afTER thy | loving-|kindness; || so shall I KEEP the | testimony | of thy | mouth.

LAMED.

89 FOR | ever, O | Lord, || THY | word is | settled in | heaven.

90 Thy faithfulness is unto ALL | gener|ations: || thou hast establishED the | earth, and | it a|bideth.

91 They continue this day accordING | to thine | ordinances: || FOR | all are | thy | servants.

92 Unless thy law had BEEN | my de|lights, || I should THEN have | perished in | mine af|fliction.

(113.)   *Goodenough.*

93 I will nevER for|get thy | precepts: || for with THEM | thou hast | quickened | me.

94 I am THINE, | save | me: || FOR | I have | sought thy | precepts.

95 The wicked have waited for ME | to de|stroy-me: || but I | will con|sider thy | testimonies.

96 I have seen an END of | all per|fection: || but thy com-mandMENT | is ex|ceeding | broad.

MEM.

97 O HOW love | I thy | law! || it is my MEDI|tation | all the | day.

98 Thou, through thy commandments, hast made me wisER | than mine | enemies; || FOR | they are | ever with | me.

99 I have more understandING than | all my | teachers: || for thy testimonIES | are my | medi|tation.

100 I understand MORE | than the | ancients, || BE|cause I | keep thy | precepts.

101 I have refrained my feet from eveRY | evil | way, || THAT | I might | keep thy | word.

102 I have not departED | from thy | judgments: || FOR | thou hast | taught | me.

103 How sweet are thy WORDS | unto my | taste! || yea, sweetER than | honey | to my | mouth!

104 Through thy precepts I GET | under|standing: || therefore I | hate every | false | way.

M   179

114.

NUN.

105 Thy word is a LAMP | unto my | feet, || AND a | light un|to my | path.

106 I have SWORN, and I | will per|form-it, || that I will | keep thy | righteous | judgments.

107 I am afflictED | very | much : || quicken me, O LORD, ac|cording | unto thy | word.

108 Accept, I beseech thee, the free-will-offerINGS of my | mouth, O | Lord, || AND | teach | me thy | judgments.

109 My soul is continualLY | in my | hand; || yet do I | not for|get thy | law.

110 The wicked have LAID a | snare for | me; || yet I | erred not | from thy | precepts.

111 Thy testimonies have I takEN as an | heritage for | ever: || for they ARE the re|joicing | of my | heart.

112 I HAVE in|clined mine | heart || to perform thy statutes alWAY, | even | unto the | end.

SAMECH.

113 I HATE | vain | thoughts : || but THY | law | do I | love.

114 Thou art my hiding-PLACE | and my | shield: || I | hope | in thy | word.

115 Depart from ME, ye | evil-|doers: || for I will KEEP the com|mandments | of my | God.

116 Uphold me according unto thy WORD, that | I may | live: || and let me NOT be a|shamed | of my | hope.

117 Hold thou me UP, and I | shall be | safe: || and I will have reSPECT | unto thy | statutes con|tinually.

118 Thou hast trodden down all them that ERR | from thy | statutes: || FOR | their de|ceit is | falsehood.

119 Thou puttest away all the wickED of the | earth like | dross: || thereFORE I | love thy | testi|monies.

120 My flesh tremBLETH for | fear of | thee; || and I AM a|fraid | of thy | judgments.

AIN.

121 I have DONE | judgment and | justice: || LEAVE me | not to | mine op|pressors.

122 Be surety for THY | servant for | good: || LET | not the | proud op|press-me.

123 Mine eyes FAIL for | thy sal|vation, || AND | for the | word-of thy | righteousness.

124 Deal with thy servant accordING | unto thy | mercy, || AND | teach | me thy | statutes.

125 I am thy servant; GIVE me | under|standing, || THAT | I may | know thy | testimonies.

126 It is time for THEE, | Lord, to | work: || FOR they | have made | void thy | law.

127 Therefore I LOVE | thy com|mandments || above GOLD; | yea, above | fine | gold.

128 Therefore I esteem all thy precepts concerning all THINGS | to be | right; || and I HATE | every | false | way.

115.

PE.

129 Thy testimonIES are | wonder|ful : ‖ thereFORE | doth my | soul | keep-them.

130 The entrance of thy WORDS | giveth | light; ‖ it giveth unDER|standing | unto the | simple.

131 I openED my | mouth, and | panted: ‖ for I | longed for | thy com|mandments.

132 Look thou upon me, and be merciFUL | unto | me, ‖ as thou usest to DO unto | those that | love thy | name.

133 Order my STEPS | in thy | word; ‖ and let not any iniquiTY | have do|minion | over-me.

134 Deliver me FROM the op|pression of | man : ‖ SO | will I | keep thy | precepts.

135 Make thy face to SHINE up|on thy | servant; ‖ AND | teach | me thy | statutes.

136 Rivers of waters RUN | down mine | eyes, ‖ beCAUSE | they keep | not thy | law.

TSADDI.

137 RightEOUS art | thou, O | Lord, ‖ AND | upright | are thy | judgments.

138 Thy testimonies that THOU | hast com|manded ‖ ARE | righteous and | very | faithful.

139 My ZEAL | hath con|sumed-me ; ‖ because mine ene-MIES | have for|gotten thy | words.

140 Thy WORD is | very | pure: ‖ thereFORE thy | servant | loveth | it.

(115.)   *E. J. Hopkins.*

141 I am SMALL | and de|spised; || yet do NOT | I for|get thy | precepts.

142 Thy righteousness is an evER|lasting | righteousness, || AND | thy law | is the | truth.

143 Trouble and anguish have takEN | hold on | me; || yet THY com|mandments are | my de|lights.

144 The righteousness of thy testimonIES is | ever|lasting: || give me unDER|standing, and | I shall | live.

KOPH.

145 I CRIED with my | whole | heart; || hear me, O LORD: | I will | keep thy | statutes.

146 I CRIED | unto | thee; || save ME, and | I shall | keep thy | testimonies.

147 I prevented the dawnING of the | morning, and | cried: || I | hoped | in thy | word.

148 Mine EYES pre|vent the | night-watches, || that I MIGHT | meditate | in thy | word.

149 Hear my voice according unto THY | loving-|kindness: || O Lord, quicken ME ac|cording | to thy | judgment.

150 They draw nigh that folLOW | after | mischief: || THEY are | far | from thy | law.

151 THOU art | near, O | Lord; || and ALL | thy com-|mandments are | truth.

152 Concerning THY | testi|monies, || I have known of old that THOU hast | founded | them for | ever.

116.

RESH.

153 Consider mine afflicTION, | and de|liver-me: || for I do | not for|get thy | law.

154 Plead my CAUSE, | and de|liver-me: || quicken ME ac-| cording | to thy | word.

155 Salvation is FAR | from the | wicked: || FOR | they seek | not thy | statutes.

156 Great are thy tenDER | mercies, O | Lord: || quicken ME ac|cording | to thy | judgments.

157 Many are my persecuTORS | and mine | enemies; || yet do I not deCLINE | from thy | testi|monies.

158 I beheld the transgresSORS, | and was | grieved; || be-CAUSE | they kept | not thy | word.

159 Consider how I | love thy | precepts: || quicken me, O Lord, accordING | to thy | loving-|kindness.

160 Thy word is TRUE | from the-be|ginning: || and every one of thy rightEOUS | judgments en|dureth for | ever.

SCHIN.

161 Princes have persecuted ME with|out a | cause: || but my HEART | standeth in | awe of-thy | word.

162 I reJOICE | at thy | word, || AS | one that | findeth great | spoil.

163 I HATE and ab|hor | lying: || BUT thy | law | do I | love.

164 Seven times a DAY | do I | praise-thee || beCAUSE | of thy | righteous | judgments.

165 Great peace have THEY which | love thy | law; || AND | nothing | shall of|fend-them.

166 Lord, I have hopED for | thy sal|vation, || AND | done | thy com|mandments.

167 My SOUL hath | kept thy | testimonies; || and I | love | them ex|ceedingly.

168 I have kept thy preCEPTS | and thy | testimonies: || for ALL my | ways | are be|fore-thee.

TAU.

169 Let my cry come near beFORE | thee, O | Lord: || give me understandING ac|cording | to thy | word.

170 Let my supplicaTION | come-before | thee: || deliver ME ac|cording | to thy | word.

171 My LIPS shall | utter | praise, || when THOU hast | taught | me thy | statutes.

172 My TONGUE shall | speak-of thy | word: || for ALL | thy com|mandments are | righteousness.

173 LET | thine hand | help-me: || FOR | I have | chosen thy | precepts.

174 I have longed for THY sal|vation, O | Lord; || and THY | law is | my de|light.

175 Let my soul LIVE, and | it shall | praise-thee; || AND | let thy | judgments | help-me.

176 I have gone astray like a lost SHEEP; | seek thy | servant: || for I do | not for|get thy-com|mandments.

GLORY BE, ETC.

117.

PSALM CXX.

IN | my dis|tress ‖ I cried unto the LORD, | and he | heard | me.

2 Deliver my soul, O LORD, from | lying | lips, ‖ AND | from a-de|ceitful | tongue.

3 What shall be givEN | unto | thee? ‖ or what shall be done unTO | thee, thou | false | tongue?

4 Sharp arROWS | of the | mighty, ‖ WITH | coals of | juni|per.

5 Wo is me that I so|journ in | Mesech, ‖ that I DWELL | in the | tents of | Kedar!

6 My SOUL | hath long | dwelt ‖ WITH | him that | hateth | peace.

7 I | am for | peace: ‖ but WHEN I | speak, they | are for | war.　　　　　　　　　　　　GLORY BE, ETC.

PSALM CXXI.

I WILL lift up mine EYES | unto the | hills, ‖ FROM | whence | cometh my | help.

2 My help comETH | from the | Lord, ‖ WHICH | made | heaven and | earth.

3 He will not sufFER thy | foot to-be | moved: ‖ HE that | keepeth thee | will not | slumber.

4 Behold, HE that | keepeth | Israel ‖ SHALL | neither | slumber nor | sleep.

5 The LORD | is thy | keeper: ‖ the Lord IS thy | shade upon | thy right | hand.

(117.)   E. J. Hopkins.

6 The sun shall not SMITE | thee by | day, ‖ NOR | … the | moon by | night.

7 The Lord shall preserve THEE | from all | evil : ‖ HE | shall pre|serve thy | soul.

8 The Lord shall preserve thy going OUT, and thy | coming | in, ‖ from this time FORTH, and | even for | ever|more.

GLORY BE, ETC.

PSALM CXXII.

I WAS glad when they SAID | unto | me, ‖ Let us GO | into the | house of-the | Lord.

2 OUR | feet shall | stand ‖ within THY | gates, | O Jer|usalem.

3 Jerusalem is buildED | as a | city ‖ THAT | is com|pact to|gether;

4 Whither the tribes go up, the tribes of the Lord, unto the testimoNY of | Isra|el, ‖ to give thanks unTO the | name | of the | Lord.

5 For there are SET | thrones of | judgment, ‖ the THRONES | of the | house of | David.

6 Pray for the PEACE | of Jer|usalem : ‖ THEY shall | prosper that | love | thee.

7 Peace BE with|in thy | walls, ‖ and prosperiTY with|in thy | pala|ces.

8 For my brethREN and com|panions' | sakes, ‖ I will now SAY, | Peace | be with|in-thee.

9 Because of the HOUSE of the | Lord our | God ‖ I | will | seek thy | good.   GLORY BE, ETC.

118.

PSALM CXXIII.

UNTO thee lift I | up mine | eyes, ‖ O THOU that | dwellest | in the | heavens.

2 Behold, as the eyes of servants look unto the hand of their masters, and as the eyes of a maiden unto the HAND | of her | mistress; ‖ so our eyes wait upon the Lord our God, unTIL that | he have | mercy up|on-us.

3 Have mercy upon us, O LORD, have | mercy up|on-us: ‖ for we are exceedingLY | filled | with con|tempt.

4 Our soul is exceedingly filled with the scorning of THOSE that | are at | ease, ‖ and WITH the con|tempt | of the | proud.   GLORY BE, ETC.

PSALM CXXIV.

IF it had not been the LORD who was | on our | side, ‖ NOW | may | Israel | say;

2 If it had not been the LORD who was | on our | side, ‖ WHEN | men rose | up a|gainst-us:

3 Then they had swallowED | us up | quick, ‖ when THEIR | wrath was | kindled a|gainst-us:

4 Then the waTERS had | over|whelmed-us, ‖ the STREAM | had gone | over our | soul:

5 THEN the | proud | waters ‖ HAD | gone | over our | soul.

6 BlessED | be the | Lord, ‖ who hath not given US as a | prey | to their | teeth.

(118.)   *E. J. Hopkins.*

7 Our soul is escaped as a bird out of the SNARE | of the | fowlers: ‖ the snare is brokEN, | and we | are es|caped.

8 Our help is IN the | name of-the | Lord, ‖ WHO | made | heaven and | earth.   Glory be, etc.

PSALM CXXV.

THEY that trust in the Lord shall BE | as mount | Zion, ‖ which cannot be removED, | but a|bideth for | ever.

2 As the mountains are ROUND a|bout Jer|usalem, ‖ so the Lord is round about his peoPLE from | henceforth, | even for | ever.

3 For the rod of the wicked shall not rest upON the | lot of-the | righteous; ‖ lest the righteous put FORTH their | hands | unto in|iquity.

4 Do good, O Lord, unto THOSE | that be | good, ‖ and to THEM that are | upright | in their | hearts.

5 As for such as turn aside unto their crooked ways, the Lord shall lead them forth with the workERS | of in|iquity: ‖ but PEACE shall | be upon | Isra|el.   Glory be, etc.

PSALM CXXVI.

WHEN the Lord turned AGAIN the cap|tivity of | Zion, ‖ WE | were like | them that | dream.

2 Then was our mouth filled with laughTER, and our | tongue with | singing: ‖ then said they among the heathen, The LORD hath | done great | things for | them.

3 The Lord hath done GREAT | things for | us, ‖ WHERE-| of | we are | glad.

119.

4 Turn again OUR cap|tivity, O | Lord, ‖ AS the | streams | in the | south.

5 THEY that | sow in | tears ‖ SHALL | reap | in | joy.

6 He that goeth forth and weepeth, bearING | precious | seed, ‖ shall doubtless come again with rejoicING, | bringing his | sheaves | with-him. GLORY BE, ETC.

PSALM CXXVII.

EXCEPT the Lord build the house, they laBOUR in | vain that | build-it: ‖ except the Lord keep the city, the watch-MAN | waketh | but in | vain.

2 It is vain for you to rise up early, to sit up late, to EAT the | bread of | sorrows; ‖ for so he givETH | his be|loved | sleep.

3 Lo, children are an heriTAGE | of the | Lord; ‖ and the FRUIT of the | womb is | his re|ward.

4 As arrows are in the HAND of a | mighty | man; ‖ SO are | children | of the | youth.

5 Happy is the man that hath his quiVER | full of | them: ‖ they shall not be ashamed, but they shall SPEAK with the | enemies | in the | gate. GLORY BE, ETC.

PSALM CXXVIII.

BLESSED is every ONE that | feareth the | Lord; ‖ THAT | walketh | in his | ways.

2 For thou shalt eat the laBOUR | of thine | hands: ‖ happy shalt thou BE, and it | shall be | well with | thee.

3 Thy wife shall be as a fruitful VINE by the | sides-of

(119.) E. J. Hopkins.

thine | house; ‖ thy children like olive PLANTS | round a|bout thy | table.

4 Behold, that THUS shall the | man be | blessed ‖ THAT | fear|eth the | Lord.

5 The Lord shall bless THEE | out of | Zion: ‖ and thou shalt see the good of JerusaLEM | all the | days of-thy | life.

6 Yea, thou shalt SEE thy | children's | children, ‖ AND peace upon | Isra|el.   GLORY BE, ETC.

PSALM CXXIX.

MANY a time have they afflicted ME | from my | youth, ‖ MAY | Isra|el now | say:

2 Many a time have they afflicted ME | from my | youth; ‖ yet THEY have | not pre|vailed a|gainst-me.

3 The ploughers ploughED up|on my | back: ‖ THEY | made | long their | furrows.

4 THE | Lord is | righteous: ‖ he hath cut asunDER the | cords | of the | wicked.

5 Let them ALL | be con|founded ‖ and turnED | back that | hate | Zion.

6 Let them be as the GRASS up|on the | house-tops, ‖ which witherETH a|fore it | groweth | up;

7 Wherewith the mower fillETH | not his | hand, ‖ nor HE that | bindeth | sheaves his | bosom.

8 Neither do they which go by say, The blessing of the LORD | be up|on-you: ‖ we bless YOU in the | name | of the | Lord.   GLORY BE, ETC.

120.

PSALM CXXX.

OUT | of the | depths ‖ have I CRIED | unto | thee, O | Lord.

    2 LORD, | hear my | voice: ‖ let thine ears be attenTIVE to the | voice of-my | suppli|cations.

    3 If thou, Lord, shouldest MARK in|iqui|ties, ‖ O | Lord, | who shall | stand?

    4 But there IS for|giveness with | thee, ‖ THAT | thou | mayest be | feared.

    5 I wait for the LORD, my | soul doth | wait, ‖ and IN | his word | do I | hope.

    6 My soul waiteth for the Lord more than they that WATCH | for the | morning: ‖ I say, more than THEY that | watch | for the | morning.

    7 Let IsraEL | hope in-the | Lord: ‖ for with the Lord there is merCY, and with | him is | plenteous re|demption.

    8 And he shall reDEEM | Isra|el ‖ from ALL | his in|iqui|ties.

                                                                                             GLORY BE, ETC.

PSALM CXXXI.

LORD, my heart is not haughTY, nor mine | eyes | lofty; ‖ neither do I exercise myself in great matTERS, or in | things too | high for | me.

    2 Surely I have behaved and quieted myself, as a child that is weanED | of his | mother: ‖ my soul is EVEN | as a | weaned | child.

    3 Let IsraEL | hope in-the | Lord ‖ FROM | henceforth | and for | ever.   GLORY BE, ETC.

PSALM CXXXII.

LORD, re|member | David, ‖ AND | all | his af|flictions:

2 How he SWARE | unto the | Lord, ‖ and vowED unto the | mighty | God of | Jacob;

3 Surely I will not come into the tabernaCLE | of my | house, ‖ nor GO | up in|to my | bed;

4 I will not give SLEEP | to mine | eyes, ‖ OR | slumber | to mine | eyelids,

5 Until I find out a PLACE | for the | Lord, ‖ an habitaTION for the | mighty | God of | Jacob.

6 Lo, we heard of IT | at Eph|ratah: ‖ we found IT in the | fields | of the | wood.

7 We will go into HIS | taber|nacles: ‖ WE will | worship | at his | footstool.

8 Arise, O LORD, | into thy | rest; ‖ THOU, and the | ark | of thy | strength.

9 Let thy PRIESTS be | clothed with | righteousness; ‖ and LET thy | saints | shout for | joy.

10 For thy serVANT | David's | sake ‖ turn not AWAY the | face of | thine a|nointed.

11 The Lord hath sworn in truth unto David; he will NOT | turn from | it; ‖ Of the fruit of thy body will I | set up|on thy | throne.

12 If thy children will keep my covenant and my testiMONY that | I shall | teach-them, ‖ their children shall also sit upon THY | throne for | ever|more.

121.

13 For the LORD hath | chosen | Zion; ‖ he hath desirED it | for his | habi|tation.

14 THIS is my | rest for | ever: ‖ here will I DWELL; | for I | have de|sired-it.

15 I will abundantly BLESS | her pro|vision; ‖ I will | satisfy her | poor with | bread:

16 I will also clothe her PRIESTS | with sal|vation; ‖ and her SAINTS shall | shout a|loud for | joy.

17 There will I make the HORN of | David to | bud: ‖ I have ordainED a | lamp for | mine a|nointed.

18 His enemies will I | clothe with | shame: ‖ but upon him-SELF | shall his | crown | flourish.   GLORY BE, ETC.

PSALM CXXXIII.

BEHOLD, how GOOD and how | pleasant it | is ‖ for brethREN to | dwell to|gether in | unity!

2 It is like the precious ointment upon the head, that ran down upon the BEARD, even | Aaron's | beard; ‖ that went DOWN | to the | skirts of-his | garments;

3 As the dew of Hermon, and as the dew that descended upON the | mountains of | Zion: ‖ for there the Lord commanded the blessING, even | life for | ever|more.   GLORY BE, ETC.

PSALM CXXXIV.

BEHOLD, bless ye the Lord, all ye serVANTS | of the | Lord, ‖ which by NIGHT | stand in-the | house of-the | Lord.

(121.)  H. Smart.

---

2 Lift up your HANDS | in the | sanctuary, ‖ AND | bless | ... the | Lord.

3 The Lord, that MADE | heaven and | earth, ‖ BLESS | thee | out of | Zion. GLORY BE, ETC.

PSALM CXXXV.

PRAISE | ye the | Lord. ‖ Praise ye the name of the Lord; praise him, O ye | servants | of the | Lord.

2 Ye that STAND in the | house of-the | Lord, ‖ IN the | courts of-the | house-of our | God,

3 Praise the LORD; for the | Lord is | good: ‖ sing praises unto HIS | name; for | it is | pleasant.

4 For the Lord hath chosen JACOB | unto him|self, ‖ and IsraEL for | his pe|culiar | treasure.

5 For I KNOW that the | Lord is | great, ‖ and that OUR | Lord is-a|bove all | gods.

6 WhatsoevER the | Lord | pleased, ‖ that did he in heaven, and in EARTH, in the | seas, and | all deep | places.

7 He causeth the vapours to asCEND from the | ends of-the | earth; ‖ he maketh lightnings for the rain; he bringETH the | wind out | of his | treasuries.

8 Who smote the FIRST-|born of | Egypt, ‖ BOTH | of | man and | beast.

9 Who sent tokens and wonders into the MIDST of | thee, O | Egypt, ‖ upon PhaRAOH, | and upon | all his | servants.

10 WHO | smote great | nations, ‖ AND | slew | mighty | kings:

11 Sihon king of the Amorites, and OG | king of | Bashan, ‖ AND | all the | kingdoms of | Canaan:

122.

12 And gave their LAND | for an | heritage, ‖ an heritage unTO | Isra|el his | people.

13 Thy name, O LORD, en|dureth for | ever; ‖ and thy memorial, O LORD, through|out all | gener|ations.

14 For the LORD will | judge his | people; ‖ and he will rePENT him|self con|cerning his | servants.

15 The idols of the heaTHEN are | silver and | gold, ‖ THE | work of | men's | hands.

16 They have MOUTHS, | but they | speak-not; ‖ EYES | have they, | but they | see-not;

17 They have EARS, | but they | hear-not; ‖ neiTHER is there | any breath | in their | mouths.

18 They that make them are LIKE | unto | them : ‖ so is eveRY | one that | trusteth in | them.

19 Bless the Lord, O HOUSE of | Isra|el : ‖ BLESS the | Lord, O | house of | Aaron :

20 Bless the LORD, O | house of | Levi : ‖ ye that FEAR the | Lord, | bless the | Lord.

21 Blessed be the LORD | out of | Zion, ‖ which dwelleth at JerusaLEM. | Praise | ye the | Lord.   GLORY BE, ETC.

PSALM CXXXVI.

O GIVE thanks unto the LORD; for | he is | good : ‖ FOR his | mercy en|dureth for | ever.

2 O give thanks unTO the | God of | gods : ‖ FOR his | mercy en|dureth for | ever.

Attwood.

3 O give thanks unTO the | Lord of | lords: ‖ FOR his | mercy en|dureth for | ever.

4 To him who ALONE | doeth great | wonders: ‖ FOR his | mercy en|dureth for | ever.

5 To him that by wisDOM | made the | heavens: ‖ FOR his | mercy en|dureth for | ever.

6 To him that stretched out the EARTH a|bove the | waters: ‖ FOR his | mercy en|dureth for | ever.

7 To HIM that | made great | lights: ‖ FOR his | mercy en|dureth for | ever:

8 The SUN to | rule by | day: ‖ FOR his | mercy en|dureth for | ever:

9 The moon and STARS to | rule by | night: ‖ FOR his | mercy en|dureth | for ever.

10 To him that smote EGYPT | in their | first-born: ‖ FOR his | mercy en|dureth for | ever:

11 And brought out IsraEL | from a|mong-them: ‖ FOR his | mercy en|dureth for | ever:

12 With a strong hand, and WITH a | stretched-out | arm: ‖ FOR his | mercy en|dureth for | ever.

13 To him which divided the Red SEA | into | parts: ‖ FOR his | mercy en|dureth for | ever:

14 And made Israel to pass THROUGH the | midst of | it: ‖ FOR his | mercy en|dureth for | ever:

15 But overthrew Pharaoh and his HOST in the | Red | sea: ‖ FOR his | mercy en|dureth for | ever.

16 To him which led his peoPLE | through the | wilderness: ‖ FOR his | mercy en|dureth for | ever.

123.

17 To HIM which | smote great | kings: ‖ FOR his | mercy en|dureth for | ever:

18 And SLEW | famous | kings: ‖ FOR his | mercy en|dureth for | ever:

19 SIHON | king of-the | Amorites: ‖ FOR his | mercy en-|dureth for | ever:

20 And OG the | king of | Bashan: ‖ FOR his | mercy en-|dureth for | ever:

21 And gave their LAND | for an | heritage: ‖ FOR his | mercy en|dureth for | ever:

22 Even an heritage unTO | Israel his | servant: ‖ FOR his | mercy en|dureth for | ever.

23 Who remembered US in our | low es|tate: ‖ FOR his | mercy en|dureth for | ever:

24 And hath redeemed US | from our | enemies: ‖ FOR his | mercy en|dureth for | ever.

25 Who giveth FOOD | to all | flesh: ‖ FOR his | mercy en-|dureth for | ever.

26 O give thanks unTO the | God of | heaven: ‖ FOR his | mercy en|dureth for | ever.   GLORY BE, ETC.

PSALM CXXXVII.

BY the rivers of Babylon, THERE | we sat | down; ‖ yea, we WEPT when | we re|membered | Zion.

2 WE | hanged our | harps ‖ upon the wilLOWS | in the | midst there|of.

3 For there they that carried us away captive requirED of |

us a | song; || and they that wasted us required of us mirth, saying, SING us | one of-the | songs of | Zion.

4 How shall we SING the | Lord's | song || IN | ... a | strange | land ?

5 If I forget THEE, | O Jer|usalem, || let my RIGHT | hand for|get her | cunning.

6 If I do not remember thee, let my tongue CLEAVE to the | roof-of my | mouth; || if I prefer not JerusaLEM a|bove my | chief | joy.

7 Remember, O Lord, the children of EDOM in the | day-of Jer|usalem; || who said, Rase it, rase it, EVEN | to-the foun-| dation there|of.

8 O daughter of Babylon, who ART to | be de|stroyed; || happy shall he be that rewardeth THEE as | thou hast | served | us.

9 HAPPY | shall he | be || that taketh and dasheth thy litTLE | ones a|gainst the | stones.　　GLORY BE, ETC.

PSALM CXXXVIII.

I WILL praise thee WITH my | whole | heart : || before the GODS will | I sing | praise unto | thee.

2 I will worship toward thy holy temple, and praise thy name for thy loving-kindNESS and | for thy | truth : || for thou hast magnifiED thy | word-above | all thy | name.

3 In the day when I CRIED thou | answeredst | me, || and strengthenedst ME with | strength | in my | soul.

4 All the kings of the earth shall PRAISE | thee, O | Lord, || WHEN they | hear the | words of-thy | mouth.

124.

5 Yea, they shall SING in the | ways of-the | Lord : || for GREAT is the | glory | of the | Lord.

6 Though the Lord be high, yet hath he reSPECT | unto the | lowly: || but the PROUD he | knoweth a|far | off.

7 Though I walk in the midst of trouBLE, thou | wilt re-| vive-me : || thou shalt stretch forth thine hand against the wrath of mine eneMIES, and | thy right | hand shall | save-me.

8 The Lord will perfect THAT which con|cerneth | me: || thy mercy, O Lord, endureth for ever: forsake NOT the | works of | thine own | hands.   GLORY BE, ETC.

PSALM CXXXIX.

O LORD, thou hast searchED | me, and | known-me. || Thou knowest my down-sitting, and mine up-rising; thou understandEST my | thought a|far | off.

2 Thou compassest my PATH, and my | lying | down, || and ART ac|quainted with | all my | ways.

3 For there is not a WORD | in my | tongue, || but, lo, O LORD, thou | knowest it | alto|gether.

4 Thou hast beset ME be|hind and-be|fore, || AND | laid thine | hand up|on-me.

5 Such knowledge is TOO | wonderful | for-me; || it is HIGH, I | cannot at|tain un|to-it.

6 Whither shall I GO | from thy | Spirit? || or whither shall I | flee | from thy | presence?

7 If I ascend up into heavEN, | thou art | there: || if I make my bed in HELL, be|hold, | thou art | there.

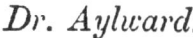

8 If I take the wings of the morning, and dwell in the utterMOST | parts of-the | sea; ‖ even there shall thy hand lead ME, and | thy right | hand shall | hold-me.

9 If I say, SureLY the | darkness shall | cover-me; ‖ even the NIGHT | shall be | light a|bout-me.

10 Yea, the darkness hideth not from thee; but the night shinETH | as the | day: ‖ the darkness and the LIGHT are | both a|like to | thee.

11 For thou HAST pos|sessed my | reins: ‖ thou hast covered ME | in my | mother's | womb.

12 I will praise thee; for I am fearfulLY and | wonderfully | made: ‖ marvellous are thy works; and THAT my | soul | knoweth right | well.

13 My substance was not hid from thee, when I was | made in | secret, ‖ and curiously WROUGHT in the | lowest | parts of-the | earth.

14 Thine eyes did see my subSTANCE, yet | being un|perfect; ‖ and in thy book all my members were written, which in continuance were fashioned, when as YET | there was | none of | them.

15 How precious also are thy THOUGHTS unto | me, O | God! ‖ how GREAT | is the | sum of | them!

16 If I should count them, they are more in numBER | than the | sand: ‖ when I AWAKE, | I am | still with | thee.

17 Surely thou wilt SLAY the | wicked, O | God: ‖ depart from ME | therefore, ye | bloody | men.

18 For they SPEAK a|gainst thee | wickedly, ‖ and thine eneMIES | take thy | name in | vain.

125.

19 Do not I hate THEM, O | Lord, that | hate-thee? ‖ and am not I grievED with | those that | rise up-a|gainst-thee?

20 I hate THEM with | perfect | hatred; ‖ I | count | them mine | enemies.

21 Search me, O GOD, and | know my | heart; ‖ TRY | me, and | know my | thoughts;

22 And see if there be any wickED | way in | me, ‖ and lead ME | in the | way ever|lasting. GLORY BE, ETC.

PSALM CXL.

DELIVER me, O LORD, from the | evil | man : ‖ preserve ME | from the | violent | man;

2 Which imagine misCHIEFS | in their | heart : ‖ continually are THEY | gathered to|gether for | war.

3 They have sharpened their TONGUES | like a | serpent : ‖ adDERS' | poison is | under their | lips.

4 Keep me, O LORD, from the | hands of-the | wicked; ‖ preserve me from the violent man, who have purposED to | over-| throw my | goings.

5 The proud have hid a SNARE for | me, and | cords; ‖ they have spread a net by the way-SIDE ; | they have | set gins | for-me.

6 I said unto the Lord, THOU | art my | God : ‖ hear the voice of my SUPpli|cations, | O | Lord.

7 O God the Lord, the STRENGTH of | my sal|vation, ‖ thou hast covered my HEAD | in the | day of | battle.

8 Grant not, O Lord, the deSIRES | of the | wicked : ‖ further not his wicked deVICE, | lest they-ex|alt them|selves.

John Marsh.

9 As for the head of those that comPASS | me a|bout, || let the misCHIEF of | their own | lips | cover-them.

10 Let burning coals fall upon them: let them be CAST | into the | fire; || into deep PITS, that they | rise not | up a|gain.

11 Let not an evil-speaker be establishED | in the | earth: || evil shall hunt the vioLENT | man to | over|throw-him.

12 I know that the Lord will maintain the CAUSE | of the-af|flicted, || AND the | right | of the | poor.

13 Surely the righteous shall give THANKS | unto thy | name: || the upRIGHT shall | dwell | in thy | presence.   GLORY BE, ETC.

PSALM CXLI.

LORD, I CRY | unto | thee: || make haste unto me; give ear unto my VOICE, | when I | cry unto | thee.

2 Let my prayer be set FORTH before | thee as | incense; || and the lifting up of my HANDS | as the | evening | sacrifice.

3 Set a watch, O LORD, be|fore my | mouth; || KEEP the | door | of my | lips.

4 Incline not my heart to any evil thing, to practise wicked works with MEN that | work in|iquity: || and LET me | not eat | of their | dainties.

5 Let the righteous smite me; it shall be a kindness: and let him reprove me; it shall be an excellent oil, which shall NOT | break my | head: || for yet my prayer alSO shall | be in | their ca|lamities.

6 When their judges are overTHROWN in | stony | places, || they shall HEAR my | words; for | they are | sweet.

126.

7 Our bones are scatterED at the | grave's | mouth, ‖ as when one cutteth and cleavETH | wood up|on the | earth.

8 But mine eyes are unto THEE, O | God the | Lord: ‖ in thee is my trust; LEAVE | not my | soul | destitute.

9 Keep me from the snares which THEY have | laid for | me, ‖ and the GINS of the | workers | of in|iquity.

10 Let the wicked FALL into | their own | nets, ‖ WHILST that | I with|al es|cape. GLORY BE, ETC.

PSALM CXLII.

I CRIED unto the LORD | with my | voice; ‖ with my voice unto the LORD did I | make my | suppli|cation.

2 I poured out MY com|plaint be|fore-him; ‖ I | showed-before | him my | trouble.

3 When my spirit was overwhelmed within me, THEN thou | knewest my | path: ‖ in the way wherein I walked have they priviLY | laid a | snare | for-me.

4 I looked on my right hand, and beheld, but there was no MAN | that would | know-me: ‖ refuge failed me; no MAN | cared | for my | soul.

5 I CRIED unto | thee, O | Lord: ‖ I said, Thou art my refuge and my porTION in the | land | of the | living.

6 Attend unto my cry; for I am BROUGHT | very | low: ‖ deliver me from my persecutORS; for | they are | stronger than | I.

7 Bring my soul out of prison, that I may | praise thy | name: ‖ the righteous shall compass me ABOUT; for | thou shalt-deal | bountifully | with-me. GLORY BE, ETC.

W. H. Smyth.

PSALM CXLIII.

HEAR my prayer, O Lord; give EAR to my | suppli|cations: |⁕ in thy faithfulNESS answer | me, and | in thy | righteousness.

2 And enter not into judgMENT | with thy | servant: ‖ for in thy SIGHT shall | no man | living be | justified.

3 For the enemy hath persecuted my soul; he hath smitten my LIFE | down to-the | ground; ‖ he hath made me to dwell in darkness, as THOSE that | have been | long | dead.

4 Therefore is my spirIT over|whelmed with|in-me; ‖ MY | heart with|in-me is | desolate.

5 I rememBER the | days of | old; ‖ I meditate on all thy WORKS; I | muse on-the | work-of thy | hands.

6 I stretch forth my HANDS | unto | thee: ‖ my soul thirsteth after THEE, | as a | thirsty | land.

7 Hear me speedily, O LORD; my | spirit | faileth: ‖ hide not thy face from me, lest I be like unto THEM that | go down | into the | pit.

8 Cause me to hear thy loving-kindness in the morning; for in THEE | do I | trust: ‖ cause me to know the way wherein I should walk; for I lift UP my | soul | unto | thee.

9 Deliver me, O LORD, | from mine | enemies: ‖ I FLEE | unto | thee to | hide-me.

10 Teach me to do thy will; FOR thou | art my | God: ‖ thy Spirit is good, LEAD me | into the | land-of up|rightness.

11 Quicken me, O LORD, for | thy name's | sake: ‖ for thy righteousness' sake BRING | my soul | out of | trouble.

127.

12 And of thy merCY cut | off mine | enemies, ‖ and destroy all them that afflict my SOUL: | for I | am thy | servant.

Glory be, etc.

PSALM CXLIV.

BLESSED be the | Lord my | strength, ‖ which teacheth my hands to WAR, | and my | fingers to | fight.

2 My goodness, and my fortress; my high tower, and my deliverer; my shield, and HE in | whom I | trust; ‖ WHO sub|dueth my | people | under-me.

3 Lord, what is man, that thou takEST | knowledge of | him! ‖ or the son of man, that THOU | makest ac|count of | him!

4 MAN is | like to | vanity: ‖ his DAYS are as a | shadow that | passeth a|way.

5 Bow thy heavens, O LORD, | and come | down: ‖ TOUCH the | mountains, and | they shall | smoke.

6 Cast FORTH | lightning, and | scatter-them: ‖ shoot OUT thine | arrows, | and de|stroy-them.

7 Send thine HAND | from a|bove; ‖ rid me, and deliver me out of great waTERS, from the | hand of | strange | children;

8 Whose MOUTH | speaketh | vanity; ‖ and their right HAND | is-a right | hand of | falsehood.

9 I will sing a new SONG unto | thee, O | God: ‖ upon a psaltery and an instrument of ten strings will I SING | praises | unto | thee.

10 It is he that giveth salvaTION | unto | kings; ‖ who delivereth David his serVANT | from the | hurtful | sword.

11 Rid me, and deliver me from the hand of strange children,

R. Cooke.

whose MOUTH | speaketh | vanity, ‖ and their right HAND | is-a right | hand of | falsehood:

12 That our sons may be as plants grown UP | in their | youth; ‖ that our daughters may be as corner-stones, polished afTER the si|militude | of a | palace;

13 That our garners may be full, affording ALL | manner of | store; ‖ that our sheep may bring forth thousands and TEN | thousands | in our | streets;

14 That our oxen MAY be | strong to | labour; ‖ that there be no breaking in, nor going out; that there be NO com|plaining | in our | streets.

15 Happy is that people that IS in | such a | case; ‖ yea, happy is that peoPLE whose | God | is the | Lord.   GLORY BE, ETC.

PSALM CXLV.

I WILL extol THEE, my | God, O | King; ‖ and I will BLESS thy | name for | ever and | ever.

2 Every DAY | will I | bless-thee; ‖ and I will PRAISE thy | name for | ever and | ever.

3 Great is the Lord, and greatLY | to be | praised; ‖ AND his | greatness | is un|searchable.

4 One generation shall praise thy WORKS | to an|other, ‖ and SHALL de|clare thy | mighty | acts.

5 I will speak of the glorious honOUR | of thy | majesty, ‖ AND | of thy | wondrous | works.

6 And men shall speak of the MIGHT of thy | terrible | acts; ‖ AND I | will de|clare thy | greatness.

128.

7 They shall abundantly utter the memoRY of | thy great | goodness, || AND shall | sing of | thy | righteousness.

8 The Lord is graCIOUS, and | full-of com|passion; || slow to anGER, | and of | great | mercy.

9 The LORD is | good to | all; || and his tender merCIES are | over | all his | works.

10 All thy works shall PRAISE | thee, O | Lord; || AND thy | saints shall | bless | thee.

11 They shall speak of the gloRY | of thy | kingdom, || AND | talk | of thy | power;

12 To make known to the sons of MEN his | mighty | acts, || and the gloriOUS | majesty | of his | kingdom.

13 Thy kingdom is an evER|lasting | kingdom, || and thy dominion endurETH through|out all | gener|ations.

14 The Lord upholdETH | all that | fall, || and raiseth up all THOSE | that be | bowed | down.

15 The eyes of ALL | wait-upon | thee; || and thou givest THEM their | meat in | due | season.

16 THOU | openest thine | hand, || and satisfiest the deSIRE of | every | living | thing.

17 The Lord is rightEOUS in | all his | ways, || AND | holy in | all his | works.

18 The Lord is nigh unto all THEM that | call-upon | him, || to ALL that | call-upon | him in | truth.

19 He will fulfil the deSIRE of | them that | fear-him: || he also will HEAR their | cry, | and will | save-them.

(128.) *Attwood.*

20 The Lord preserveth ALL | them that | love-him: ‖ but ALL the | wicked will | he de|stroy.

21 My mouth shall SPEAK the | praise of-the | Lord: ‖ and let all flesh bless his hoLY | name for | ever and | ever.

Glory be, etc.

PSALM CXLVI.

PRAISE | ye the | Lord. ‖ PRAISE the | Lord, | O my | soul.

2 While I LIVE will I | praise the | Lord: ‖ I will sing praises unto my GOD while | I have | any | being.

3 Put not your trust in princes, nor IN the | son of | man, ‖ IN | whom there | is no | help.

4 His breath goeth forth, he returnETH | to his | earth; ‖ in that veRY | day his | thoughts | perish.

5 Happy is he that hath the God of JACOB | for his | help, ‖ whose HOPE is | in the | Lord his | God;

6 Which made heaven, and earth, the sea, and ALL that | therein | is; ‖ WHICH | keepeth | truth for | ever;

7 Which executeth judgMENT | for the-op|pressed; ‖ WHICH | giveth | food to-the | hungry.

8 The Lord looseth the prisoners: the Lord openETH the | eyes of-the | blind: ‖ the Lord raiseth them that are bowed DOWN: the | Lord | loveth the | righteous:

9 The Lord preserveth the strangers; he relievETH the | fatherless and | widow: ‖ but the way of the wickED he | turneth | upside | down.

10 The LORD shall | reign for | ever, ‖ even thy God, O Zion, unto all generaTIONS. | Praise | ye the | Lord. Glory be, etc.

129.

PSALM CXLVII.

PRAISE | ye the | Lord : || for it is good to sing praises unto our God; FOR it is | pleasant; and | praise is | comely.

2 The Lord doth BUILD | up Jer|usalem : || he gathereth togethER the | outcasts-of | Isra|el.

3 He healETH the | broken in | heart, || AND | bindeth | up their | wounds.

4 He telleth the numBER | of the | stars; || he calleth THEM | all | by their | names.

5 Great is our LORD, and | of great | power : || HIS | under-| standing is | infinite.

6 The Lord liftETH | up the | meek : || he casteth the wickED | down | to the | ground.

7 Sing unto the LORD | with thanks|giving; || sing praise upON the | harp un|to our | God:

8 Who covereth the heaven with clouds, who prepareth RAIN | for the | earth, || who maketh GRASS to | grow up|on the | mountains.

9 He givETH to the | beast his | food, || and TO the | young | ravens which | cry.

10 He delighteth NOT in the | strength of-the | horse: || he taketh not pleaSURE | in the | legs of-a | man.

11 The Lord taketh pleaSURE in | them that | fear-him, || IN | those that | hope in-his | mercy.

12 Praise the LORD, | O Jer|usalem; || PRAISE | thy | God, O | Zion :

13 For he hath strengthenED the | bars-of thy | gates; || HE hath | blessed thy | children with|in-thee.

14 He maketh PEACE | in thy | borders, || and filleth THEE with the | finest | of the | wheat.

15 He sendeth forth his commandMENT | upon | earth; || his WORD | runneth | very | swiftly.

16 He givETH | snow like | wool : || he scatterETH the | hoar-|frost like | ashes.

17 He casteth FORTH his | ice like | morsels: || WHO can | stand be|fore his | cold?

18 He sendeth OUT his | word, and | melteth-them: || he causeth his wind to BLOW, | and the | waters | flow.

19 He showeth his WORD | unto | Jacob, || his statutes and HIS | judgments | unto | Israel.

20 He hath not dealt SO with | any | nation: || and as for his judgments, they have not known THEM. | Praise | ye the | Lord. GLORY BE, ETC.

PSALM CXLVIII.

PRAISE | ye the | Lord. || Praise ye the Lord from the heavENS: | praise him | in the | heights.

2 Praise ye HIM, | all his | angels: || PRAISE ye | him, | all his | hosts.

3 Praise ye HIM, | sun and | moon: || PRAISE him, | all ye | stars of | light.

4 Praise HIM, ye | heavens of | heavens, || and ye waTERS that | be a|bove the | heavens.

130.

5 Let them PRAISE the | name of-the | Lord : || for he commandED, | and they | were cre|ated.

6 He hath also stablished THEM for | ever and | ever : || he hath MADE a de|cree which | shall not | pass.

7 Praise the LORD | from the | earth, || YE | dragons, | and all | deeps:

8 Fire, and HAIL; | snow, and | vapours; || STORMY | wind ful|filling his | word;

9 MounTAINS, | and all | hills; || fruitFUL | trees, and | all | cedars;

10 BEASTS, | and all | cattle; || creepING | things, and | flying | fowl;

11 Kings of the EARTH, | and all | people; || princes, and ALL | judges | of the | earth;

12 Both YOUNG | men and | maidens; || OLD | men | and | children:

13 Let them PRAISE the | name of-the | Lord: || for his name alone is excellent; his gloRY is a|bove the | earth and | heaven.

14 He also exalteth the horn of his people, the PRAISE of | all his | saints; || even of the children of Israel, a people near unto HIM. | Praise | ye the | Lord.   GLORY BE, ETC.

PSALM CXLIX.

PRAISE | ye the | Lord. || Sing unto the Lord a new song, and his PRAISE in the | congre|gation of | saints.

2 Let Israel reJOICE in | him that | made-him : || let the children of ZION be | joyful | in their | King.

(130.)

3 Let them praise his NAME | in the | dance: || let them sing praises unto HIM | with the | timbrel and | harp.

4 For the Lord taketh pleaSURE | in his | people: || he will beautiFY the | meek | with sal|vation.

5 Let the SAINTS be | joyful in | glory: || let them SING a|loud up|on their | beds.

6 Let the high praises of GOD be | in their | mouth, || and a two-edgED | sword | in their | hand;

7 To execute venGEANCE up|on the | heathen, || AND | punishments-up|on the | people;

8 To BIND their | kings with | chains, || AND their | nobles with | fetters of | iron;

9 To execute upon THEM the | judgment | written: || this honour have all his SAINTS. | Praise | ye the | Lord.

GLORY BE, ETC.

PSALM CL.

PRAISE | ye the | Lord. || Praise God in his sanctuary: praise HIM in the | firmament | of his | power.

2 Praise him FOR his | mighty | acts: || praise him accordING | to his | excellent | greatness.

3 Praise HIM with the | sound of-the | trumpet: || PRAISE him | with the | psaltery and | harp.

4 Praise him WITH the | timbrel and | dance: || praise him with stringED | instru|ments and | organs.

5 Praise him upON the | loud | cymbals: || praise him upON the | high-|sounding | cymbals.

131.

6 Let every THING | that hath | breath ‖ praise the LORD. | Praise | ye the | Lord.

GLORY BE TO THE FATHER, AND | TO THE | SON, ‖ AND | TO THE | HOLY | GHOST;

AS IT WAS IN THE BEGINNING, IS NOW, AND | EVER | SHALL-BE, ‖ WORLD | WITHOUT | END. A|MEN.

(131.) *Rev. W. H. Havergal.*

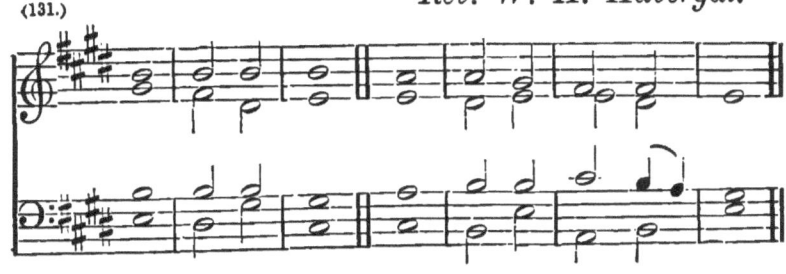

EXODUS XV.

I WILL sing unto the Lord, for HE hath | triumphed | gloriously: || the horse and his ridER hath | he thrown | into the | sea.

The Lord is my strength and song, and he is beCOME | my sal|vation: || he is my God, and I will prepare him an habitation; my father's GOD, | and I | will ex|alt-him.

The LORD is a | man of | war: || THE | Lord | is his | name.

Pharaoh's chariots and his host hath he CAST | into the | sea: || his chosen captains alSO are | drowned in-the | Red | sea.

The DEPTHS have | covered | them: || they sank inTO the | bottom | as a | stone.

Thy right hand, O Lord, is beCOME | glorious in | power: || thy right hand, O LORD, hath | dashed in | pieces the | enemy.

And in the greatness of thine excellency thou hast overthrown THEM that | rose up-a|gainst-thee: || thou sentest forth thy WRATH, which con|sumed | them as | stubble.

And with the blast of thy nostrils the waTERS were | gathered to|gether, || the floods stood upright as an heap, and the depths were congealED | in the | heart of-the | sea.

The enemy said, I will pursue, I will overtake, I WILL di|vide the | spoil; || my lust shall be satisfied upon them; I will draw my SWORD, | my hand | shall de|stroy-them.

Thou didst blow with thy wind, the SEA | covered | them: || they SANK as | lead in-the | mighty | waters.

Who is like unto thee, O LORD, a|mong the | gods? || who

132.

is like thee, glorious in holiness, fearFUL in | praises, | doing | wonders?

Thou stretchedst OUT | thy right | hand, || THE | earth | swallowed | them.

Thou in thy mercy hast led forth the peoPLE which | thou hast-re|deemed: || thou hast guided them in thy strength unto THY | holy | habi|tation.

Thou shalt bring them in, and plant them in the mounTAIN of | thine in|heritance, || in the place, O Lord, which thou hast made for thee to dwell in, in the Sanctuary, O LORD, which | thy hands | have es|tablished.

THE | Lord shall | reign || FOR | ever | and | ever.

GLORY BE, ETC.

ECCLESIASTES XII.

REMEMBER now thy CreaTOR in the | days-of thy | youth, || while the evil days come not, nor the years draw nigh, when thou shalt SAY, I | have no | pleasure | in-them;

While the sun, or the light, or the moon, or the STARS, | be not | darkened, || nor the CLOUDS re|turn | after the | rain:

In the day when the keepers of the house shall tremble, and the strong MEN shall | bow them|selves, || and the grinders cease because they are few, and THOSE that look | out-of the | windows be | darkened,

And the doors shall be shut in the streets, when the SOUND of the | grinding is | low, || and he shall rise up at the voice of the bird, and all the daughTERS of | musick shall | be brought | low;

Rev. W. Fitzherbert.

Also when they shall be afraid of that which is high, and FEARS shall | be in-the | way, || and the almond tree shall flourish, and the grasshopper shall be a burDEN, | and de|sire shall | fail:

Because man goETH to | his long | home, || and the mourn-ERS | go a|bout the | streets:

Or ever the silver cord be loosed, or the goldEN | bowl be | broken, || or the pitcher be broken at the fountain, or the WHEEL | broken | at the | cistern.

Then shall the dust return to the EARTH | as it | was: || and the spirit shall reTURN | unto | God who | gave-it.

ISAIAH XII.

O LORD, | I will | praise-thee: || though thou wast angry with me, thine anger is turned AWAY, | and thou | comfortedst | me.

Behold, God is my salvation; I will TRUST, and | not be-a|fraid: || for the Lord Jehovah is my strength and my song; he alSO | is-become | my sal|vation.

Therefore with JOY shall | ye draw | water || out OF the | wells | of sal|vation.

And in that day shall ye SAY, | Praise the | Lord, || call upon his name, declare his doings among the people, make menTION that | his name | is ex|alted.

Sing unto the Lord; for he hath DONE | excellent | things: || THIS is | known in | all the | earth.

Cry out and SHOUT, thou in|habitant of | Zion: || for great is the Holy One of IsraEL | in the | midst of | thee.

GLORY BE, ETC.

133.

ISAIAH XL.

COMFORT ye, comfort ye my peoPLE, | saith your | God. ‖
Speak ye comfortably to Jerusalem, and cry unto her, that her warfare is accomplished, that HER in|iqui|ty is | pardoned:

FOR she | hath re|ceived ‖ of the Lord's HAND | double for | all her | sins.

The voice of him that criETH | in the | wilderness, ‖ Prepare ye the way of the Lord, make straight in the deSERT a | highway | for our | God.

Every valley shall be exalted, and every mountain and HILL shall | be made | low: ‖ and the crooked shall be made STRAIGHT, | and the | rough places | plain:

And the glory of the Lord shall be revealed, and all FLESH shall | see-it to|gether: ‖ FOR the | mouth of-the | Lord hath | spoken-it.

The voice said, Cry. And he SAID, | What-shall I | cry? ‖ All flesh is grass, and all the goodliness thereof is AS the | flower | of the | field:

The grass witherETH, the | flower | fadeth: ‖ because the spirit of the Lord bloweth upon IT: | surely the | people is | grass.

The grass witherETH, the | flower | fadeth: ‖ but the WORD of our | God shall | stand for | ever.

O ZION, that | bringest good | tidings, ‖ get thee UP | into the | high | mountain;

O Jerusalem, that bringest good tidings, lift UP thy | voice with | strength; ‖ lift it up, be not afraid; say unto the citIES of | Judah, Be|hold your | God!

(133.)   *G. Wood.*

Behold, the Lord God will come with strong hand, and his ARM shall | rule for | him: ‖ behold, his reward is with HIM, | and his | work be|fore-him.

He shall feed his FLOCK | like a | shepherd: ‖ he shall gather the lambs with his arm, and carry them in his bosom, and shall gently LEAD | those that | are with | young.

Hast thou not KNOWN? hast | thou not | heard, ‖ that the everlasting God, the Lord, the Creator of the ends of the earth, fainteth not, neither is weary? there is no searchING | of his | under|standing.

He giveth powER | to the | faint; ‖ and to them that have no MIGHT | he in|creaseth | strength.

Even the YOUTHS shall | faint-and be | weary, ‖ and the YOUNG | men shall | utterly | fall:

But they that wait upon the LORD shall re|new their | strength; ‖ they shall mount up with wings as eagles; they shall run, and not be weaRY; and | they shall | walk,-and not | faint.

                                                         GLORY BE, ETC.

ISAIAH LIII.

WHO hath believED | our re|port? ‖ and to WHOM is the | arm of-the | Lord re|vealed?

For he shall grow up before him as a tender plant, and as a root out OF a | dry | ground: ‖ he hath no form nor comeliness; and when we shall see him, there is no beauTY | that we | should de|sire-him.

He is despisED and re|jected of | men; ‖ a man of sorROWS, | and ac|quainted with | grief:

134.

And we hid as it WERE our | faces | from-him; ‖ he was despisED, and | we es|teemed him | not.

Surely he hath borne our GRIEFS, and | carried our | sorrows: ‖ yet we did esteem him strickEN, | smitten of | God, and-af|flicted.

But he was woundED for | our trans|gressions, ‖ HE was | bruised for | our in|iquities:

The chastisement of our PEACE | was up|on-him; ‖ and WITH | his stripes | we are | healed.

All we like SHEEP have | gone a|stray; ‖ we have turned eveRY | one to | his own | way;

And the LORD hath | laid on | him ‖ THE in|iquity | of us | all.

He was oppressED, and | he-was af|flicted, ‖ YET he | opened | not his | mouth:

He is BROUGHT as a | lamb to-the | slaughter, ‖ and as a sheep before her shearers is DUMB, so he | openeth | not his | mouth.

He was taken from prisON | and from | judgment: ‖ and WHO shall de|clare his | gener|ation?

For he was cut off out OF the | land-of the | living: ‖ for the transgresSION of my | people | was he | stricken.

And he MADE his | grave with-the | wicked, ‖ and WITH the | r͡ich | in his | death;

Because HE had | done no | violence, ‖ neither was ANY de|c͡eit | in his | mouth.

Yet it pleasED the | Lord to | bruise-him; ‖ HE | hath put | him to | grief:

220

When thou shalt make his SOUL an | offering for | sin, || he shall see his SEED, | he shall-pro|long his | days,

AND the | pleasure of-the | Lord || SHALL | prosper | in his | hand.

He shall see of the travail of his SOUL, and | shall be | satisfied : || by his knowledge shall my righteous servant justify MANY; for he | shall bear | their in|iquities.

Therefore will I divide him a porTION | with the | great, || and he SHALL di|vide the | spoil with-the | strong;

Because he hath poured OUT his | soul unto | death: || and HE was | numbered | with-the trans|gressors;

And he BARE the | sin of | many, || and made inTER-|cession for | the trans|gressors. GLORY BE, ETC.

ISAIAH LX.

ARISE, SHINE; for thy | light is | come, || and the gloRY of the | Lord is | risen up|on-thee.

For, behold, the darkness shall cover the earth, and GROSS | darkness the | people: || but the Lord shall arise upon thee, and his gloRY | shall be | seen up|on-thee.

And the GenTILES shall | come to-thy | light, || and KINGS to the | brightness | of thy | rising.

Lift up thine eyes round about, and see: all they gather themselves togethER, they | come to | thee: || thy sons shall come from far, and thy daughTERS | shall be | nursed at-thy | side.

Then thou shalt see, and flow together, and thine heart shall

135.

FEAR, and | be en|larged; || because the abundance of the sea shall be converted unto thee, the forcES of the | Gentiles shall | come unto | thee.

The glory of LebaNON shall | come unto | thee, || the fir tree, the pine TREE, | and the | box to|gether,

To beautiFY the | place-of my | sanctuary; || and I will MAKE the | place of | my feet | glorious.

The sons also of them that afflicted thee shall come bendING | unto | thee; || and all they that despised thee shall bow themselves DOWN | at the | soles of-thy | feet;

And they shall call THEE, The | city of-the | Lord, || The ZION of the | Holy | One of | Israel.

Violence shall no more be heard in thy land, wasting nor destrucTION with|in thy | borders; || but thou shalt call thy WALLS Sal|vation, and | thy gates | Praise.

The sun shall be no more thy light by day; neither for brightness shall the MOON give | light unto | thee: || but the Lord shall be unto thee an everlasting LIGHT, | and thy | God thy | glory.

Thy sun shall no more go down; neither shall thy MOON with|draw it|self: || for the Lord shall be thine everlasting light, and the DAYS of thy | mourning | shall be | ended.

GLORY BE, ETC.

HABAKKUK III.

O LORD, revive thy WORK in the | midst of-the | years, || in the midst of the years make KNOWN; in | wrath re-| member | mercy.

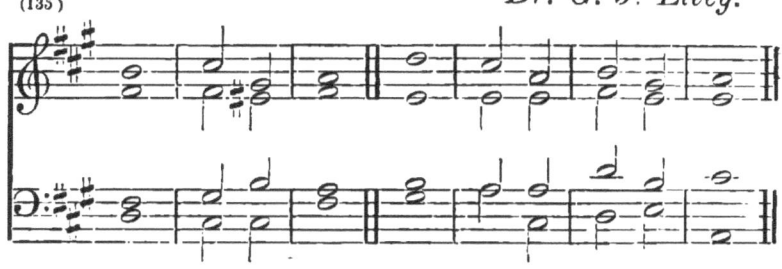

GOD | came from | Teman, ‖ AND the | Holy One | from mount | Paran.

His gloRY | covered the | heavens, ‖ AND the | earth was | full-of his | praise.

And his brightNESS was | as the | light; ‖ he had horns coming out of his hand; and there WAS the | hiding | of his | power.

Before HIM | went the | pestilence, ‖ and burnING | coals went | forth at-his | feet.

He STOOD, and | measured the | earth: ‖ he beHELD, and | drove a|sunder the | nations;

And the everlasting mountains were scattered, the perpetuAL | hills did | bow: ‖ HIS | ways are | ever|lasting.

The mountains saw THEE, | and they | trembled: ‖ the overflowING of the | water | passed | by:

The DEEP | uttered his | voice, ‖ and liftED | up his | hands on | high.

The sun and moon stood STILL in their | habi|tation : ‖ at the light of thine arrows they went, and at the shinING | of thy | glittering | spear.

Thou didst march through the LAND in | indig|nation, ‖ THOU didst | thresh the | heathen in | anger.

Thou wentest forth for the salvaTION | of thy | people, ‖ even FOR sal|vation with | thine a|nointed.

Although the fig TREE | shall not | blossom, ‖ neiTHER shall | fruit be | in the | vines;

The laBOUR of the | olive shall | fail, ‖ AND the | fields shall | yield no | meat;

136.

The flock shall be cut OFF | from the | fold, ‖ and there SHALL be | no herd | in the | stalls:

Yet I will reJOICE | in the | Lord, ‖ I will JOY in the | God of | my sal|vation.

GLORY BE, ETC.

LUKE I., v. 46.

MY soul doth MAGni|fy the | Lord, ‖ and my spirit HATH re|joiced in | God my | Saviour.

For HE | hath re|garded ‖ the LOW es|tate of | his hand-|maiden:

FOR, be|hold, from | henceforth ‖ ALL gener|ations shall | call me | blessed.

For he that is mighty hath DONE to | me great | things; ‖ AND | holy | is his | name.

And his merCY is on | them that | fear-him ‖ FROM gener-|ation to | gener|ation.

He hath shewED | strength with-his | arm; ‖ he hath scattered the proud in the IMAGin|ation | of their | hearts.

He hath put down the MIGHTY | from their | seats, ‖ and exaltED | them of | low de|gree.

He hath filled the hunGRY | with good | things; ‖ and the RICH he | hath sent | empty a|way.

He hath holpEN his | servant | Israel, ‖ IN re|membrance | of his | mercy;

As he SPAKE | to our | fathers, ‖ to AbraHAM, and | to his | seed for | ever.

GLORY BE, ETC.

Prof^{r.} Herbert S. Oakeley.

LUKE I., v. 68.

BLESSED be the LORD | God of | Israel; ‖ for he hath visitED | and re|deemed his | people,

And hath raised up an HORN of sal|vation | for-us ‖ IN the | house of-his | servant | David;

As he spake by the MOUTH of his | holy | prophets, ‖ which have BEEN | since the | world be|gan:

That we should be savED | from our | enemies, ‖ and FROM the | hand of | all that | hate-us;

To perform the mercy promisED | to our | fathers, ‖ and TO re|member his | holy | covenant;

The oath which he sware to OUR | father | Abraham, ‖ THAT | he would | grant unto | us,

That we being delivered out OF the | hand-of our | enemies ‖ MIGHT | serve him | without | fear,

In holiness and RIGHTeous|ness be|fore-him, ‖ ALL the | days | of our | life.

And thou, child, shalt be called the proPHET | of the | Highest: ‖ for thou shalt go before the FACE of the | Lord to-pre|pare his | ways;

To give knowledge of salvaTION | unto his | people ‖ BY the re|mission | of their | sins,

Through the tender merCY | of our | God; ‖ whereby the dayspring FROM on | high hath | visited | us,

To give light to them that sit in darkness and IN the | shadow of | death, ‖ to guide our FEET | into the | way of | peace. GLORY BE, ETC.

137.

I. CORINTHIANS XV., v. 20.

NOW is Christ risEN | from the | dead, ‖ and beCOME the | firstfruits - of | them that | slept.

For SINCE by | man came | death, ‖ by man came also the RESUR|rection | of the | dead.

For AS in | Adam all | die, ‖ even so in CHRIST shall | all be | made a|live.

But every man in his own orDER: | Christ the | firstfruits; ‖ afterward THEY that | are Christ's | at his | coming.

Then cometh the end, when he shall have delivered up the kingdom to GOD, | even the | Father; ‖ when he shall have put down all RULE and | all au|thority and | power.

For he must reign, till he hath put all eneMIES | under his | feet. ‖ The last eneMY that | shall be-de|stroyed is | death.

BEHOLD, I | shew-you a | mystery; ‖ We shall not all SLEEP, but | we shall | all be | changed,

In a moment, in the twinkling of an EYE, | at-the last | trump: ‖ for the trumpet shall sound, and the dead shall be raised incorruptiBLE, | and we | shall be | changed.

For this corruptible must put ON | incor|ruption, ‖ and this morTAL must | put on | immor|tality.

So when this corruptible shall have put ON | incor|ruption, ‖ and this mortal shall HAVE | put on | immor|tality,

Then shall be brought to pass the sayING | that is | written, ‖ DEATH is | swallowed | up in | victory.

O DEATH, | where-is thy | sting? ‖ O GRAVE, | where | is thy | victory?

The STING of | death is | sin; ‖ AND the | strength of | sin is-the | law.

BUT | thanks be-to | God, ‖ which giveth us the victoRY | through our | Lord Jesus | Christ.   GLORY BE, ETC.

WE PRAISE THEE, O GOD.—(*Te Deum laudamus.*)

WE PRAISE | thee, O | God; ‖ we acknowLEDGE | thee to | be the | Lord.

All the EARTH doth | worship | thee, ‖ THE | Father | ever|lasting.

To thee all anGELS | cry a|loud, ‖ the heavENS, and | all the | powers there|in;

To THEE | cherubin and | seraphin ‖ CON|tinual|ly do | cry, HOLY, | holy, | holy, ‖ LORD | God of | Saba|oth:

HeavEN and | earth are | full ‖ OF the | majesty | of thy | glory.

The glorious compaNY | of the-a|postles ‖ PRAISE | ... ... | ... ... | thee:

The goodly fellowSHIP | of the | prophets ‖ PRAISE | ... ... | ... ... | thee:

The noBLE | army of | martyrs ‖ PRAISE | ... ... | ... ... | thee:

The holy church throughOUT | all the | world ‖ DOTH | ... ac|knowledge | thee,

The FA| ... ... | ther ‖ OF an | infinite | majes|ty;

Thine honourable, TRUE, and | only | Son; ‖ alSO the | Holy | Ghost, the | Comforter.

THOU | art the | King ‖ OF | glo|ry, O | Christ;

138.

Thou art the evER|lasting | Son, || THE | Son | of the | Father.

When thou tookest upon THEE to de|liver | man, || thou didst NOT ab|hor the | virgin's | womb.

When thou hadst overCOME the | sharpness of | death, || thou didst open the kingDOM of | heaven to | all be|lievers.

Thou sittest at the RIGHT | hand of | God, || IN the | glory | of the | Father.

We beLIEVE that | thou shalt | come || TO | be | our | Judge:

We therefore pray THEE, | help thy | servants, || whom thou hast redeemED | with thy | precious | blood;

Make them to be numberED | with thy | saints, || IN | glory | ever|lasting.

O LORD, | save thy | people, || AND | bless ... | ...thine | heritage:

GO| ... vern | them, || AND | lift them | up for | ever.

DAY | by | day || WE | magni|fy | thee,

AND we | worship thy | name || evER | world | without | end.

VOUCH|safe, O | Lord, || to keep US | this day | without | sin.

O LORD, have | mercy up|on-us, || HAVE | mer|cy up|on-us.

O Lord, let thy merCY | lighten up|on-us; || as OUR | trust | is in | thee.

O LORD, in | thee have-I | trusted: || LET me | never | be con|founded.

Prof^{r.} Herbert S. Oakeley.

GLORY BE TO GOD ON HIGH.

GLORY be to God on high, and in earth peace, good will towards men.

We praise Thee, we bless Thee, we worship Thee, we glorify Thee, we give thanks to Thee for Thy great glory, O Lord God, heavenly King, God the Father Almighty.

O Lord, the only-begotten Son Jesus Christ; O Lord God, Lamb of God, Son of the Father, that takest away the sins of the world, have mercy upon us.

Thou that takest away the sins of the world, have mercy upon us.

Thou that takest away the sins of the world, receive our prayer.

Thou that sittest at the right hand of God the Father, have mercy upon us.

For Thou only art holy; Thou only art the Lord; Thou only, O Christ, with the Holy Ghost, art most high in the glory of God the Father. Amen.

139.

O ALL YE WORKS OF THE LORD.

Benedicite, Omnia Opera.

O ALL ye Works of the LORD, | bless ye the | Lord : ‖ praise HIM, and | magnify | him for | ever.

2 O ye Angels of the LORD, | bless ye the | Lord : ‖ praise HIM, and | magnify | him for | ever.

3 O ye HEAV'NS, | bless ye the | Lord : ‖ praise HIM, and | magnify | him for | ever.

4 O ye waters that be above the firmaMENT, | bless ye the | Lord : ‖ praise HIM, and | magnify | him for | ever.

5 O all ye powers of the LORD, | bless ye the | Lord : ‖ praise HIM, and | magnify | him for | ever.

6 O ye Sun and MOON, | bless ye the | Lord : ‖ praise HIM, and | magnify | him for | ever.

7 O ye Stars of HEAV'N, | bless ye the | Lord : ‖ praise HIM, and | magnify | him for | ever.

8 O ye Showers and DEW | bless ye the | Lord : ‖ praise HIM, and | magnify | him for | ever.

9 O ye Winds of GOD, | bless ye the | Lord : ‖ praise HIM, and | magnify | him for | ever.

10 O ye Fire and HEAT, | bless ye the | Lord : ‖ praise HIM, and | magnify | him for | ever.

11 O ye Winter and SumMER, | bless ye the | Lord : ‖ praise HIM, and | magnify | him for | ever.

(139.)   *A. H. D. Troyte.*

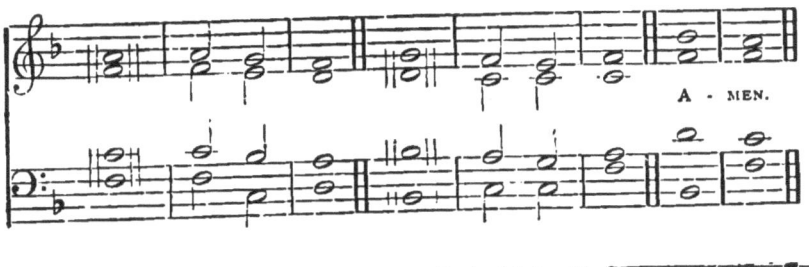

12 O ye Dews and FROSTS, | bless ye the | Lord: || praise HIM, and | magnify | him for | ever.

13 O ye Frost and COLD, | bless ye the | Lord: || praise HIM, and | magnify | him for | ever.

14 O ye Ice and SNOW, | bless ye the | Lord: || praise HIM, and | magnify | him for | ever.

15 O ye Nights and DAYS, | bless ye the | Lord: || praise HIM, and | magnify | him for | ever.

16 O ye Light and DarkNESS, | bless ye the | Lord: || praise HIM, and | magnify | him for | ever.

17 O ye Lightnings and CLOUDS, | bless ye the | Lord: || praise HIM, and | magnify | him for | ever.

18 O let the EARTH | bless the | Lord: || yea, let it praise HIM, and | magnify | him for | ever.

19 O ye Mountains and HILLS, | bless ye the | Lord: || praise HIM, and | magnify | him for | ever.

20 O all ye Green Things upon the EARTH, | bless ye the | Lord: || praise HIM, and | magnify | him for | ever.

21 O ye WELLS, | bless ye the | Lord: || praise HIM, and | magnify | him for | ever.

22 O ye Seas and FLOODS, | bless ye the | Lord: || praise HIM, and | magnify | him for | ever.

23 O ye Whales, and all that move in the WATERS, | bless ye the | Lord: || praise HIM, and | magnify | him for | ever.

24 O all ye Fowls of the AIR, | bless ye the | Lord: || praise HIM, and | magnify | him for | ever.

140.—Single Chant. *Prof^{r.} Herbert S. Oakeley.*

25 O all ye Beasts and CATTLE, | bless ye the | Lord: ‖ praise HIM, and | magnify | him for ever.

26 O ye Children of MEN | bless ye the | Lord: ‖ praise HIM, and | magnify | him for | ever.

27 O let IsRA'L | bless the | Lord: ‖ praise HIM, and | magnify | him for | ever.

28 O ye Priests of the LORD, | bless ye the | Lord: ‖ praise HIM, and | magnify | him for | ever.

29 O ye Servants of the LORD, | bless ye the | Lord: ‖ praise HIM, and | magnify | him for | ever.

30 O ye Spirits and Souls of the RightEOUS, | bless ye the | Lord: ‖ praise HIM, and | magnify | him for | ever.

31 O ye holy and humble Men of HEART, | bless ye the | Lord: ‖ praise HIM, and | magnify | him for | ever.

32 O Ananias, Azarias, and MisaEL, | bless ye the | Lord: ‖ praise HIM, and | magnify | him for | ever.

Glory be to the FaTHER, | and to the | Son: ‖ AND | to the | Holy | Ghost;

As it was in the beginning, is NOW, and | ever | shall be: ‖ WORLD | without | end. A|men.

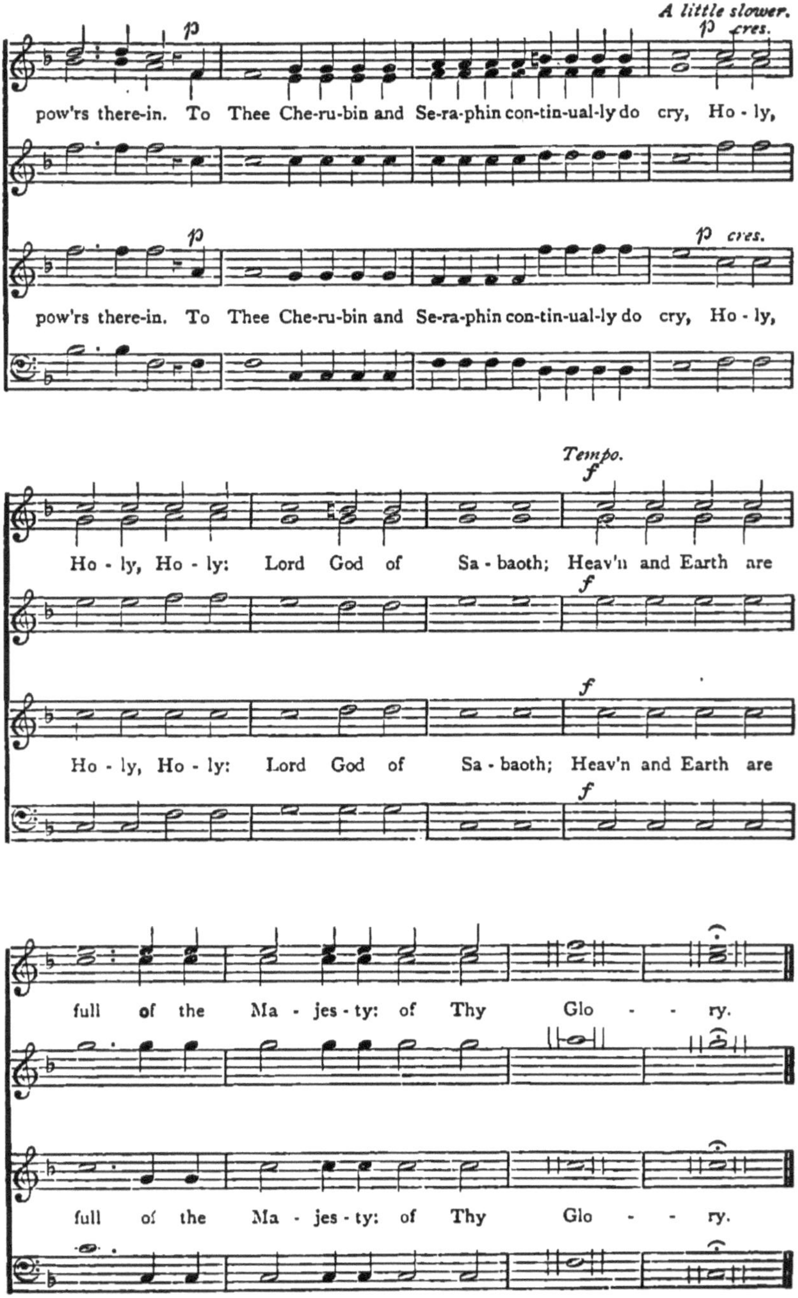
A little slower.
p
p cres.
pow'rs there-in. To Thee Che-ru-bin and Se-ra-phin con-tin-ual-ly do cry, Ho - ly,
p
p cres.
pow'rs there-in. To Thee Che-ru-bin and Se-ra-phin con-tin-ual-ly do cry, Ho - ly,
Tempo.
f
Ho - ly, Ho - ly: Lord God of Sa - baoth; Heav'n and Earth are
f
f
Ho - ly, Ho - ly: Lord God of Sa - baoth; Heav'n and Earth are
f
full of the Ma - jes - ty: of Thy Glo - - ry.
full of the Ma - jes - ty: of Thy Glo - - ry.

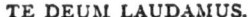

TE DEUM LAUDAMUS.

235

TE DEUM LAUDAMUS.

TE DEUM LAUDAMUS.

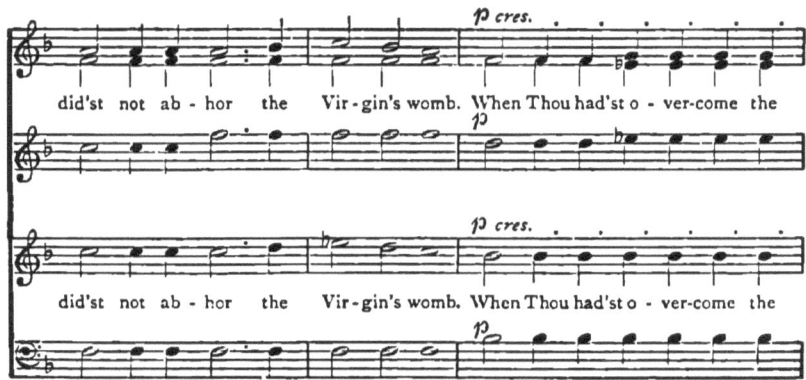

TE DEUM LAUDAMUS.

TE DEUM LAUDAMUS.

TE DEUM LAUDAMUS.

TE DEUM LAUDAMUS.

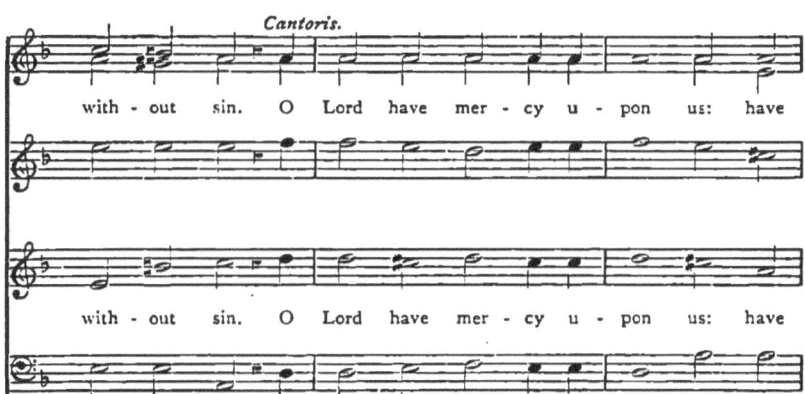

TE DEUM LAUDAMUS.

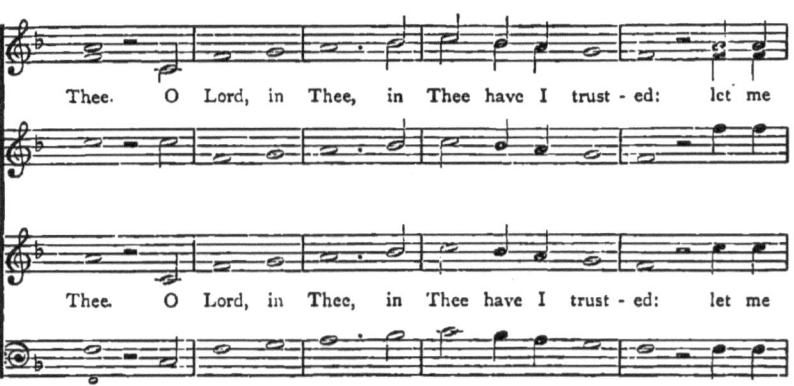

(Inserted by Permission of Messrs. Novello, Ewer & Co., by whom it is Sold in a separate form).

TE DEUM LAUDAMUS.

TE DEUM LAUDAMUS.

245

TE DEUM LAUDAMUS.

TE DEUM LAUDAMUS.

TE DEUM LAUDAMUS.

TE DEUM LAUDAMUS.

TE DEUM LAUDAMUS.

TE DEUM LAUDAMUS.

ANTHEMS.

No. 1. I WILL ARISE.
LUKE XV. 18, 19.
(MUSIC BY REV. R. CECIL.)

I will arise, and go to my Father, and will say unto Him, Father, I have sinned against Heav'n, and before Thee, and am no more worthy to be called Thy son.

No. 2. O PRAISE THE LORD.
PSALM CXLVII. 1, 5.
(MUSIC BY JOHN WELDON.)

O praise the Lord: for it is a good thing to sing praises unto our God; yea, a joyful and pleasant thing it is to be thankful.

Great is the Lord, and great is His power: yea, and His wisdom is infinite.

No. 3. O PRAISE GOD IN HIS HOLINESS.
PSALM CL. 1-4, 6.
(MUSIC BY JOHN WELDON.)

O praise God in His holiness: praise Him in the firmament of His pow'r.

Praise Him in His noble acts: praise Him according to His excellent greatness.

Praise Him in the sound of the trumpet: praise Him upon the lute and harp.

Praise Him in the cymbals and dances: praise Him upon the strings and pipe.

Let ev'rything that hath breath praise the Lord.

No. 4. HOW BEAUTIFUL UPON THE MOUNTAINS.
ISAIAH LII. 7.
(MUSIC BY R. A. SMITH.)

How beautiful upon the mountains are the feet of him that bringeth good tidings, that publisheth peace; that bringeth good tidings of good, that publisheth salvation; that saith unto Zion, Thy God reigneth!

Break forth into joy, sing together, ye waste places of Jerusalem : for the Lord hath comforted His people, He hath redeemed Jerusalem.

Hallelujah! Praise ye the Lord.

No. 5.   TEACH ME, O LORD.
PSALM CXIX. 33.
(MUSIC BY THOMAS ATTWOOD.)

Teach me, O Lord, the way of Thy statutes; and I shall keep it unto the end.

No. 6.   HEAR MY PRAYER, O LORD.
PSALM CXLIII. 1.
(ADAPTED FROM WINTER, BY W. SHORE.)

Hear my pray'r, O Lord, give ear to my supplications: in Thy faithfulness answer me, and in Thy righteousness.

No. 7.   ARISE, SHINE; FOR THY LIGHT IS COME.
ISAIAH LX. 1-3.
(MUSIC BY DR. G. J. ELVEY.)

Arise, shine; for thy light is come, and the glory of the Lord is risen upon thee.

For, behold, the darkness shall cover the earth, and gross darkness the people; but the Lord shall arise upon thee, and His glory shall be seen upon thee. And the Gentiles shall come to thy light, and kings to the brightness of thy rising.

No. 8.   ENTER NOT INTO JUDGMENT.
PSALM CXLIII. 2.
(MUSIC BY THOMAS ATTWOOD.)

Enter not into judgment with Thy servant, O Lord: for in Thy sight shall no man living be justified.

No. 9. THINE, O LORD, IS THE GREATNESS.
1 CHRON. XXIX. 11.
(MUSIC BY JAMES KENT.)

Thine, O Lord, is the greatness, and the pow'r, and the glory, and the victory, and the majesty: for all that is in the heav'n and the earth are Thine; Thine is the kingdom, O Lord, and Thou art exalted as head over all.

No. 10.   I WILL LIFT UP MINE EYES.
PSALM CXXI.
(MUSIC BY DR. J. CLARKE WHITFELD.)

I will lift up mine eyes unto the hills, from whence cometh my help. My help cometh even from the Lord, who hath made heav'n and earth.

The Lord himself is thy keeper: the Lord is thy defence upon thy right hand; so that the sun shall not burn thee by day, neither the moon by night.

The Lord shall preserve thee from all evil; yea, it is He that shall keep thy soul. The Lord shall preserve thy going out and coming in from this time forth, for evermore.

Hallelujah. Amen.

No. 11. MY SOUL DOTH MAGNIFY THE LORD.

LUKE I. 46-55.

(MUSIC BY DR. ARNOLD.)

My soul doth magnify the Lord, and my spirit hath rejoiced in God my Saviour. For He hath regarded the low estate of His handmaiden: for, behold, from henceforth all generations shall call me blessed. For He that is mighty hath magnified me; and holy is His name. And His mercy is on them that fear Him throughout all generations.

He hath shewed strength with His arm; He hath scattered the proud in the imagination of their hearts. He hath put down the mighty from their seat, and hath exalted the humble and meek. He hath filled the hungry with good things; and the rich He hath sent empty away.

He, remem'bring His mercy, hath holpen His servant Israel; as He promised to our forefathers, Abraham, and his seed, for ever.

Glory be to the Father, and to the Son, and to the Holy Ghost; as it was in the beginning, is now, and ever shall be, world without end. Amen.

No. 12. LORD, NOW LETTEST THOU THY SERVANT.

LUKE II. 29-32.

(MUSIC BY DR. ARNOLD.)

Lord, now lettest Thou Thy servant depart in peace, according to Thy word: for mine eyes have seen Thy salvation, which Thou hast prepared before the face of all people; to be a light to lighten the Gentiles, and to be the glory of Thy people Israel.

Glory be to the Father, and to the Son, and to the Holy Ghost; as it was in the beginning, is now, and ever shall be, world without end. Amen.

No. 13. O TASTE AND SEE.

PSALM XXXIV. 8-11.

(MUSIC BY JOHN GOSS.)

O taste and see how gracious the Lord is: blessed is the man that trusteth in Him. O fear the Lord, ye that are His saints: for they that fear Him lack nothing.

The lions do lack, and suffer hunger; but they who seek the Lord shall want no manner of thing that is good.

No. 14. O LORD MY GOD.

1 KINGS VIII. 28-30.

(MUSIC BY THE REV. C. MALAN, D.D., OF GENEVA.)

O Lord my God, hear Thou the prayer Thy servant prayeth: have Thou respect unto his prayer.

Hear Thou in heav'n Thy dwelling-place; and when Thou hearest, Lord, forgive.

No. 15. REND YOUR HEART.
JOEL II. 13.

(MUSIC BY J. BAPTISTE CALKIN.)

Rend your heart, and not your garments, and turn unto the Lord your God: for He is gracious and merciful, slow to anger, and of great kindness, and repenteth Him of the evil.

No. 16. I WILL ALWAY GIVE THANKS.
PSALM XXXIV. 1-6.

(MUSIC BY J. BAPTISTE CALKIN.)

I will alway give thanks unto the Lord: His praise shall ever be in my mouth. My soul shall make her boast in the Lord: the humble shall hear thereof, and be glad. O praise the Lord with me, and let us magnify His name together.

I sought the Lord and He heard me; yea, and delivered me out of all my fears. They had an eye unto Him, and were lightened; and their faces were not ashamed.

Lo, the poor crieth, and the Lord heareth him: yea, and saveth him out of all his troubles.

No. 17. COME UNTO ME.
MATT. XI. 28-30.

(MUSIC BY JOHN STAFFORD SMITH.)

Come unto Me, all ye that labour and are heavy laden, and I will give you rest.

Take My yoke upon you, and learn of Me; for I am meek and lowly in heart; and ye shall find rest unto your souls.

For My yoke is easy, and My burden is light.

No. 18. PRAISE THE LORD, O JERUSALEM.
PSALM CXLVII. 12; CXLVIII. 2, 4.

(MUSIC BY JOHN SCOTT.)

Praise the Lord, O Jerusalem; praise God, O Zion.

Praise Him all ye angels: praise Him all His host: praise Him, sun and moon: praise Him, stars and light.

O that men would therefore praise the Lord for His goodness, and declare the wonders that He doth for the children of men.

Hallelujah. Amen.

No. 19. LORD, FOR THY TENDER MERCIES' SAKE.

(MUSIC BY RICHARD FARRANT.)

Lord, for Thy tender mercies' sake, lay not our sins to our charge; but forgive that is past, and give us grace to amend our sinful lives: to decline from sin, and incline to virtue: that we may walk with a perfect heart before Thee now and evermore.

No. 20. BLESSED FOR EVER.
(MUSIC FROM SPOHR.)

Blessed for ever are they that die trusting in God; yea, blessed for ever are they that die in the Lord.

From henceforth they rest from their labours: for them that sleep in Jesus, God will bring with Him.

No. 21. THE LORD DESCENDED FROM ABOVE.
PSALM XVIII. OLD VERSION.
(MUSIC BY PHILIP HAYES.)

The Lord descended from above,
And bow'd the heav'ns most high;
And underneath His feet He cast
The darkness of the sky.

On cherubs and on cherubims
Full royally He rode,
And on the wings of mighty winds
Came flying all abroad.

No. 22. HEAR THE VOICE AND PRAYER.
2 CHRON. VI. 19.
(MUSIC BY J. L. HOPKINS.)

Hear the voice and prayer of Thy servants, which they make before Thee this day: that Thine eyes may be open towards this house day and night, ever towards this place, of which Thou hast said, My name shall be there. And when Thou hearest, have mercy upon them.

No. 23. CHRIST IS RISEN FROM THE DEAD.
(MUSIC BY DR. G. J. ELVEY.)

Christ is risen from the Dead—Hallelujah! In that He died, He died unto sin once; but in that He liveth, He liveth unto God.

No. 24. O LORD GOD.
PSALM CXL. 7; XXXI. 5.
(MUSIC BY JOHN GOSS.)

O Lord God, Thou strength of my health, Thou hast covered my head in the day of battle.

Into Thy hands I commend my spirit: for Thou hast redeemed me, O Lord, Thou God of truth. Amen.

No. 25.   MY GOD, LOOK UPON ME.

PSALM XXII. 1-3.

(MUSIC BY JOHN REYNOLDS.)

My God, look upon me: why hast Thou forsaken me, and art so far from my health, and from the words of my complaint?
O my God, I cry in the daytime, but Thou hearest not; and in the night season also I take no rest.
But Thou continuest holy, O Thou worship of Israel.

No. 26.   THE LORD IS MY SHEPHERD.

PSALM XXIII.

(MUSIC BY HENRY SMART.)

The Lord is my shepherd; I shall not want.
He maketh me to lie down in green pastures: He leadeth me beside the still waters.
He restoreth my soul: He leadeth me in the paths of righteousness for His name's sake.
Yea, though I walk through the valley of the shadow of death, I will fear no evil: for Thou art with me; Thy rod and Thy staff they comfort me.
Thou preparest a table before me in the presence of mine enemies: Thou anointest my head with oil; my cup runneth over.
Surely goodness and mercy shall follow me all the days of my life: and I will dwell in the house of the Lord for ever.

No. 27.   O SING UNTO THE LORD.

PSALM XCVIII.

(MUSIC BY JACKSON OF EXETER.)

O sing unto the Lord a new song: for He hath done marvellous things. With His own right hand, and with His holy arm: hath He gotten Himself the victory.
The Lord declar'd His salvation: His righteousness hath He openly show'd in the sight of the heathen. He hath remember'd His mercy and truth toward the house of Israel: and all the ends of the world have seen the salvation of our God.
Show yourselves joyful unto the Lord, all ye lands: sing, rejoice, and give thanks.
Praise the Lord upon the harp: sing to the harp with a Psalm of thanksgiving. With trumpets also and shawms: O show yourselves joyful before the Lord the King.
Let the sea make a noise, and all that therein is: the round world, and they that dwell therein.
Let the floods clap their hands, and let the hills be joyful together before the Lord: for He cometh to judge the earth. With righteousness shall He judge the world: and the people with equity.
Glory be to the Father, and to the Son, and to the Holy Ghost; as it was in the beginning, is now, and ever shall be: world without end. Amen.

No. 28. GOD BE MERCIFUL UNTO US.
PSALM LXVII.
(MUSIC BY JACKSON OF EXETER.)

God be merciful unto us, and bless us: and show us the light of His countenance, and be merciful unto us; that Thy way may be known upon earth: Thy saving health among all nations.

Let the people praise Thee, O God: yea, let all the people praise Thee.

O let the nations rejoice and be glad: for Thou shalt judge the folk righteously, and govern the nations upon earth.

Let the people praise Thee, O God: yea, let all the people praise Thee. Then shall the earth bring forth her increase: and God, ev'n our own God, shall give us His blessing. God shall bless us: and all the ends of the world shall fear Him.

Glory be to the Father, and to the Son, and to the Holy Ghost; as it was in the beginning, is now, and ever shall be: world without end. Amen.

No. 29. HOW DEAR ARE THY COUNSELS.
PSALM CXXXIX. 17, 23, 24.
(MUSIC BY DR. CROTCH.)

How dear are Thy counsels unto me, O God: O how great is the sum of them!

Try me, prove me, examine my thoughts, and seek the ground of my heart.

Look well if there be any way of wickedness in me, and lead me in the way everlasting.

No. 30. PONDER MY WORDS, O LORD.
PSALM V. 1, 2.
(MUSIC BY LANGDON COLBORNE.)

Ponder my words, O Lord; consider my meditation.

O hearken Thou to the voice of my calling, my King and my God; for unto Thee will I make my pray'r.

No. 31. O PRAISE THE LORD, ALL YE HEATHEN.
PSALM CXVII.
(MUSIC BY THE EARL OF WILTON.)

O praise the Lord, all ye heathen: praise Him, all ye nations.

For His merciful kindness is ever more and more towards us, and the truth of the Lord endureth for ever. O praise the Lord. Amen.

No. 32. O HOLY GHOST, INTO OUR MINDS.
(MUSIC BY G. A. MACFARREN.)

O Holy Ghost, into our minds send down Thy heav'nly light,
Kindle our hearts with fervent zeal, to serve God day and night.
Thou art the very Comforter, in grief and all distress,
The heavenly gift of God most high, no tongue can it express.

Such measures of Thy pow'rful grace, grant to us, Lord, we pray,
That Thou may'st be our Comforter at the last awful day.
O Holy Ghost, into our hearts send down Thy heav'nly light,
Kindle our hearts with fervent zeal, to serve God day and night.
Amen.

No. 33. HOW GOODLY ARE THY TENTS.
NUMBERS XXIV. 5, 6.
(MUSIC BY THE REV. SIR FREDERICK A. GORE OUSELEY, BART.)

How goodly are thy tents, O Jacob! and thy tabernacles, O Israel. As the valleys are they spread forth, as gardens by the river side.

No. 34. LET US NOW GO EVEN UNTO BETHLEHEM.
LUKE II. 10, 11.
(MUSIC BY E. J. HOPKINS.)

Let us now go even unto Bethlehem, and see this thing which is come to pass, which the Lord hath made known unto us.

For the Angel said unto us, Fear not: for, behold, I bring you good tidings of great joy, which shall be to all people.

For unto you is born this day, in the city of David, a Saviour, which is Christ the Lord.

No. 35. BLESSED IS HE THAT CONSIDERETH.
(MUSIC BY DR. NARES.)

Blessed is he that considereth the poor and needy, the Lord shall deliver him in the time of trouble.

No. 36. THOU KNOWEST, LORD.
(MUSIC BY HENRY PURCELL.)

Thou knowest, Lord, the secrets of our hearts; shut not Thy merciful ears unto our prayers; but spare us, Lord most holy. O God most mighty, O holy and most merciful Saviour, Thou most worthy Judge eternal, suffer us not at our last hour for any pains of death to fall from Thee. Amen.

No. 37. SAVIOUR, SOURCE OF EV'RY BLESSING.
(MUSIC BY MOZART.)

Saviour, source of ev'ry blessing!
Tune my heart to grateful lays:
Streams of mercy, never ceasing,
Call for endless songs of praise.

By Thy hand restor'd, defended,
Safe through life thus far I've come;
Safe, O Lord! when life is ended,
O bring me to my heav'nly home.

No. 38. LIKE AS THE HART.
PSALM XLII.
(MUSIC BY VINCENT NOVELLO.)

Like as the hart desireth the water-brooks, so longeth my soul after Thee, O God.

Why art thou so full of heaviness, O my soul, and why art thou so disquieted within me?

O put thy trust in God.

No. 39. THE LORD IS LOVING.

Psalm cxlv. 9-13.

(MUSIC BY DR. G. M. GARRETT.)

The Lord is loving unto ev'ry man, and His mercy is over all His works.
All Thy works praise Thee, O God, and Thy saints give thanks unto Thee.
They show the glory of Thy kingdom, and talk of Thy pow'r, that Thy pow'r, Thy glory, and the mightiness of Thy kingdom might be known unto men.
Thy kingdom is an everlasting kingdom, and Thy law is the truth.
Amen.

No. 40. O GIVE THANKS.

Psalm cv. 1-3.

(MUSIC BY DR. G. J. ELVEY.)

O give thanks unto the Lord, and call upon His name: tell the people what things He hath done. O give thanks unto the Lord.
O let your songs be of Him, and praise Him, and let your talking be of all His wondrous works.
Rejoice in His holy name: let the heart of them rejoice that seek the Lord. Amen.

No. 41. THIS IS THE DAY.

Psalm cxviii. 24; 1 Cor. xv. 20-22, 57.

(MUSIC BY JOHN SEWELL.)

This is the day which the Lord hath made; we will rejoice and be glad in it.
For now is Christ risen from the dead, and become the first-fruits of them that slept.
For since by man came death, by man came also the resurrection of the dead.
For as in Adam all die, even so in Christ shall all be made alive.
Thanks be to God which giveth us the victory, through our Lord Jesus Christ. Hallelujah! Amen.

No. 42. O LOVE THE LORD.

Psalm xxxii. 23, 24.

(MUSIC BY ARTHUR S. SULLIVAN.)

O love the Lord, all ye His saints, for the Lord preserveth them that are faithful, and plenteously rewardeth the proud doer.
Be strong, and He shall establish your heart, all ye that put your trust in the Lord. O love the Lord. Amen.

No. 43. O COME, YE SERVANTS.

(MUSIC BY DR. CHRISTOPHER TYE.)

O come, ye servants of the Lord;
And praise His holy name.
From early morn to setting sun,
His might on earth proclaim.

His laws are just, and glad the heart;
He makes His mercies known:
Ye princes come, ye people too,
And bow before His throne.

No. 44. O LORD, WE TRUST ALONE IN THEE.

PSALM CXLI. 8.

(MUSIC BY HANDEL.)

O Lord, we trust alone in Thee.

No. 45. BLESSED BE THE LORD GOD.

PSALM LXXII. 18, 19.

(MUSIC BY DR. NARES.)

Blessed be the Lord God, ev'n the God of Israel, which only doth wondrous things.
And blessed be the name of His Majesty for ever and ever.
And all the earth shall be fill'd with His Majesty. Amen.

No. 46. THE LORD IS KING.

PSALM XCVII. 1; CXVIII. 14, 24, 29.

(MUSIC BY JOSIAH PITTMAN.)

The Lord is King, let the earth now be glad; yea, let the Isles rejoice now before Him.
The Lord is my song, God is my strength and my salvation.
Give thanks to the Lord, for He is gracious, His mercy endureth for ever.
This is the day which the Lord hath made; we will rejoice and be glad in it.
Hymns of praise, then, let us sing, unto Christ our Heav'nly King, who endur'd the cross and grave, sinners to redeem and save. Hallelujah, Amen.

No. 47. O HOW AMIABLE ARE THY DWELLINGS.

(MUSIC BY V. RICHARDSON.)

O how amiable are Thy dwellings, Thou Lord of hosts! My soul hath a desire and longing to enter into the house of the Lord; my heart and my flesh rejoice in the living God.
Blessed are they that dwell in Thy house; they will alway be praising Thee. Hallelujah.

No. 48.   REJOICE, O YE PEOPLE.
(MUSIC BY MENDELSSOHN.)

Rejoice! O ye people of earth, sing and praise the Lord; for the Saviour has appeared, whom the Lord had promised; He, His truth and His justice to the world hath proclaimed. Hallelujah.

No. 49.   THOU LORD OUR REFUGE.
(MUSIC BY MENDELSSOHN.)

Thou Lord our refuge hast been from age to age. Ere Thou hadst brought forth the mountains or the earth hadst formed, or the world created, Thou art God from everlasting, world without end. Hallelujah.

No. 50.   LORD, ON OUR OFFENCES.
(MUSIC BY MENDELSSOHN.)

Lord, on our offences in justice look not, but in mercy, Lord, look Thou upon us; Lord, who art our Redeemer, O send us Thine aid, deliver us, and forgive us now all our sins in mercy, for Thy great glory and Thy name's sake.

No. 51.   FOR OUR OFFENCES, JESUS.
(MUSIC BY MENDELSSOHN.)

For our offences, Jesus took upon Him humility, and unto death, ev'n upon the cross, became He obedient: God therefore Him hath exalted, and on Him a name hath bestowed high above ev'ry mortal name. Amen.

No. 52.   HALLELUJAH.
Revelation xix. 6; xi. 15; xix. 16.
(MUSIC BY HANDEL.)

HALLELUJAH! for the Lord God Omnipotent reigneth.
The kingdom of this world is become the kingdom of our Lord, and of His Christ; and He shall reign for ever and ever—
KING OF KINGS, AND LORD OF LORDS. HALLELUJAH!

www.ingramcontent.com/pod-product-compliance
Lightning Source LLC
Chambersburg PA
CBHW032000230426
43672CB00010B/2218